东南大学建筑学院国际联合教学丛书
International Joint Teaching Series of SEU–ARCH

AQUA-URBANISM

A Swedish CITYLAB Guided Joint Research & Teaching Studio
in Changzhou Tianning, China

水 域 都 市

中瑞联合可持续性城市发展
研究与教学·常州天宁

张彤 Ronald Wennersten 顾震弘 徐瑾 殷铭 著

东南大学出版社·南京

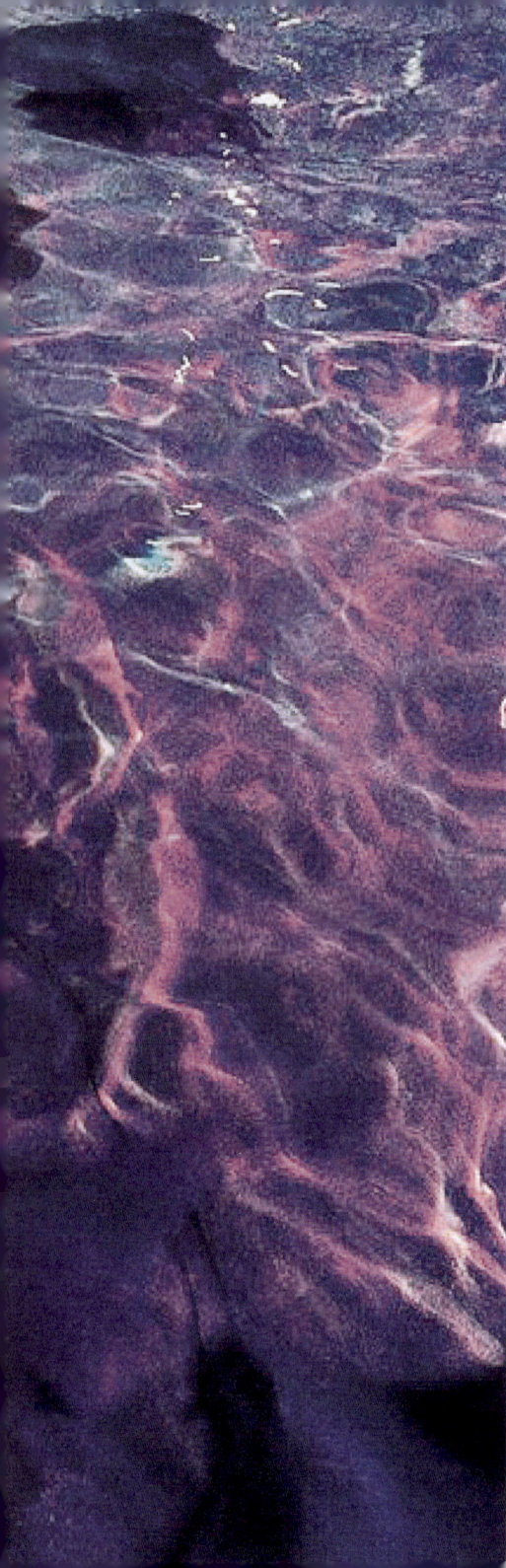

组织机构
东南大学建筑学院
瑞典绿色建筑委员会
江苏省城镇化和城乡规划研究中心
常州市规划局天宁分局
常州市规划设计研究院
指导老师
罗纳德·维纳斯坦、张彤、殷铭、刘泓伶、徐瑾、顾震弘、权亚玲
助　教
季云竹、段一行
参与学生
赵紫彬、周圆圆、牟思聪
林逸风、邹立君、邹闻婷
蒋茂源、程孟晴、屈佳慧
曹云琥、戴金贝、陆　垠
樊中山、施昊希、汪　琦

Organizers
School of Architecture, Southeast University
Sweden Green Building Council
Urbanization and Urban Rural Planning Research Center of Jiangsu
Changzhou Urban Planning Bureau Tianning Branch
Changzhou City Planning and Design Institute
Supervisors
Ronald Wennersten, Zhang Tong, Yin Ming, Liu Hongling, Xu Jin,
Gu Zhenhong, Quan Yaling
Teaching Assistants
Ji Yunzhu, Duan Yixing
Participating Students
Zhao Zibin, Zhou Yuanyuan, Mou Sicong
Lin Yifeng, Zou Lijun, Zou Wenting
Jiang Maoyuan, Cheng Mengqing, Qu Jiahui
Cao Yunhu, Dai Jinbei, Lu Yin
Fan Zhongshan, Shi Haoxi, Wang Qi

概　述

中国城市在前所未有的尺度上经历了以空间扩张为主要标志的城市化过程，整个国家的城市建成区面积在过去 20 年中增加了两倍以上。这种以土地和人口规模为指标的城市化不可避免地带来资源浪费和对均衡环境的损害。位于江南水网地带的常州，拥有悠久的历史和迷人的河城文化，也是中国经济最为发达的城市之一。迅猛的经济增长与城市化疾速改变着常州的城市规模和面貌，从而使得这座历史名城的结构、肌理和公共生活面临割裂、差异和碎片化。

瑞典在可持续性城市发展方面一直居于全球引领地位。瑞典绿色建筑委员会于 2009 年开始构建可持续发展城市实验室（CITYLAB），作为一个合作、共享和创新的平台，它为城市可持续发展建设和运营提供一系列导则、工具和评价方法。

本次联合研究和教学，由东南大学建筑学院与瑞典绿色建筑委员会、江苏省城镇化和城乡规划研究中心、常州市规划局天宁分局、常州市规划设计研究院五方合作开展，针对常州市天宁区五个具有典型问题的地块，运用瑞典绿色建筑委员会可持续发展城市实验室的理念与方法，进行实验性的研究和教学，探讨系统网络的重构与耦合、城市资源的循环利用、水岸空间的开放共享以及河城文化的再造与复兴，试图为存量时代的城市更新探索一条均衡有序的可持续性发展路径。

Introduction

Chinese cities have experienced urbanization on an unprecedented scale marked by spatial expansion, and the urban built-up area of the whole country has more than tripled in the past two decades. Such urbanization, which is based on land and population size, inevitably leads to waste of resources and damage to the balanced environment. Located in the water network area south of the Yangtze River, Changzhou has a long history and charming river city culture. It is also one of the most economically developed cities in China. Rapid economic growth and urbanization have changed the size and appearance of changzhou city, but caused the structure, texture and public life of this historic city to be split, different and fragmented.

Sweden has been a global leader in sustainable urban development. The Sweden Green Building Council started building CITYLAB in 2009 as a platform for collaboration, sharing and innovation, providing a series of guidelines, tools and evaluation methods for the construction and operation of sustainable urban development.

Joint Research & Teaching Studio was carried out by the School of Architecture at Southeast University and the Sweden Green Building Council, the Urbanization and Urban Rural Planning Research Center of Jiangsu, the Changzhou Urban Planning Bureau Tianning Branch, and the Changzhou City Planning and Design Institute. Five plots with typical problems in Tianning District, using the ideas and methods of the Sustainable Development City Laboratory of Sweden Green Building Council, conducting experimental research and teaching, exploring the reconstruction and coupling of system networks, recycling of urban resources, the open sharing of waterfront space and the re-creation and revival of Hecheng culture seek to explore a balanced and orderly sustainable development path for urban renewal in the stock era.

目 录

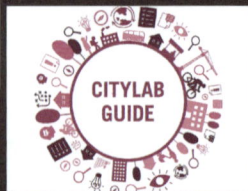

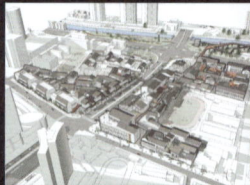

4 水·公共服务
WATER + PUBLIC SERVICE

水·混合社区·工业遗产
WATER + MIXED COMMUNITY
+ INDUSTRIAL HERITAGE

2

3 水·铁路设施
WATER + RAILWAY FACILITY

1
水·历史文化
WATER + HISTORY CULTURE

5 水·城中村
WATER + URBAN VILLAGE

N

0
250

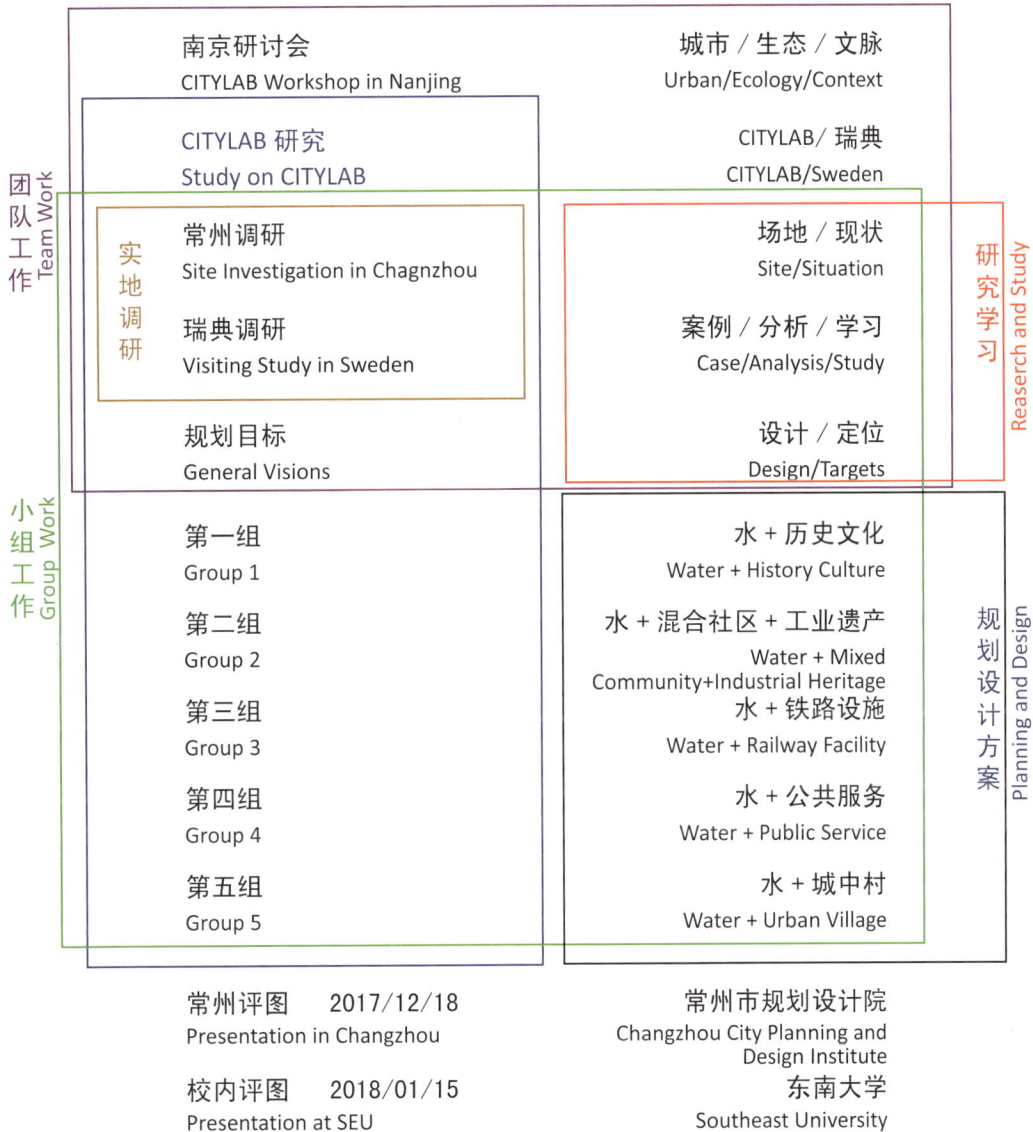

团队工作
Team Work

小组工作
Group Work

实地调研

研究学习
Reaserch and Study

规划设计方案
Planning and Design

南京研讨会
CITYLAB Workshop in Nanjing

城市 / 生态 / 文脉
Urban/Ecology/Context

CITYLAB 研究
Study on CITYLAB

CITYLAB/ 瑞典
CITYLAB/Sweden

常州调研
Site Investigation in Chagnzhou

场地 / 现状
Site/Situation

瑞典调研
Visiting Study in Sweden

案例 / 分析 / 学习
Case/Analysis/Study

规划目标
General Visions

设计 / 定位
Design/Targets

第一组
Group 1

水 + 历史文化
Water + History Culture

第二组
Group 2

水 + 混合社区 + 工业遗产
Water + Mixed
Community+Industrial Heritage

第三组
Group 3

水 + 铁路设施
Water + Railway Facility

第四组
Group 4

水 + 公共服务
Water + Public Service

第五组
Group 5

水 + 城中村
Water + Urban Village

常州评图　　2017/12/18
Presentation in Changzhou

常州市规划设计院
Changzhou City Planning and
Design Institute

校内评图　　2018/01/15
Presentation at SEU

东南大学
Southeast University

CITYLAB 南京研讨会
CITYLAB Workshop in Nanjing

由东南大学建筑学院、瑞典绿色建筑委员会、江苏省城镇化和城乡规划研究中心主办，东南大学建筑学院承办的"CITYLAB 南京研讨会"于 2018 年 6 月 6 日—6 月 8 日召开。

研讨会的主题是介绍瑞典 CITYLAB 体系的相关情况，并探讨其在中国建设背景下应用的可能性。过去 7 年间，CITYLAB 在数千名瑞典专业人士参与下，服务于可持续城市理念，已发展成为一整套完整的规划支撑体系。在瑞典，超过 20 个城市的可持续发展项目受益于 CITYLAB 机制。CITYLAB 不会取代地方政府的现有规划系统，而是支持不同参与者和项目之间的合作及经验交流，并为此制定了行动指南。本次研讨会致力于通过经验和技术交流，在瑞典 CITYLAB、东南大学建筑学院、江苏省规划研究机构和地方政府之间建立强有力的伙伴关系与协作机制，从而使各方在可持续城市发展领域的工作中受益。研讨会选取江苏正在进行的相关项目作为案例，讨论 CITYLAB 用于支持中国可持续城市规划的途径。

"CITYLAB Workshop in Nanjing" organized by the School of Architecture at Southeast University and the Sweden Green Building Council, the Urbanization and Urban Rural Planning Research Center of Jiangsu was held from June 6 to June 8, 2018.

The general theme in the workshop is to introduce CITYLAB and to discuss how it could be used in a Chinese context. CITYLAB has been developed by thousands of actors in Sweden during 7 years into a system to support in planning of more sustainable city areas. More than 20 city projects have been involved in CITYLAB in Sweden. CITYLAB does not replace existing planning systems in municipalities but rather supports the cooperation and experience exchange between different actors and projects. For this purpose, a Guideline has been developed. The purpose of the first workshop is to find mechanisms to develop a strong partnership between CITYLAB in Sweden, the School of Architecture at SEU, the planning research institutes in Jiangsu Province, and the local governments. This partnership should lead to benefit for all partners in the work for more sustainable urban development. The workshop chose some on going projects in Jiangsu where a more detailed discussion about how and what from CITYLAB can be used to support Chinese planning.

与会人员 Participants

Sweden 瑞典

Tomas Gustafsson, Senior Advisor, CITYLAB Action, Sweden Green Building Council
托马斯·古斯塔夫松，CITYLAB 高级顾问，瑞典绿色建筑委员会
Sigrid Walve, Head of CITYLAB, Sweden Green Building Council
西格丽德·沃尔夫，CITYLAB 主任，瑞典绿色建筑委员会
Liu Hongling, Project Coordinator, CITYLAB Action, Sweden Green Building Council
刘泓伶，CITYLAB 项目协调员，瑞典绿色建筑委员会
Ann-Kristin Belkert, Senior Expert, CITYLAB Action, Sweden Green Building Council
安-克里斯汀·贝尔克特，CITYLAB 高级专家，瑞典绿色建筑委员会
Jenni Brink, Sustainability Coordinator, Täby Municipality Government
珍妮·布林克，可持续发展协调员，瑞典泰比市政府

Government Actors 政府管理部门

Chen Xiaohui, Professor, Director of National Resources Department of Jiangsu, Director of Urbanization and Urban Rural Planning Research Center of Jiangsu
陈小卉，教授，江苏省自然资源厅处长，江苏省城镇化和城乡规划研究中心主任
Luo Haiming, Director of Master Planning Office, Nanjing Urban Planning Bureau
罗海明，处长，总规处，南京市规划局

Planning Institute 规划机构

Ye Xingping, Chief Planner, Urbanization and Urban Rural Planning Research Center of Jiangsu
叶兴平，总规划师，江苏省城镇化和城乡规划研究中心
Dai Guowen, Director of the Institute of Ecology, China Eco-city Academy
戴国雯，生态所所长，中国生态城市研究院

SEU 东南大学

Zhang Tong, Professor, Dean, Architecture Department, SEU-ARCH
张彤，教授，院长，建筑系，东南大学建筑学院
Ronald Wennersten, Professor, Architecture Internationalization Demonstration School, SEU
罗纳德·维纳斯特，教授，东南大学建筑国际化示范学院
Jiang Hong, Associate Professor, Deputy Director, Department of Urban Planning, SEU-ARCH
江泓，副教授，城市规划系副系主任，东南大学建筑学院
Fang Rong, Architect, Architecture Design and Research Institute of SEU
方榕，建筑师，东南大学建筑设计研究院
Xue Song, National registered planner, Director of No.3 Planning Office, Urban Planning Research Institute of SEU
薛松，国家注册规划师，规划三所所长，东南大学城市规划设计研究院

Wu Jinxiu, Professor, Department of Landscape Architecture, SEU-ARCH
吴锦绣，教授，景观学系，东南大学建筑学院
Zhang Meiying, Associate Professor, Architecture Department, SEU-ARCH
张玫英，副教授，建筑系，东南大学建筑学院
Quan Yaling, Lecturer, Department of Urban Planning, SEU-ARCH
权亚玲，讲师，城市规划系，东南大学建筑学院
Yin Ming, Lecturer, Department of Urban Planning, SEU-ARCH
殷铭，讲师，城市规划系，东南大学建筑学院
Zhou Xin, Lecturer, Institute of Building Technology and Science, SEU-ARCH
周欣，讲师，建筑技术与科学研究所，东南大学建筑学院
Xu Jin, Lecturer, Department of Urban Planning, SEU-ARCH
徐瑾，讲师，城市规划系，东南大学建筑学院

CITYLAB 研究
Study on CITYLAB

瑞典是世界上在可持续城市规划和建设方面走在世界前列的国家。许多成功的可持续城市建设案例给瑞典带来了深远的影响和瞩目的国际声誉。

瑞典绿色建筑委员会（SGBC）是一家会员制的非政府组织。现有 350 家会员单位，包括公司、政府和科研机构等，涵盖了从研究、规划、设计、建筑施工以及后期使用维护等与城市建设全过程相关的各个领域。瑞典绿色建筑委员会主要提供绿色建筑的评定和认证以及与各种认证体系相关的课程和培训。

Sweden is the leading country in the world of sustainable urban planning and construction. Many successful examples of sustainable urban development have brought far-reaching influence and impressive international reputation to Sweden.

The Sweden Green Building Council (SGBC) is a membership-based NGO. The existing 350 member units, including companies, government and scientific research institutions, cover various fields related to the whole process of urban construction, from research, planning, design, construction and post-use maintenance. SGBC mainly provides assessment and certification of green buildings, as well as courses and training related to various certification systems.

图片来源：CITYLAB 行动导则

CITYLAB 是一系列辅助可持续城市规划与建设的工具
CITYLAB is a range of tools to assist in sustainable urban planning and development.

第三方质量认证
Third-party quality certification

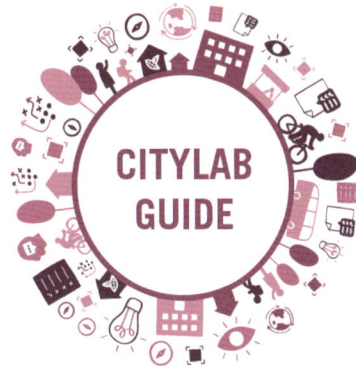

可持续规划指南
Guidance of sustainable development

信息和解决方案分享平台
Information and solution sharing platform

课程培训
Course training

CITYLAB 是瑞典绿色建筑委员会开发创立的可持续城市规划、建设与评估的辅助工具和经验交流平台，包括 CITYLAB 行动和 CITYLAB 网络。CITYLAB 行动主要用于支持具有可持续目标的城市开发项目，以及在城市规划中实现这些可持续目标。CITYLAB 网络举办可持续城市开发的研讨，并定期举行会议。任何人都可以加入 CITYLAB 网络，成为会员并建立与业内人士或机构的联系。

CITYLAB 涵盖了城市规划、建设与使用维护的整个过程，可以为可持续城市建设提供全方位的技术支持。

CITYLAB is a auxiliary tool and an experience exchange platform for sustainable urban planning, construction and evaluation. Initiated by Sweden Green Building Council (SGBC), CITYLAB consists of CITYLAB Action and CITYLAB Network. CITYLAB primarily supports urban development projects in formulating sustainability targets and ensuring that those targets are achieved within the urban planning process. CITYLAB Network holds inspirational seminars in sustainable urban development and regular meetings. Anyone can join the CITYLAB Network, and establish contacts with people or institutions in the industry by becoming a member.

CITYLAB covers the entire process of urban planning, construction and maintenance, and provides comprehensive technical support for sustainable urban development.

图片来源：CITYLAB 行动导则

CITYLAB 行动导则主要组成
The Main Components of The CITYLAB Guide

CITYLAB GUIDE

	简介	Introduction
	总体可持续发展目标	Overall Sustainability Development Goals
	现状描述	Description of Existing Conditions
	项目愿景	Project Vision
	项目目标	Project Goals
	流程管理	Process Management
	重点领域	Focus Areas
	概念界定	List of Definitions

图片来源：CITYLAB 行动导则

CITYLAB GUIDE

基本原则
BASIC PRINCIPLE

因地制宜	Local Conditions
系统的流程管理	System Process Management
定性的而非对细节的控制	Qualitative Targeting Before Micro-management
透明和鼓励分享的环境	Sharing Culture and Transparency
平等和参与	Inclusive Interaction
有利于创新的环境	Innovation-driven Development
相互促进的投资	Mutually Reinforcing Investment

流程管理
PROCESS MANAGEMENT

组织结构	Organization Structure
合作机制	Cooperation Mechanism
各方的广泛参与	Broad Participation of all Parties
信息交流机制	Information Exchange Mechanism
创造有利于创新的环境	Create an Environment Conducive to Innovation

重点领域
FOCUS AREAS

功能	Function
开发结构	Development Structure
场地	Place
学习环境	Learning Setting
文化遗产	Cultural Heritage
本地服务和就业	Local Supplier and Labor
交通	Transportation
信息通信技术	Information and Communication Technology
空气	Air
照明	Lighting
噪声	Sound
蓝绿结构	Blue and Green Structure
气候适应性	Climate Adaptation
物质流动	Material Flow
产品	Product
水	Water
能源	Energy

总体可持续发展目标
OVERALL SUSTAINABILITY DEVELOPMENT GOALS

健康与幸福感	Good Health and Well-being
性别平等、机会均等与社会凝聚力	Gender Equality, Equal Opportunities, and Social Cohesion
高度参与和影响	Participation and Influence
安全的生活环境	Safe Living Environment
良好的就业条件	Good Conditions for Employment
有吸引力的城市生活	Attractive City Life
良好的资源管理	Resource Management
对气候没有负面影响	No Negative Impact on the Climate
对环境没有负面影响	No Negative Impact on the Environment
良好的弹性和灵活性	Resilience and Flexibility

图片来源：CITYLAB 行动导则

1.Function
功能

17.Energy
能源

2.Development
Structure
开发结构

16.Water
水

3.Place
场地

15.Product
产品

4.Learning
Setting
学习环境

**CITYLAB´S 10 OVERALL
SUSTAINABILITY GOALS**
10 个总体可持续发展目标

1. Good health and well-being 健康和幸福感
2. Gender equality, equal opportunities, and social cohesion
性别平等、机会均等和良好的社会凝聚力
3. Participation and influence 高度参与和影响
4. Safe living environment 安全的生活环境
5. Good conditions for employment 良好的就业条件
6. Attractive city life 有吸引力的城市生活
7. Resource management 良好的资源管理
8. No negative impact on the climate
对气候没有负面影响
9. No negative impact on the environment
对环境没有负面影响
10. Resilience and flexibility
良好的弹性和灵活性

14.Material Flow
物质流动

5.Cultural
Heritage
文化遗产

13.Climate
Adaptation
气候适应性

6.Local
Supplier and
Labor
本地服务
和就业

12.Blue and
Green Structure
蓝绿结构

7.Transportation
交通

11.Sound
噪声

8.ICT
信息通信技术

10.Lighting
照明

9.Air
空气

图片来源：CITYLAB 行动导则

Rosendal
Uppsala

Masthuggskajen
Göteborg

Stadsläkning
Lagersdal, Eskilstuna

Norrtälje Hamn
Norrtälje

DrottningH
Helsingborg

Täby Park
Täby

Barkarbystaden TRE
Järfälla

Solna Business Park
Solna

Arninge Ullna
Täby

Borlänge Västra
Borlänge

Kista Strukturplan
Stockholm

Kungens kurva
Huddinge

Kristineberg
Vallentuna

NEXT
Norrköping

Nydala Sjöstad
Umeå

Sege Park
Malmö

图片来源：CITYLAB 行动导则

常州调研
Site Investigation in Changzhou

一座拥有 2600 多年历史的国家历史文化名城。
A national historical heritage city with more than 2600 years' history.

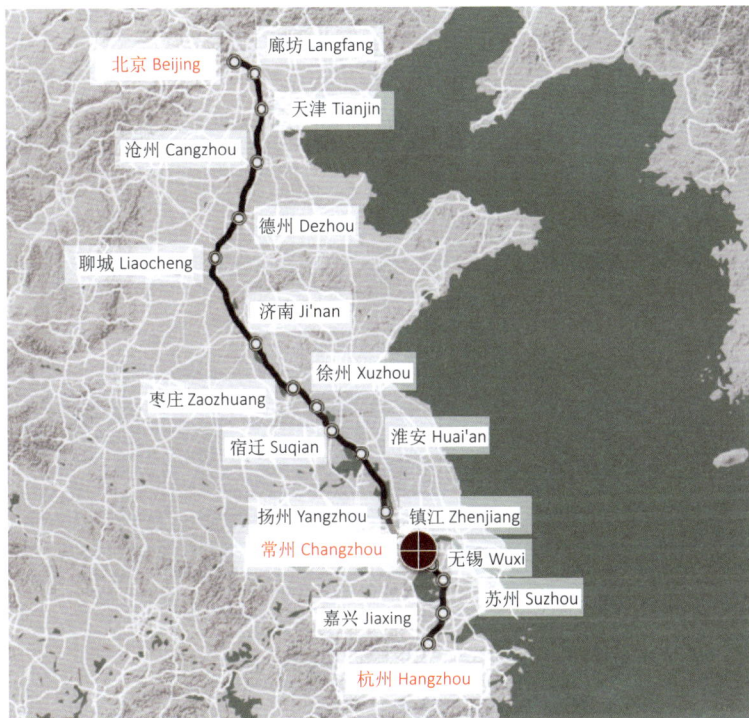

常州内城水系
The canal system of inner Changzhou city

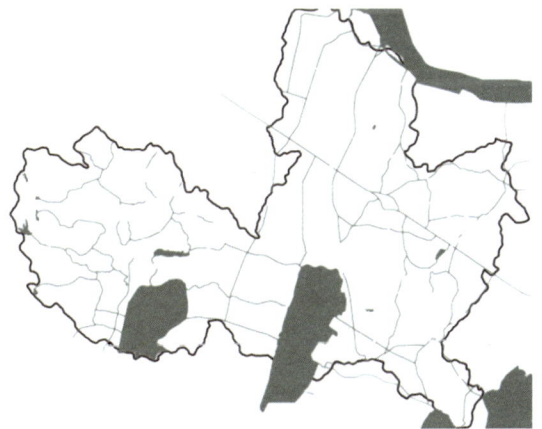

常州水系
Networks of water, Changzhou area

京杭大运河建于 6 世纪，从杭州到北京，总长 1747 公里，是世界上最长最古老的运河，贯穿 18 个城市。常州是唯一一座运河穿过内城的城市。

The Grand Canal, built in 6th century, from Hangzhou to Beijing with the total distance of 1747 km, is the longest and oldest canal in the world, running through 18 cities. Changzhou is the only one that the canal passes through its inner city.

自公元 581 年（隋朝）开始，因为经济上和政治上的原因，中国南方和北方迫切希望加强联系，常州作为在运河旁边的城市开始繁荣起来。在宋朝和清朝，常州已经成为运河上的交通枢纽城市。

常州古城因河而生，因河而兴，逐渐形成以"古运河、明运河、关河"围合的"内子城、外子城、罗城、新城"城河相套的"三河四城"格局。

From the Sui Dynasty A.D. 581, when south and north China were eager to strengthen ties for economic and political reasons, Changzhou flourished as a city on the side of a canal. During the Song and Qing Dynasties, Changzhou became a transportation hub on the canal.

The ancient city of Changzhou was born and flourished because of rivers. The pattern of "Three Rivers and Four Cities" gradually formed, which consists of "Inner Zicheng, Outer Zicheng, Luocheng and New Town" surrounded by "Old Canal, Ming Canal and Guan River".

运河的历史沿革 Evolution of the canal

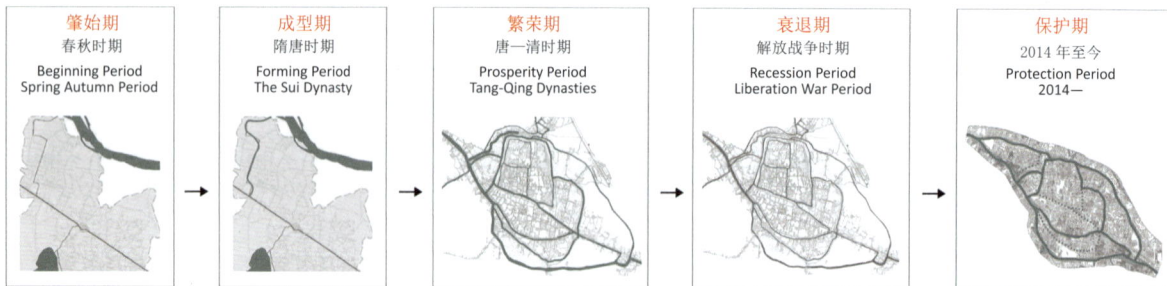

肇始期	成型期	繁荣期	衰退期	保护期
春秋时期	隋唐时期	唐—清时期	解放战争时期	2014 年至今
Beginning Period Spring Autumn Period	Forming Period The Sui Dynasty	Prosperity Period Tang-Qing Dynasties	Recession Period Liberation War Period	Protection Period 2014—

主要河道演变 Evolution of main rivers

卧龙湾
护城河
锁桥湾
顾塘河
唐家湾
古运河
大运河

1913　　　1958　　　2012

——既有的河道
┅┅消失的河道

天宁——老城区 Tianning—The Old District

天宁区位于常州市区东北部，常州与无锡交接之地，东、北部与常州新北区、无锡江阴市接壤，南与武进、经开区横山桥镇相邻，西接钟楼区。辖区面积 154 平方公里。大运河穿城而过，拥有青果巷、前后北岸等历史文化街区。

中心老城区板块（人文老城）：由 4 个半街道组成，它们是茶山街道、红梅街道、天宁街道、兰陵街道，以及青龙街道部分。老城区面积 37.6 平方公里。

天宁城区内水网较多，区域内骨干河道 7 条，支河 8 条，总长度 52.5 公里，骨干河道功能以引水、排水、行洪、生态景观为主。

Tianning District is located in the northeast of Changzhou City, near the junction between Changzhou and Wuxi. The east and north of this district is next to Xinbei District and Wuxi Jiangyin City. The south of Tianning is next to Wujin and Hengshanqiao Town in Jingkai District. The west of Tianning is next to Zhonglou District. Tianning district covers 154 square kilometers. The Grand Canal passes through the city. This district also has some historical and cultural blocks such as Qingguo Lane and Qianhoubei'an.

Central Old District (humanistic old town): it consists of four and a half streets, which are Chashan Street, Hongmei Street, Tianning Street, Lanling Street and Qinglong Street. The old district is about 37.6 square kilometers.

There are many water networks in Tianning District. There are 7 main rivers and 8 branch rivers with a total length of 52.5 kilometers. The main functions of rivers are water diversion, drainage, flood discharge and ecological landscape.

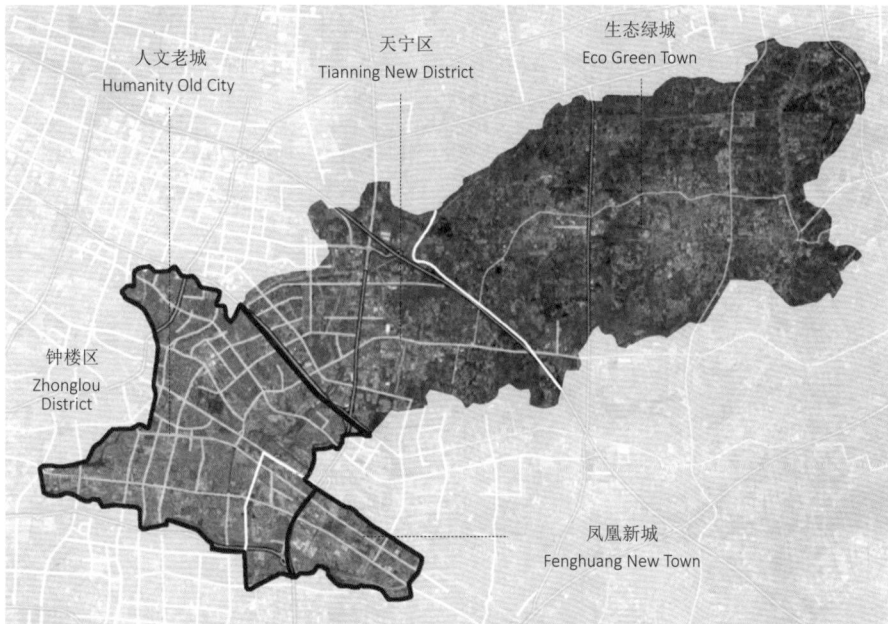

常州天宁区
Tianning District, Changzhou

人文老城
Humanity Old City

天宁区
Tianning New District

生态绿城
Eco Green Town

钟楼区
Zhonglou District

凤凰新城
Fenghuang New Town

稳定"蓝绿体系"构筑生态网络本底

Stabilize the "blue and green system"+Build an ecological network background

- 稳定 14 处大型公园，构建 50 公里线性廊道，形成天宁区 "翡翠项链"。
- 疏通河道网络，全域构建 52.5 公里滨水生态环。

· Stabilize 14 large parks and build a 50-kilometer linear corridor to form "jade necklace" in Tianning District.
· Dredge the river network and build a 52.5 kilometers waterfront ecological ring.

构建"快廊慢网"形成出行网络骨架

Construct "fast corridor & slow network"+Form network skeleton

- 打造 12 条功能复合的主要通勤廊道，满足中长距离出行需求。
- 新增 28.7 公里慢行绿道网络，提高慢行出行品质。

· This transportation system will consist of twelve main functional highways which can meet the medium and long distance travelling demand.
· A new 28.7 kilometers green transportation network will be constructed to improve the travelling standard of slow line.

塑造"活力中心"完善服务网络体系

Shape "vitality center" + Improve service network system

- 优化 8 处现状活力中心，切实提升老城区竞争力。
- 分类预控 5 处新增活力中心，构建全域活力集聚场所。

· This entertainment center system is expected to optimize the exsisted 8 entertainment centers, which will considerablely increase the competitiveness of old city center.
· It will be added five new entertainment centers to construct the entertainment facilities and sites for the whole city.

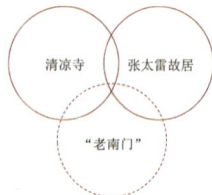

清凉寺　张太雷故居

"老南门"

延伸"日常生活"营造社区生活圈和街巷网络

Extend "daily life"+Build community life circle and street network

- 预控 13 片公共服务设施用地，形成全覆盖的社区设施体系。
- 建设全域贯通的社区滨水和慢行街巷网。

· This requires to preplan 13 sites of community facilities forming a fully functional community system.
· The government will build the community waterfront flowing through the whole city and the walkway lane system.

图片来源：江苏省城镇化和城乡规划研究中心

围绕"以人为本"要求，集成"自然生态空间、城市公共空间、城市公共服务、城市基础设施"，实现多网融合、特色引领天宁区规划。

According the "human-oriented" requirements, "natural ecological space, urban public space, urban public services, urban infrastructure" need to be combined together, so that the Tianning District planning will realize multi-network integration and be leaded by characteristics.

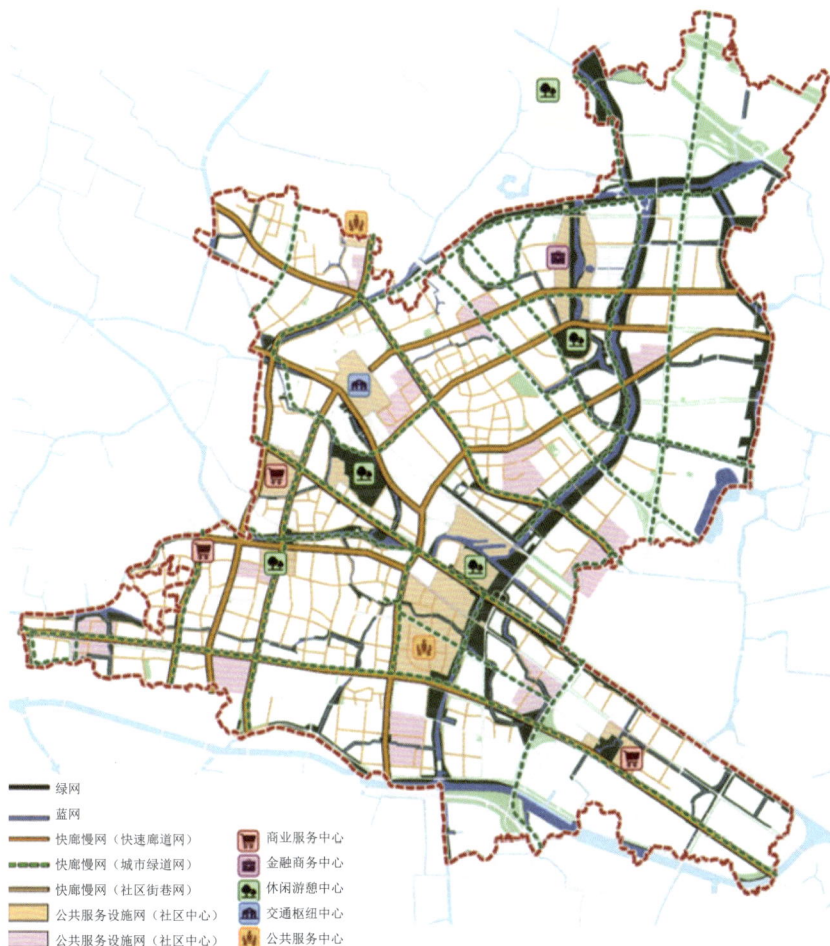

绿网
蓝网
快廊慢网（快速廊道网）
快廊慢网（城市绿道网）
快廊慢网（社区街巷网）
公共服务设施网（社区中心）
公共服务设施网（社区中心）

商业服务中心
金融商务中心
休闲游憩中心
交通枢纽中心
公共服务中心

图片来源：江苏省城镇化和城乡规划研究中心

组 1：同济桥
Group 1: Tongji Bridge

基地紧邻常州市老城与京杭大运河，位于城市发展轴和平东路上，在常州占据重要的地理位置。同济桥横跨运河连接老城厢内外，周围密集分布着商业设施和教育设施。地块中的组成因素较为复杂，有丰富的历史文化要素，如全国重点文物保护单位张太雷故居和省级重点文物保护单位清凉禅寺等，其他要素还有两所中学、城中村以及地面停车场等。周围有数码城、家居城等大型商业设施，且一南一北连接着规划地铁站同济桥和清凉寺站。

The site is close to the old city of Changzhou and the Grand Canal, located on the urban development axis and Heping East Road, occupying an important position in Changzhou. Tongji Bridge across the canal connects the old city inside and outside, surrounded by dense distribution of commercial facilities and educational facilities. There are a lot of historical and cultural elements in the plot, such as Zhang Tailei's Residence, the national cultural heritage unit and the Qingliang Temple, a provincial cultural heritage unit. Other elements include two middle schools, urban villages and ground parking lots. It is surrounded by digital city, home city and other large commercial facilities, and connected with the planned subway station Tongji Bridge and Qingliang Temple in the south and north.

南门集庆 **+** 运河文化展示带 **+** 规划市级绿道系统

常州自隋朝以来形成"三河四城""城河相套"的城市格局。基地中的核心要素是水和历史文化，因其同时兼有常州最鲜明的两个标志——老城厢与大运河。且基地位于运河文化展示带上，是滨河的重要节点"南门集庆"。同时在城市级的公共空间系统中两条重要的城市绿道经过地块。场地在历史上被称为老南门街区，而老南门地区自明清两代开始，就云集了常州的许多商家，也是常州最早的商业街区。

Since ancient times, Changzhou has been a city pattern of "three rivers and four cities" and "city and river interlaced". The core elements of the site are water and history and culture, as they combine the two most distinctive symbols of Changzhou—the old city chamber and the Grand Canal. Moreover, the base is located in the canal culture exhibition zone, which is an important node of the riverside "south gate gathering". Meanwhile, two important urban greenways pass through the plot in the urban-level public space system. The site is historically known as the Old South Gate District, and the Old South Gate District had gathered many merchants in Changzhou since the Ming and Qing Dynasties. It is also the earliest commercial district in Changzhou.

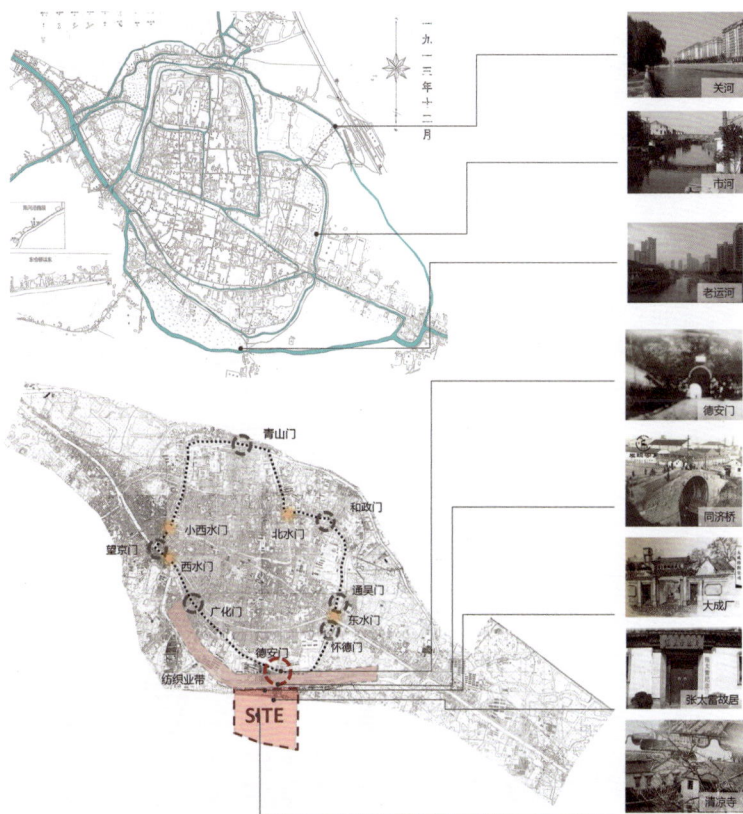

基地现状要素较为复杂，地块由两条城市级道路穿越。周边商业密布，基地内部拥有丰富的历史资源点，如全国重点文物保护单位张太雷故居及中国青运史馆常州馆和省级文物保护单位清凉禅寺，其他要素有学校、城中村、地面停车场等。

The current elements of the base are complex, and the plot is traversed by two city-level roads. Surrounded by densely commercial areas, the base has rich historical resource points inside, such as Zhang Tailei's Former Residence and the Changzhou Museum of Chinese Youth Sports History, a national cultural relic protection unit, and the Qingliang Temple, a provincial cultural relic protection unit. Other elements include schools, urban villages, and ground parking lots.

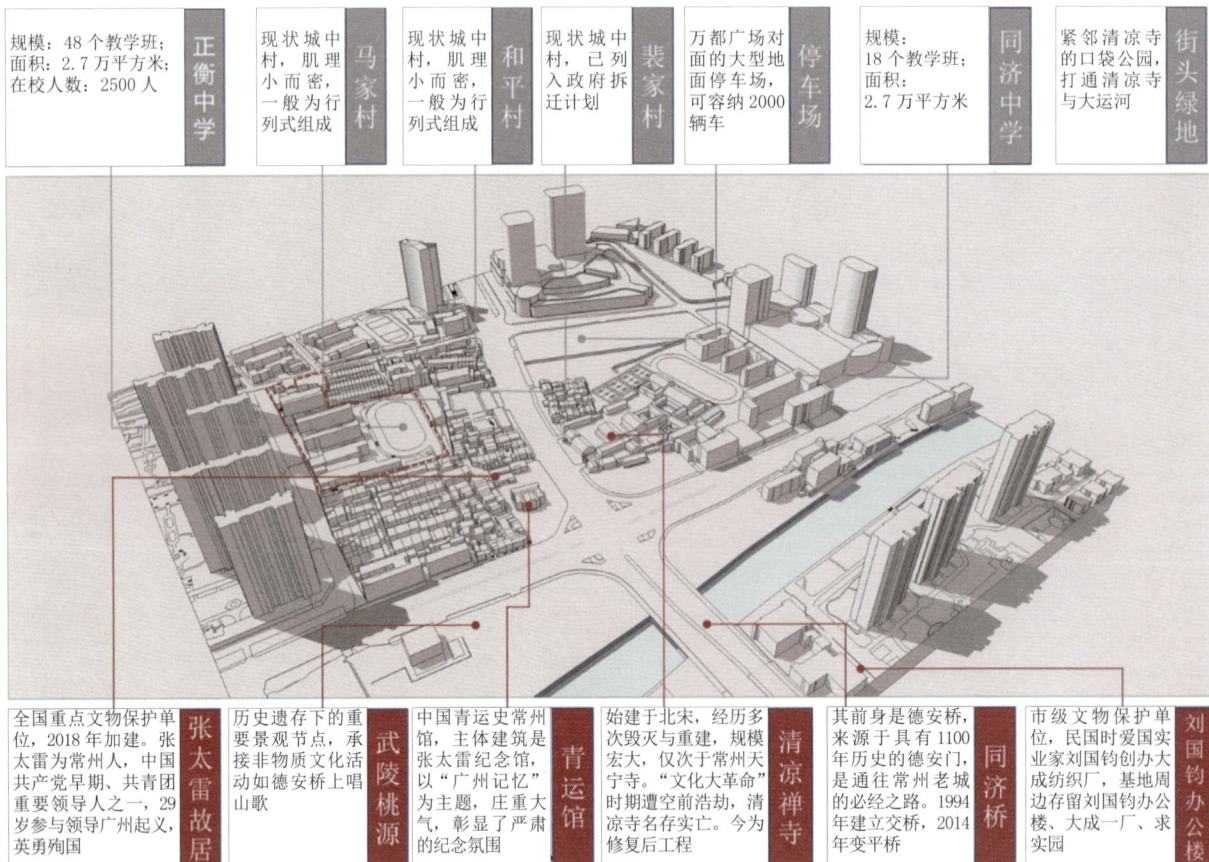

规模：48 个教学班；面积：2.7 万平方米；在校人数：2500 人 — **正衡中学**

现状城中村，肌理小而密，一般为行列式组成 — **马家村**

现状城中村，肌理小而密，一般为行列式组成 — **和平村**

现状城中村，已列入政府拆迁计划 — **裴家村**

万都广场对面的大型地面停车场，可容纳 2000 辆车 — **停车场**

规模：18 个教学班；面积：2.7 万平方米 — **同济中学**

紧邻清凉寺的口袋公园，打通清凉寺与大运河 — **街头绿地**

全国重点文物保护单位，2018 年加建。张太雷为常州人，中国共产党早期、共青团重要领导人之一，29 岁参与领导广州起义，英勇殉国 — **张太雷故居**

历史遗存下的重要景观节点，承接非物质文化活动如德安桥上唱山歌 — **武陵桃源**

中国青运史常州馆，主体建筑是张太雷纪念馆，以"广州记忆"为主题，庄重大气，彰显了严肃的纪念氛围 — **青运馆**

始建于北宋，经历多次毁灭与重建，规模宏大，仅次于常州天宁寺。"文化大革命"时期遭空前浩劫，清凉寺名存实亡。今为修复后工程 — **清凉禅寺**

其前身是德安桥，来源于具有 1100 年历史的德安门，是通往常州老城的必经之路。1994 年建立交桥，2014 年变平桥 — **同济桥**

市级文物保护单位，民国时爱国实业家刘国钧创办大成纺织厂，基地周边存留刘国钧办公楼、大成一厂、求实园 — **刘国钧办公楼**

明永乐元年（1403）移居现址，常州城外临大运河进香之地
The first year of Yongle in Ming Dynasty (1403), it moved to the current site. Outside Changzhou City, it is adjacent to the Grand Canal.

毗邻民族资本工厂（1930年代）
Adjacent to the national capital factory (1930s)

由于通航需要，同济桥改为立交桥，桥下设立花鸟虫鱼市场
Due to the need of navigation, Tongji Bridge was changed into an overpass, under which a flower, bird, insect and fish market was set up

立改平＋轨道交通（2018）
Interchange to level crossing + rail transit (2018)

宗教圣地（1403）
Religious holy land (1403)

1930年代，常州实业家刘国钧的纺织工厂在地块对侧，与清凉寺共建同济桥
In the 1930s, the textile factory of Liu Guojun, an industrialist in Changzhou, built Tongji Bridge with Qingliang temple on the opposite side of the plot

同济立交桥＋花鸟虫鱼市场（1993）
Tongji overpass + flower, bird, insect and fish market (1993)

由于轨道交通1号线的需要，同济桥需要立交改平交
Due to the need of rail transit line 1, Tongji Bridge needs to be changed from interchange to level crossing

各类文化资源整合

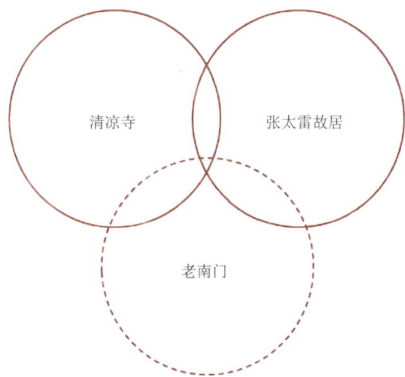

- 梵音唱响的**宗教文化**
- 千年运河的**运河文化**
- 张太雷故居的**红色文化**
- 德安歌台的**市井文化**

城河两条历史文脉
空间叙事
人文两种体验模式

营城　理水　聚人　兴文

水利景观	商业手工业			古建筑		非物质遗产	
大运河　求是园	武进陵桃源	大成纺织厂　沿街商业	万都商业　张太雷故居	清凉禅寺　刘国钧办公楼	德安山歌	龙舟竞渡	清凉法会

清凉寺　　张太雷故居

老南门

基地不仅仅有清凉寺、张太雷故居等历史文化遗产价值，更重要的是作为"老南门"地区在城市中的重要地位，复兴了人们的城市记忆。

The base not only has the value of historical and cultural heritage such as Qingliang Temple and Zhang Tailei's Former Residence, but more importantly is as the important position of the "Old South Gate" area in the city, it revived people's memory of the city.

开发结构 Development Structure

现状问题：

1. 围墙纵横。
There are many walls such as school walls and residential enclosure.
2. 各功能区块联系被割裂。
The disconnection of different functional blocks.
3 区块交通可达性差。
Poor accessibility of transportation.
4. 不同功能区的人隔离，交往极少。
The persons from different function area are isolated and have few contact.

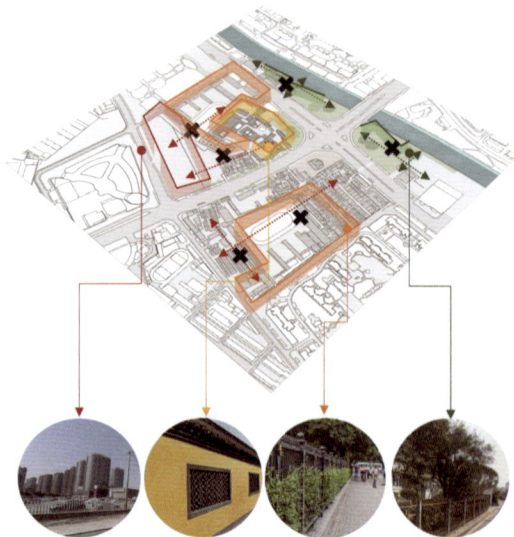

文化遗产 Culture Heritage

现状问题：

1. 基地中有丰富的历史资源点，但内涵挖掘并不深入，文化点并未因此而成为触媒。
There are rich historical resource points in the base, but the connotation mining is not in-depth, and cultural points have not become catalyst.
2. 非物质文化遗产没有得到彰显。
Intangible cultural heritage is not highlighted.
3. 不同文化点之间没有联系，相互隔绝，不能整合成一个整体。
Different cultural points are not connected with each other, isolated from each other, and cannot be integrated into a whole.

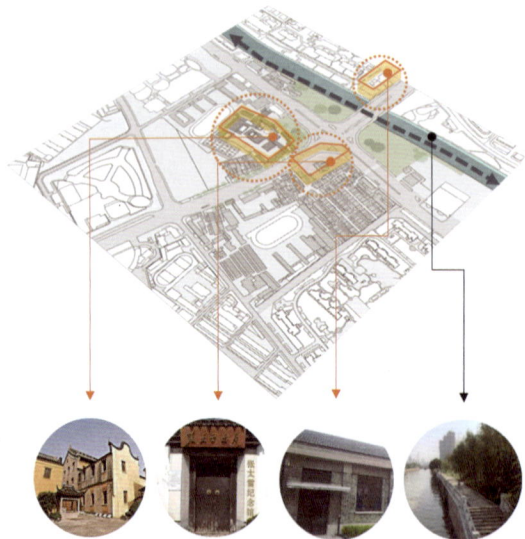

蓝绿结构 Green and Blue Structure

现状问题：

1. 绿地空间总量不足，分配不均。
The total amount of green space is insufficient and unevenly distributed.
2. 公园绿地、绿道网络难以有效串联，存在较多断点。
It is difficult to effectively connect public space networks because there are many breakpoints.
3. 运河和绿地的开放性、感知度不强，人与水的互动性较弱。
The openness and perception of canals and green spaces are not strong, and the interaction between people and water is very weak.

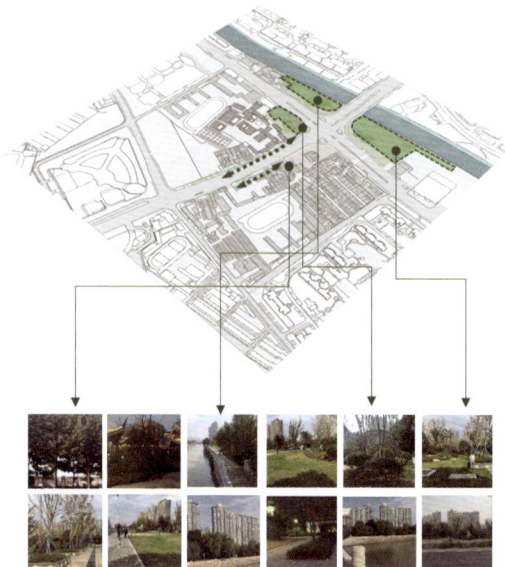

交通 Transportation

现状问题：

1. 地块被城市两条城市道路隔开，行人流线被隔断。
The plot is separated by two roads in the city, and the pedestrian flow line is interrupted.
2. 地块内公共交通资源较为充足，但可达性不好。
There are plenty of public transportation resources in the plot, but the accessibility is not good.
3. 地块内的步行不连续，各功能块之间联系不强。
The walking in the plot is not continuous, and the links between the functional blocks are not strong.
4. 学校周边的交通拥堵问题较为严重。
Traffic congestion around the school is serious.

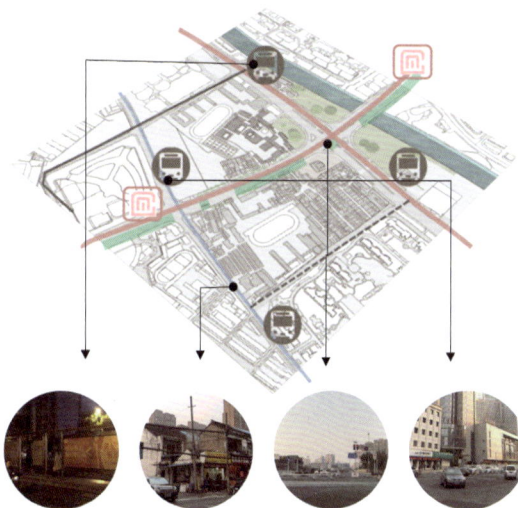

组 2：舣舟亭社区
Group 2: Yizhouting Community

舣舟亭社区位于天宁区的东北侧，毗邻东坡公园与红梅公园，是重要的文化节点与景观节点。场地北侧是延陵中路与市河，西侧的桃园路是整片场地面向城市最大的开放界面。东侧为东坡公园，是市民主要的休憩健身场所。设计场地三面环水，拥有较好的环境特质与自然景观。

但其内部所呈现的复杂性与矛盾性也是整个调研重要的关注点。场地的复杂与矛盾聚焦在不同功能、不同建造时间、不同人群、不同基础设施与社会关系呈现出的边界障碍。由工人社区、城中村、干部疗养院、工业遗迹、军事管制区、寺庙组成的舣舟亭社区存在着各种物理的边界与社会的边界，阻断了沟通，支离了场地。

The Yizhouting Community is located on the northeast side of Tianning District, Changzhou City, adjacent to Dongpo Park and Hongmei Park. It is an important cultural node and landscape node. The north side of the site is Yanling Middle Road and the city river, and the Taoyuan Road on the west side is the largest open interface facing the city. The east side is Dongpo Park, which is the main resting and fitness place for the public. The design site is surrounded by water on three sides and has good environmental characteristics and natural landscape.

However, the complexity and contradiction presented within it are also important concerns of the entire survey. The complexity and contradiction of the site focus on the boundary barriers presented by different functions, different construction time, different groups of people and different infrastructures & social relationships. The Yizhouting Community, which consists of workers' community, city villages, cadres' sanatorium, industrial relics, military control area and temples, has various physical boundaries and social boundaries, blocking communication and separating the site.

场地的航拍呈现出不同的建筑肌理。片区被道路划分成南北两个部分，南侧由大尺度的工业遗迹、工人学校与滨水景观组成，北侧为不同的居住功能组团。

The aerial photography of the site presents different architectural textures. The area is divided into two parts: the south side consists of a large number of industrial relics, workers' schools and waterfront landscapes; the north side is mainly composed of different groups of residential functions.

场地肌理历史变迁 Site Texture History Evolution

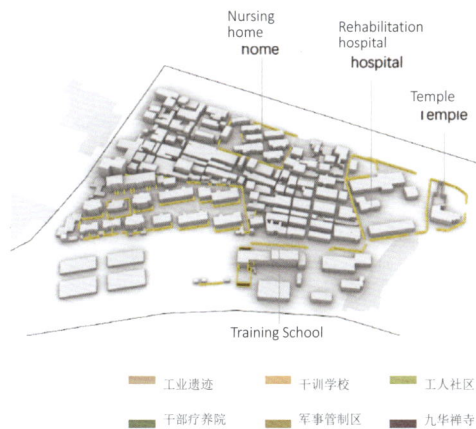

Nursing home

Rehabilitation hospital

Temple

Training School

| | 工业遗迹 | | 干训学校 | | 工人社区 |
| | 干部疗养院 | | 军事管制区 | | 九华禅寺 |

场地的边界障碍 Site Boundary Barrier

1960—1980

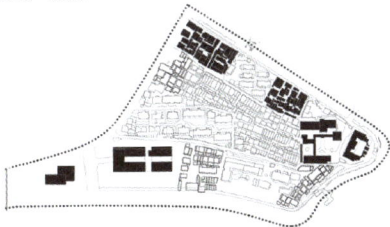

1980—2000

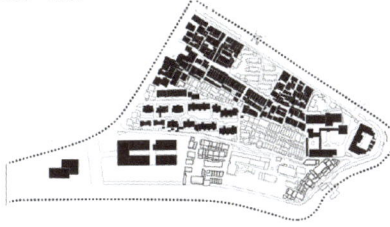

2000—2025

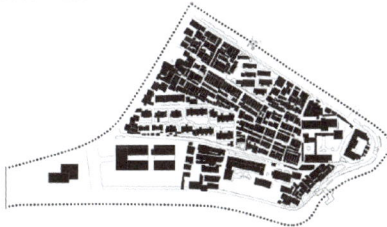

场地边界分析 Site Boundary Analysis

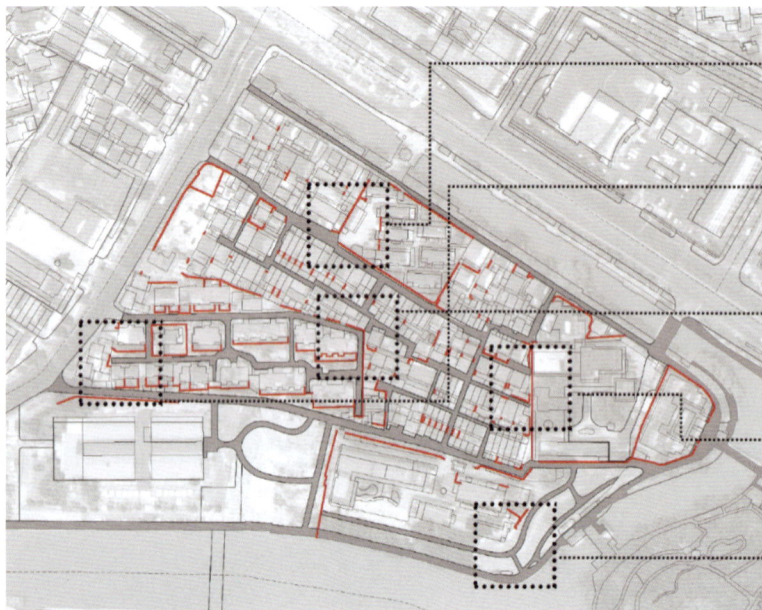

潘家村｜干休所
Panjia Village｜Cadre Recuperation

桃园二村｜街道
Taoyuan Village No. 2｜Street

潘家村｜桃园二村
Panjia Village｜Taoyuan Village No. 2

潘家村｜康复医院
Panjia Village｜Rehabilitation Hospital

干部学校｜运河
Cadre School｜Canal

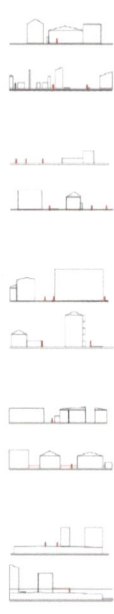

潘家村｜干休所
Panjia Village｜Cadre Recuperation

桃园二村｜街道
Taoyuan Village No. 2｜Street

潘家村｜桃园二村
Panjia Village｜Taoyuan Village No. 2

潘家村｜康复医院
Panjia Village｜Rehabilitation Hospital

干部学校｜运河
Cadre School｜Canal Landscape

潘家村围院　　　潘家村单户　　　桃园二村　　　干休所

居住组团类型
Residential Group Type

  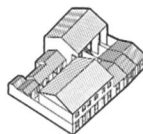 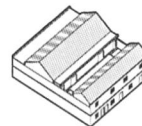

居住组团肌理
Residential Group Texture

   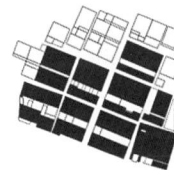

底层平面
Ground Plan

 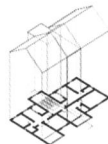  

房屋剖面
Building Section

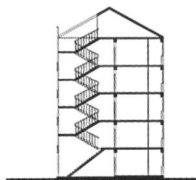  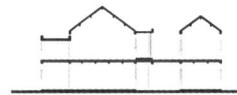

上下交通
Circulation of the Settlement

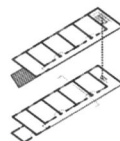  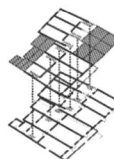 

庭院空间
Yard in the Settlement

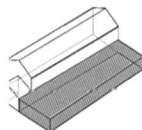 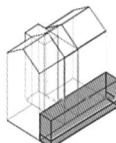 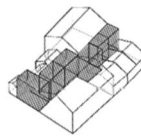 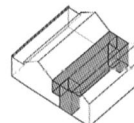

居住空间
Living Part of the Settlement

空间分类
Spatial Classification

   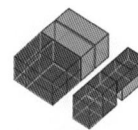
  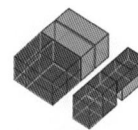

图例 Legend
居住小区 Residential
城中村 City Village
小学 Primary School
幼儿园 Kindergarden
医院 Hospital
寺庙 Temple
军事疗养院 Military sanatorium
工会学校（闲置）Trade Cadre School
公园 Park

Ⅰ 功能 Function

1. 场地与周边功能缺乏联系。2. 场地内部功能缺少联系及互动。
3. 场地内部功能衰退，缺少活力。
1. Lack of connection between site and surrounding function. 2. Lack of connection and interaction within the site .3. The internal function of the site is declining and lacks vitality

活动场地
图例 Legend
半开放的节点 Half-open Node Space
开放的节点 Open Node Space
围墙 Wall

Ⅲ 场地 Place

1. 点状空间（场地）：分散、封闭、缺乏联系，使用较少。
1. Node space : Dispersion, closure, lack of contact, low vitality, less use.

图例 Legend
垂直河岸村落肌理 Village Texture
南北向城市肌理 City Texture 1
垂直河岸城市肌理 City Texture 2
边界 Boundary

Ⅱ 开发结构 Development Structure

1. 场地内部不同发展结构相互冲突，产生很多边界。2. 场地的发展结构与城市的发展结构不匹配。
1. The different development structures within the site conflict with each other and create many boundaries. 2. The development structure of the site does not match the development structure of the city.

滨水绿廊
图例 Legend
滨水绿廊 Greenland
硬质广场 Rigid Square
围墙 Wall

Ⅲ 场地 Place

2. 滨水空间以滨水步行道及绿地为主，部分边界由围墙限定，体验单一。
2. Waterfront space is dominated by waterfront walkways and green spaces, with some boundaries limited by fences and a single experience.

街巷空间

围墙阻隔街巷　围墙阻断街巷　围墙阻断街巷　围墙限定街巷　围墙限定街巷

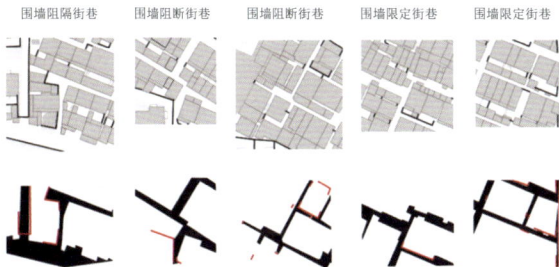

III 场地 Place

3. 由于基地内部围墙、违建的存在，街巷空间或破碎或被阻隔。

3. Because of the existence of wall and illegal construction inside the base, the space of streets and lanes is broken or blocked.

V 文化遗产 Cultural Heritage

1. 工业厂房改造为美食集中营，建筑内部大部分空置，改造后的厂房利用率低，改造成效有限。

1. The industrial plant is transformed into a food concentration camp, and most of the interior of the building is vacant. After transformation, the utilization rate of the plant is low, and the transformation effect is limited.

IV 学习环境 Learning Setting

1. 基地西侧为延陵小学，附近缺少配套服务，上学、放学时间人流、车流量大，造成拥堵。2. 基地南部有一工会干部学校，处于停课状态，教学楼闲置。

1. The west side of the base is Yanling Primary School, lack of supporting services. People flow and traffic flow during school hours cause congestion. 2. There is a trade union cadre school in the south of the base, which is in a state of suspension, and the teaching buildings and venues are idle.

VI 交通 Transportation

1. 场地内部人车混行，步行路径不畅，车行交通路线不明确，造成不便。2. 场地现有一处集中公共停车，内部沿街停车，停车位无法满足需求。

1. Inter-site pedestrians and vehicles mixed, walking path is not smooth, traffic routes are not clear, resulting in inconvenience. 2. There is a centralized public parking spaces in the site. Internal vehicles stop along the street. The parking spaces can not meet the demand.

图例 Legend

kWh/m²

2000
1805
1610
1415
1220
1025
830
635
440
245
<50

Ⅶ 采光 Lighting

1.潘家村民居的采光较差。2.潘家村内部街道阴暗潮湿。
1. The residents of the Panjia Village have poor lighting. 2. The inner streets of Panjia Village are dark and damp.

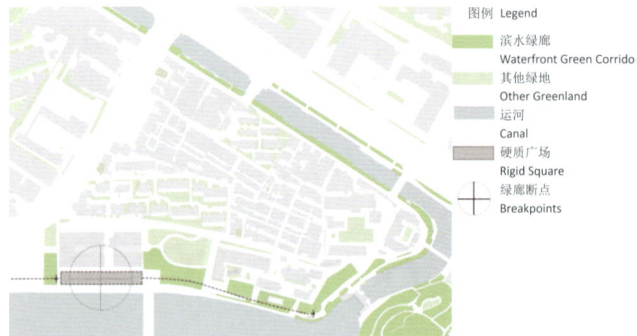

图例 Legend

滨水绿廊
Waterfront Green Corrido
其他绿地
Other Greenland
运河
Canal
硬质广场
Rigid Square
绿廊断点
Breakpoints

Ⅸ 蓝绿结构 Blue and Green Structure

1.滨水绿廊在工业厂房附近存在断点，基地东西两侧绿廊缺少绿地联系。
1. The waterfront green corridor has a breakpoint near the industrial plant, and the green corridor on the east and west sides of the base lacks green space connection.

图例 Legend

噪声
Sound
隔离绿带
Greenland

Ⅷ 噪声 Sound

1.临近桃园路城市主干道一侧噪声污染较大。
1. The noise pollution on the side of Taoyuan Road is relatively large.

图例 Legend

渗水绿地
Seepage Green Space
内涝影响范围
Scope of Waterlogging Impact

Ⅹ 气候适应性 Climate Adaptation

1.运河防洪功能减弱，大暴雨内部易内涝。
1. The canal's flood control function is weakened, and the internal rainstorm is easy.

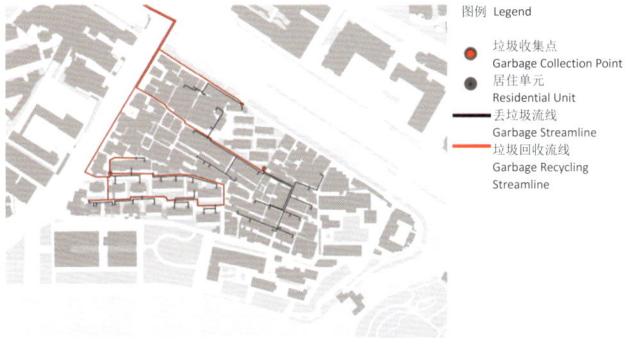

图例 Legend
垃圾收集点
Garbage Collection Point
居住单元
Residential Unit
丢垃圾流线
Garbage Streamline
垃圾回收流线
Garbage Recycling
Streamline

XI 物质流动 Material flow

1. 垃圾处理系统简单低效。2. 绿地生态功能较差。雨水统一排放导致管网压力大。

1. Garbage disposal system is simple and inefficient. 2. The ecological function of green space is poor, and the unified discharge of rainwater leads to pressure on the pipe network.

XII 水 Water

1. 城中村水管外搭现象严重。2. 排水系统不完善。3. 水回收处理欠考虑。4. 暴雨天局部地区易出现积水。

1. The urban water pipe outside the village is serious. 2. Drainage system is not perfect. 3. Water recycling treatment is not considered. 4. Partially prone to water accumulation in heavy rainy days.

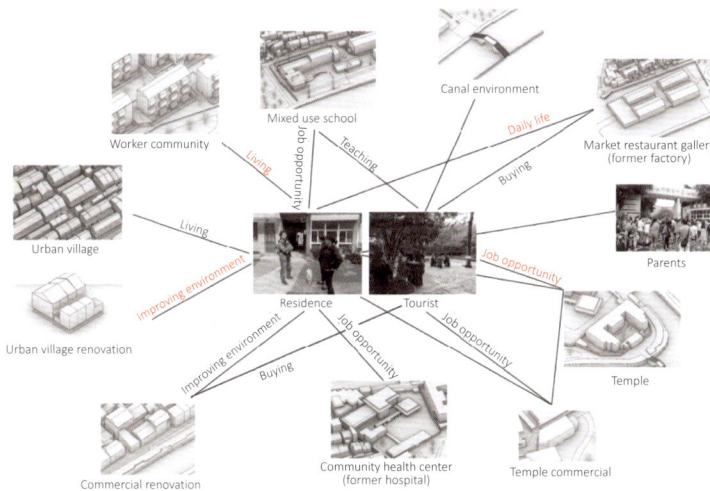

地块生态模型
Land Ecological Model

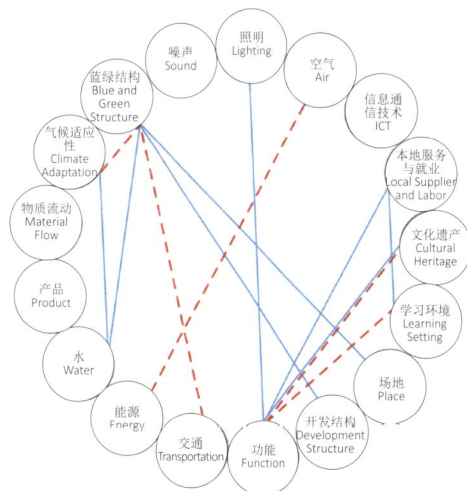

领域协同与矛盾关系
Synergy and Conflict Illustration

组 3: 东货场
Group 3: East Freight Yard

基地位于常州市老城东部，东货场是其中极为重要的组成部分。时至今日，场地内的货运功能依旧在使用，然而随着时代的变迁和城市的进程，单一的货运功能逐渐满足不了城市多元化的发展需求。

在这片土地上，承载了铁路运输、水运的历史文化，承载了纺织、印染等工业文化。这里是横塘河和运河支流交汇的节点，也是蓝绿结构中重要的节点，拥有仓库、铁路、龙门吊等具有价值的遗产。

本场地独特的岸线形式，是历史的沉淀，汇聚了常州城市的记忆。

The site is located in the the east of the old city of Changzhou, and one of its most important part is the Changzhou East Freight Yard. Today, the freight function in the site is still in use; however, with the changes of the time and urban process, the monotonous freight function would gradually fail to meet up with the development's need of urban diversification.

In this land, it carries the history and culture of railway transportation and aquatic transportation and industrial goods such as textile printing and dyeing. It is the node where the Hengtang River and the tributaries of the canal meet. It is also an important node in the blue and green structure. And it possesses valuable heritage such as warehouses, railways and gantry cranes.

The formation of the shoreline form in the site is a sediment of history, which brings together the memories of Changzhou city.

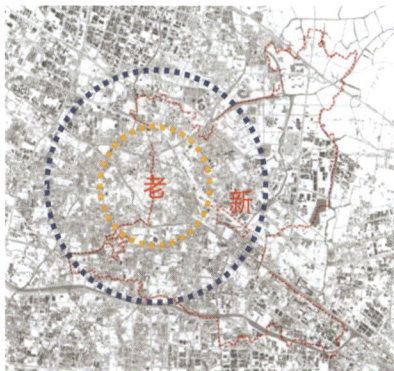

老城区外围
The out-ring of the old city

蓝绿结构交会点
The intersection of blue and green structure

两种现有交通，一种在建交通，一种可能交通
Two kind of existing transportations, one kind of under-construction transportation and one kind of a possibility

周边住区分布
Residential area around the site

周边医疗分布
Hospital area around the site

周边景区分布
Sightseeing area around the site

周边教育分布
Education area around the site

主要问题 Main problem

场地所存在的主要问题是用地权属问题。

基地中核心区域土地现属于常州市东货场，分属上海铁路局南京分局管理。东侧用地归常州市交运集团管理。如何取得土地的使用权、符合现实、合理地进行开发设计是本次城市设计中的难点。

The main problem of the site is the issue of property rights.

The core area of the site is now owned by the Changzhou East Freight Yard and is managed by the Nanjing Branch of the Shanghai Railway Bureau. The land on the east side is managed by Changzhou Transportation Group. Obtaining the right to use the land in accordance with the actual reality rational development and design is crucial in this urban design.

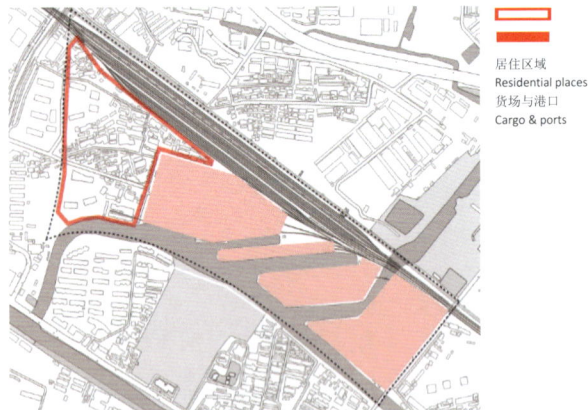

居住区域
Residential places
货场与港口
Cargo & ports

功能 Function

功能较为单一，混合度低。
The function of the base is single, and lowly mixed.
物流功能占地较大，不符合老城发展需求。
The logistics function occupy large land, it does not match the need of development of the old city.

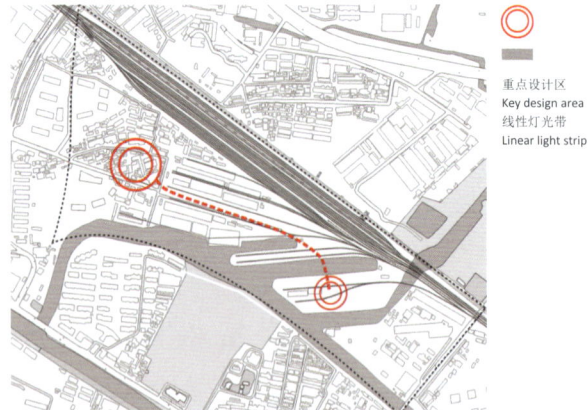

重点设计区
Key design area
线性灯光带
Linear light strip

照明 Lighting

老旧小区内光线暗淡，有安全隐患。
With dim light in the old community, there are security risks.
沿街店铺缺少灯光设计。
Street shops lack lighting design.

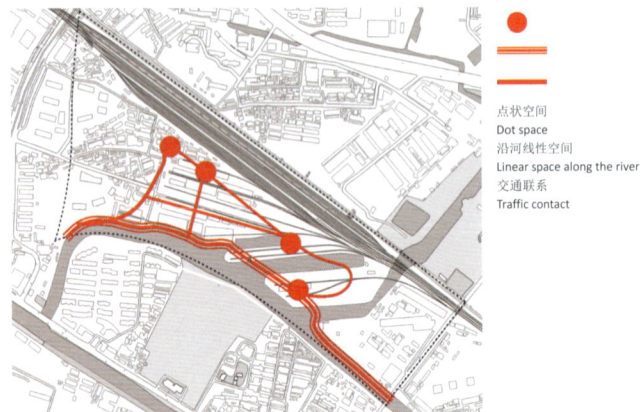

点状空间
Dot space
沿河线性空间
Linear space along the river
交通联系
Traffic contact

场地 Place

沿河公共区可达性低。
Low accessibility in public areas along the river.
好的公共空间景观没有被发掘。
Good public space landscape has not been discovered.

产品输出
Product

产品 Product

物流园区运送煤炭、钢材，对环境影响较大。
The logistics park transports coals and steel products, which has some impact on the environment.
挖沙公司采挖河沙，对运河生态造成破坏。
The dredging company mines the river sand and causes damage to the canal ecology.

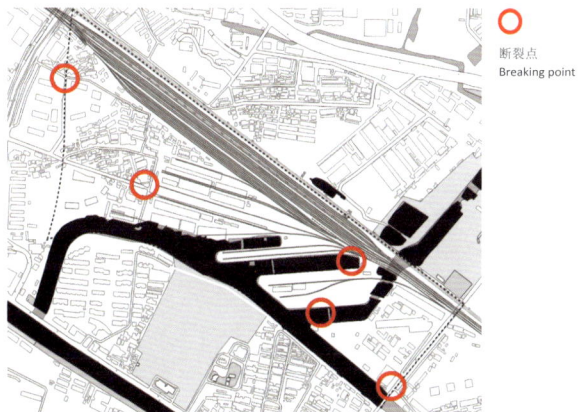

断裂点
Breaking point

开发结构 Development Structure

现有的用地功能与周边割裂较强，未能形成完整和连贯的城市区域

The existing land use function is strongly separated from the surrounding area and fails to form a complete and coherent urban area.

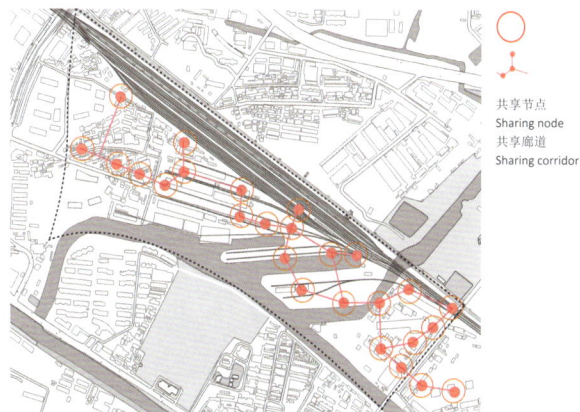

共享节点
Sharing node
共享廊道
Sharing corridor

信息通信技术 ICT

各公共资源间缺乏联系性。
Less of connection between each public resources and functions.
各资源在时间上使用的空档与高峰。
The usage valley and peak of each resources.

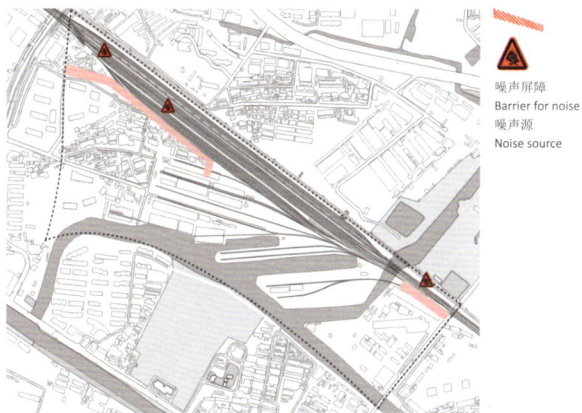

噪声屏障
Barrier for noise
噪声源
Noise source

噪声 Sound

基地北侧噪音影响严重。
Severe influence of noise from the railway on the north.

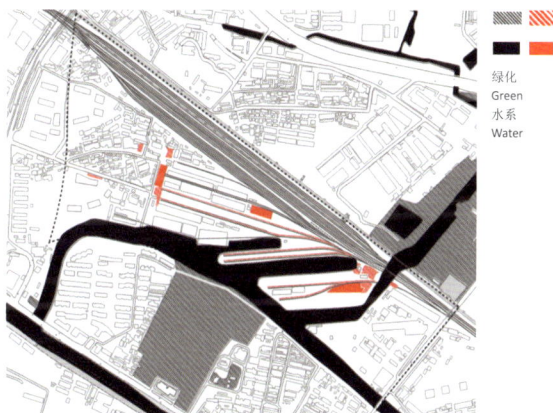

绿化
Green
水系
Water

蓝绿结构 Blue and Green Structure

基地所在地块绿化水系空间良好
The green and blue system is good surround the site.

场地内现有常州购物中心、第二人民医院等单位，南侧紧临青果巷历史文化街区。道路饱和度较高，运营车速较低，交通处于拥堵的临界区域，进一步发展机动车极易产生拥堵。由于商贸和公共服务中心的强吸引，造成周边城区内大量交通向历史城区汇集，潮汐交通明显，给历史城区的交通带来很大压力。场地位于 1、2 号地铁线交会处，将带来复杂的地下交通问题。场地内部停车问题严重，加重了交通拥堵与街道的空间体验。机动车、非机动车、人流混杂，步行环境存在安全隐患。

老城区内功能多样，包括居住生活、文化展示、休闲旅游、商业服务等，主要以公共服务为主。同时老城内城市级设施分布过于集中，基地附近医疗资源过于饱和，带来严重的交通压力。周边教育资源丰富。旅馆数量大，等级不一。地块南北两侧存在两个重要历史文化街区，场地内相应辅助功能缺失。地块内居住小区建筑

There are facilities such as Changzhou Shopping Center and the Second People's Hospital in the plot, and Qingguo Lane historical and cultural block is adjacent to the plot in the south. It has high road saturation, low operating speed, and the traffic is in the critical area of congestion, so further development of motor vehicles is very likely to cause congestion. Due to the strong attraction of the commercial and public service center, a large number of traffic within the plot converged to the historic district, and tidal traffic was obvious, which brought great pressure to the traffic in the historic district. The site is located at the intersection of metro line 1 and line 2, which will bring complex underground traffic, a large number of people and traffic problems with surrounding plots. The parking problem inside the site is serious, which aggravates traffic congestion and spatial occupation of streets. Motor vehicles, non-motor vehicles, mix the flow of people, making the walking environment safety hazard.

There are various functions in the old urban area, including residential life, cultural display, leisure tourism, business services, etc., mainly public services. At the same time, the city level facilities in the old city are too

地块位置

centralized, and the medical resources near the plot are too saturated, which brings serious traffic pressure. The surrounding educational resources are rich. There are a large number of hotels with different grades. There are two important historical and cultural blocks on the north and south sides of the plot, and the corresponding auxiliary functions in the site are missing. The residential buildings in the plot are old and the living environment is poor. There are plots with undetermined functions in and around the plot.

The historical and cultural blocks on the north and south sides of the plot are blocked with little connection, resulting in the dissection of the surrounding texture of the plot. The building height around the plot is out of control. The internal architectural style of the plot is incompatible with the historical block style before and after. The traditional ancient lane is beyond recognition and has lost its life breath and vitality.

The green space inside and outside the site is cut off, the connection is weak, and the green space inside the site lacks vitality. The famous and ancient trees around the plot are isolated and improperly protected. The city river is being forgotten, partly lost to new roads.

老旧，居住环境较差。地块及周边存在功能待定地块。

地块南北两侧历史文化街区被阻断，联系甚微，导致地块周边肌理存在断裂。周边建筑高度失控。地块内部建筑风貌与前后历史街区风貌格格不入。传统古巷面目全非，失去了往日的生活气息与活力。

场地内外绿地隔断，联系薄弱，场地内绿地活力不足。地块周边名木古树孤立，保护不当。城河因新建道路而局部消失，正在被世人遗忘。

CITYLAB 重点领域问题分析
Analysis from the View of the in Focus Areas of CITYLAB

主干道
Main Road
次干道
Secondary Road

低饱和路段
Low saturation section
中饱和路段
Medium saturation section
中高饱和路段
Medium-high saturation section
高饱和路段
High saturation section
机动车饱和交叉口
Vehicle saturation intersection
低饱和点
Low saturation point
中饱和点
Medium saturation point
高饱和点
High saturation point

常规公交线路
Conventional bus lines
专用公交线路
Dedicated bus lines
公交站点
Bus stop
待建轨道交通
Rail transit to be built
轨道交通站点
Rail transit station

严重拥堵路段
Heavily congested road section
较拥堵路段
Congested section

1号线
Line 1
2号线
Line 2

地下停车
Underground parking
非机动车停车
Non motor vehicle parking
机动车停车
Motor vehicle parking
车库出入口
Entrance of the garage

人行路线
Pedestrian route
步行断头点
Walking breakpoint
人车混行严重路段
Serious section of mixed traffic

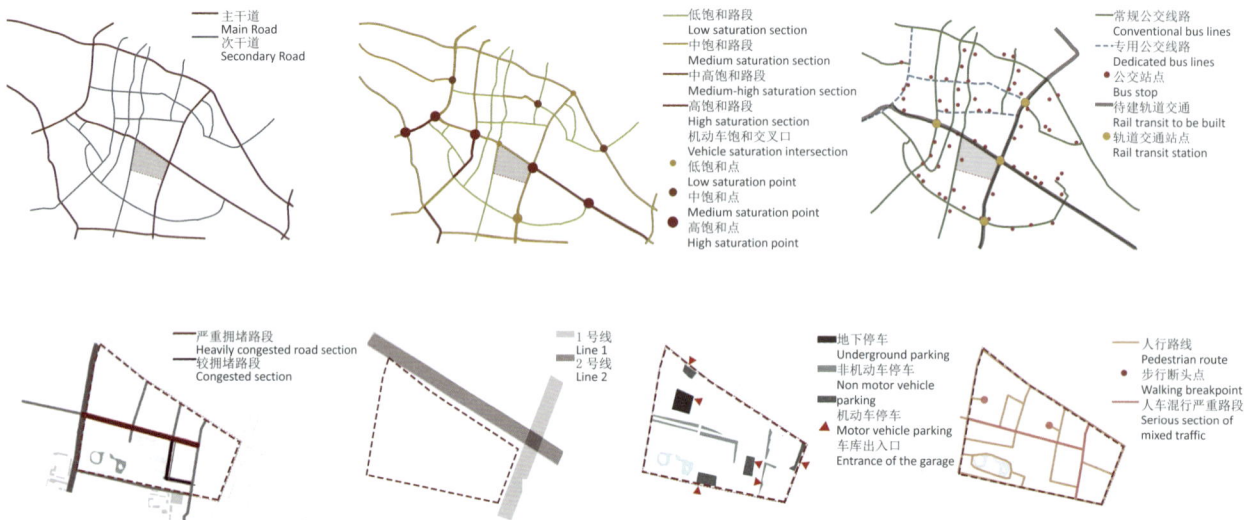

场地位于城市中最主要的主干道交会口。周边交通问题较为复杂：主干道交通饱和度较高，次干道饱和度稍低；主干道与主干道的交会口交通饱和度高，次干道的交会口饱和度较低。

场地附近有健全的公共交通系统，轨道交通和公交车站点分布密度比较高。场地有良好的公共交通条件，可达性好。

场地内部路网密度不足，存在大量断头路，内部道路拥堵现象严重，且停车设施不足，分布不合理。

场地内部人行系统不完善，存在大量人车混行路段，人行系统可达性、安全性差。

The site is located at the intersection of the city's main thoroughfare. Peripheral traffic problems are more complex. The traffic saturation of the main road is higher than that of the secondary road; the intersection of the main road and the main road is higher than that of the secondary road.

There is a sound public transportation system near the site, and the density of rail transit and bus stations is relatively high.The site has good public transportation conditions and good accessibility.

The density of the road network inside the site is insufficient, with a large number of severed roads and serious internal road congestion. There are insufficient parking facilities and unreasonable distribution inside the site.

The indoor pedestrian system of the site is not perfect, and there is a large number of mixed sections of people and vehicles, and the pedestrian system has poor accessibility and safety.

历史文化保护区 ▮▮
Historical area
历史文化展示带 ◄┅►
History display zone

1—3 层
1-3 F
1—3 层
1-3 F
1—3 层
1-3 F
10 层以上不超过
100 米
≥10 F，≤100m
100 米以上
≥100m

断裂肌理
Breaking texture

序号	名称	起止点	长（米）	宽（米）	曾用名	备注
1	劳动巷	古村一周线巷	170	1.5	雷祖庙、五富弄、小太平巷	此处旧有雷祖庙，后改名劳动巷
2	青果巷	和平南路一南大街	937	3—12	反帝东路	因位于河北岸，曾为南北果品集散地，旧称"千果巷"
3	周线巷	正素巷一打索巷	380	2.1	反修路	宋代学者周孚先、周恭先兄弟居此，卒后配祀于"先贤祠"，"贤""仙"音近，旧称"周仙巷"，后演化为周线巷
4	鲜鱼巷	兴隆巷一东大街	200	3—5	东方红西路	改巷北首原靠后河，形成鲜鱼集市，故名
5	周线里	周线巷一东大街	212	1—1.5	东方红西路	周线巷的派生地名

根据上位规划，常州老城地带要打造历史文化轴线，场地南北的青果巷历史文化街区和前后北岸历史文化街区是文化轴线上的重要节点。

老城厢地带的建筑高度大多在100米以下，以中高层建筑为主，与场地附近现存的历史文化街区极为不匹配。场地内部存在大量的高层。大量缺乏控制的高层树立在场地中导致了此片区在肌理上的断裂和不连续，为打造连续的文化长廊设置了不小的障碍。

场地内部老巷道现状不佳，地块内建筑风貌与历史街区格格不入。

According to the upper planning, Changzhou old town zone should build a historical and cultural axis. Qingguo Lane historical and cultural block and Qianhoubei'an historical and cultural block are the important nodes on the cultural axis in the north and south of the site.

The height of the buildings in the old city area is mostly below 100 m, mainly medium and high-rise buildings, which is very mismatched with the existing historical and cultural blocks near the site. A large number of high layers led to the rupture and discontinuity in the texture of the area, which sets up many obstacles for building a continuous cultural corridor.

The current situation of the old alley inside the site is not good, and the architectural style of the site is incompatible with the historical block.

功能 Function

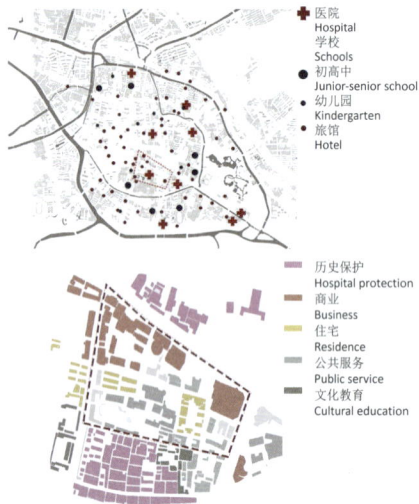

医院 Hospital
学校 Schools
初高中 Junior-senior school
幼儿园 Kindergarten
旅馆 Hotel

历史保护 Hospital protection
商业 Business
住宅 Residence
公共服务 Public service
文化教育 Cultural education

场地位于老城的中心地带，也位于地铁 1 号线和 2 号线的交会地带，周边拥有大量的商业和办公资源。

除此之外，场地内外还存有大量的医疗资源和教育设施，包括常州市第一人民医院、常州市第二人民医院、常州市中医院、常州市 102 医院等等，还有各个小学、高中，如江苏省立常州第一高级中学等等。

这些公共设施与城市核心地带所需要的公共不匹配，而且为这个地段带来了巨大的交通压力和交通负荷。在设计中需要对功能进行一定的置换和改造。

The site is located in the heart of the old city and at the intersection of metro line 1 and line 2. There are a lot of commercial and office resources around.

In addition, there are a lot of medical resources and education facilities on and off the site. There are elementary schools, high schools and so on.

These public facilities do not match the public needs of the urban core, and bring great traffic pressure and load to the area. It is necessary to replace and transform the function in the design.

开发结构 Development Structure

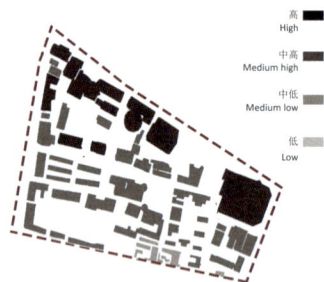

高 High
中高 Medium high
中低 Medium low
低 Low

场地内沿着主干道的区域开发强度高，建筑层数高；离主干道较远的地方开发强度低。

在设计策略中我们沿用这一开发思路，沿着地铁 1 号线和 2 号线进行高强度的开发，并且结合地下空间进行立体高强度开发。低矮的青果巷附近作为历史风貌过渡区，进行低强度开发。

The area along the main road in the site has a high development intensity and a high number of building floors. Development intensity is low farther from the main road.

In the design strategy, we use this development idea, along the metro line 1 and line 2 for high-intensity development, and combined with the underground space for three-dimensional high-intensity development. As a transitional area of historical features, the Qingguo Lane is developed with low intensity.

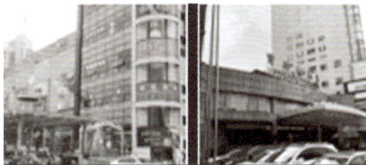

蓝绿结构 Blue and Green Structure

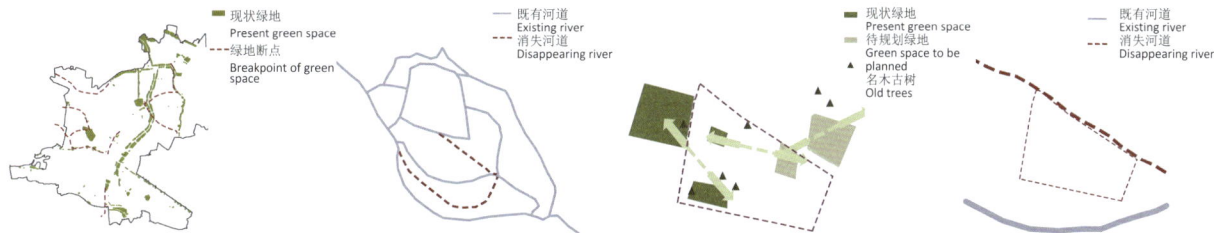

现状绿地
Present green space
绿地断点
Breakpoint of green space

既有河道
Existing river
消失河道
Disappearing river

现状绿地
Present green space
待规划绿地
Green space to be planned
名木古树
Old trees

既有河道
Existing river
消失河道
Disappearing river

根据上位规划，常州市要打造整个城市完善的蓝绿体系和生态结构。因此场地不再是一个内向的城市设计，也是整个城市蓝绿体系下的一个重要环节。基本策略是恢复古老城市河道和将场地内的现存绿地打开，与城市绿地相联系，构建城市中心区的连续绿廊和慢行空间。

According to the upper planning, Changzhou city should build a complete blue and green system and ecological structure of the whole city. Therefore, the site is no longer an introverted urban design, but also an important part of the whole urban blue and green system. The basic strategy is to restore the ancient urban riverway and open the existing green space in the site, and connect with the urban green space to build the continuous green corridor and slow-moving space in the urban center area.

场地 Place

现有公共空间
Existing public space

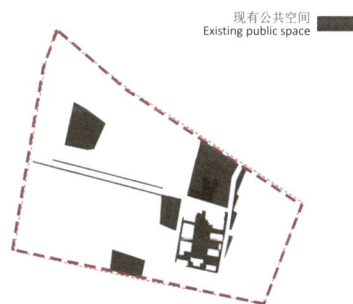

场地位于城市中心区，此地块开发强度高，用地紧张。

The site is located in the central area of the city. The development intensity of this plot is high and the land use is tight.

场地内现存的公共空间较为零散，相互之间没有联系，界面封闭，没有配套的服务功能而且可达性较差。

The existing public space in the site is scattered, with no connection between each other, closed interface, no supporting service functions and poor accessibility.

基本策略是打开封闭的界面，置换公共空间附近的功能，引导人流，激发活力。

The basic strategy is to open up the closed interface and to replace the functions near the public space, guide the flow of people and stimulate vitality.

学习环境 Learning Setting

● 初中小学
Junior and primary schools
● 高中
High school
↗ 辐射
Radiation

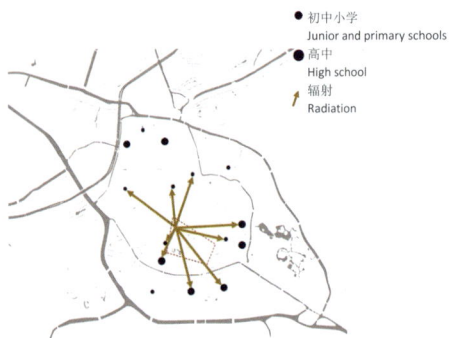

场地周边有大量的教育资源。

城市中心区不仅是一个商业办公中心，其强大的辐射能力也可以作为文化教育的中心辐射到整个老城地区。

在设计中结合学校和通俗易懂的可持续能源设计，在耳濡目染中培养人们的绿色意识。

There are a lot of educational resources around the site.

The central area of the city is not only a commercial office center, its strong radiation capacity can also be used as the center of cultural education radiation to the whole old city area.

In the design, the school and the easy to understand sustainable energy design are combined to cultivate people's green consciousness.

本地服务与就业 Local Supplier and Labor

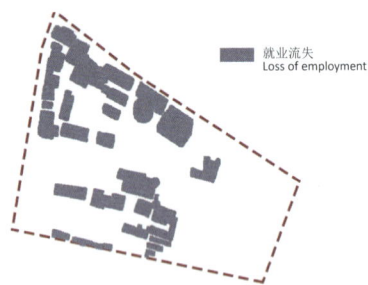

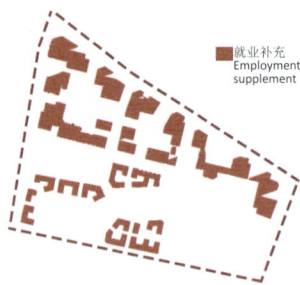

■ 就业流失
Loss of employment

■ 就业补充
Employment supplement

在改造中会流失部分商业和配套的劳动力，设计中应当考虑增补相对应的商业功能。

Part of the commercial and supporting labor will be lost in the transformation, and the corresponding commercial functions should be supplemented in the design.

噪声 Sound

〰 场外噪声
Off site noise
○ 场地内噪声
Noise in site

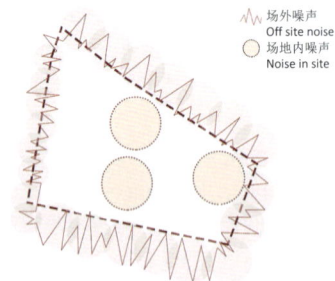

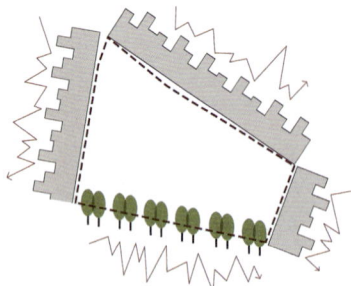

场地周边的交通噪声、施工噪声对场地内部产生了不好的影响。应当用建筑界面和绿化来减弱噪声的影响。

Traffic noise and construction noise around the site have a bad impact on the site interior. Building interface and greening should be used to reduce the impact of noise.

夜间照明强度分布
Distribution of night
lighting intensity

场地内除了基本的交通照明之外几乎没有其余的照明。

There is little lighting except for basic traffic lighting.

在设计中应当从使用者出发，增设夜间不断电的商铺照明、绿化小品的照明等等，给夜间的使用者渲染温暖、安全的感受。

In the design, we should start from the users, add the shop lighting of continuous electricity at night, the lighting of greening sketch and so on, so as to give the users at night a warm and safe feeling.

其能源可以是白天储存的太阳能或者是其他绿色能源。

Its energy can be solar energy stored in the daytime or other green energy.

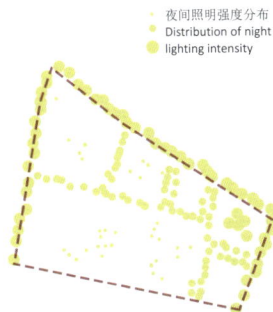

信息通信技术 Information and Communication Technology

电信设施
Telecommunication facilities
广电设施
Broadcasting and television facilities
邮政设施
Postal facilities
供电设施
Power supply facilities

场地周边有良好的通信设施、邮政设施、广电设施。

The site is surrounded by good communication facilities, postal facilities and broadcasting and television facilities.

场地可以紧密联系这些资源设施，形成完整的通信网络。

The site can be closely linked to these resources and facilities, forming a complete information and communication network.

| 水 Water | 气候适应性 Climate Adaption | 空气 Air |

结合蓝绿体系，提高气候适应性
Combine blue-green system to improve climate adaptability

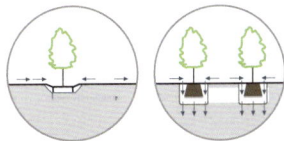

采用渗水铺装，结合地下水管增强气候适应性。

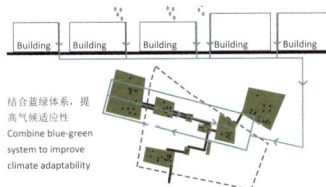

采用立面雨水收集系统，结合立体绿化增强气候适应性。

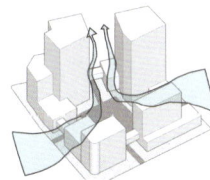

采用风环境模拟分析，改善形体和风环境增强气候适应性。

本项目设计基地位于常州市天宁区南部，中吴大道从基地南侧穿过，东侧为和平中路，基地东南角为规划地铁 1 号线、4 号线换乘站。地块处于五块基地的最南部、常州老城范围以外，属于城市快速扩张阶段产物，其性质为被城市所包围的城中村。历史上，场地北部有龙游河支流（三宝滨）通过，如今河道消失，村城隔阂。

The design base of this project is located in the south of Tianning District, Changzhou City. Zhongwu Avenue runs through the south side of the base, and the east side is Heping Middle Road. The southeast corner of the base is the transfer station of planned metro line 1 and line 4. The plot is located in the southernmost part of the five plots, outside the old city of Changzhou. It belongs to the product of rapid urban expansion, and is an urban village surrounded by the city. Historically, a tributary of Longyou River (Sanbaobin) passed through the northern part of the site, but now the river has disappeared and the village is isolated.

明清　　　民国　　　1954　　　1964　　　1974　　　1985　　　1995　　　2004

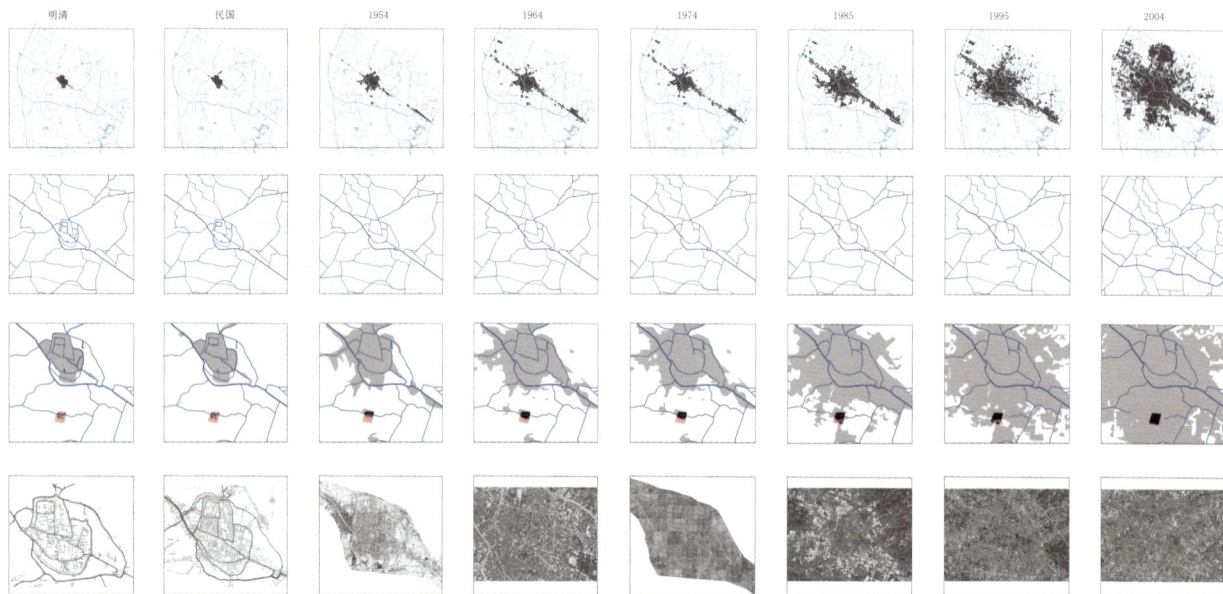

龙游河及其支流作为运河支流从明清运河改道开始，孕育了村庄，常州水系也基本形成。随着历史变迁，河流改道支流消失，快速的城市化进程让传统的村落被吞噬，终形成城中村的形态。

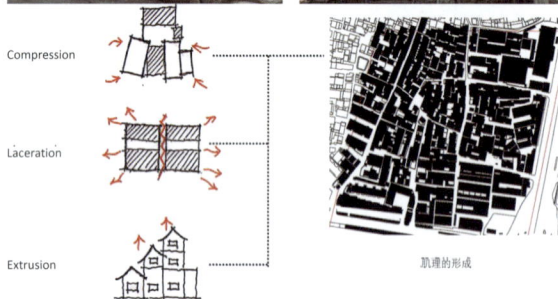

Longyou River and its tributaries began to divert from the Ming and Qing Dynasties as a tributary of the canal, and the village was born. The Changzhou water system was basically formed. With the historical changes, the tributaries of the river diversion disappeared, and the rapid urbanization process caused the traditional villages to be swallowed and eventually formed the morphology of the village in the city

城市的发展并没有改变片区内部的环境，在片区内有许多的老民居建筑，都为常州市一般不可动文物，彰显了村落的历史。但随着时代发展，老建筑不适应现代的生活要求，许多建筑已用做储藏，并在其旁边进行加建来满足居住要求。我们总结了三种加建形式来推演其肌理的形成方式。

The development of the city has not changed the environment inside the district. There are many old residential buildings in the area, which are the general immovable cultural relics of Changzhou, which shows the history of the village. However, with the development of the times, old buildings are not suitable for modern living requirements, and many buildings have been used for storage and added to the side to meet the living requirements. We have summarized three forms of addition to derive the way in which texture is formed.

Compression

Laceration

Extrusion

肌理的形成

生活与基础设施 Daily Life and Infrastructure

开发结构 Development Structure

茶山片区位于地铁规划换乘点，四周都在进行高强度开发，政府对于此片区的改造势在必行；但传统一刀切的规划方式在此片区并不适用。

The Chashan area is located at the subway planning transfer point, and high-intensity development is underway all around. The government's transformation of this area is imperative; but the traditional planning method is not applicable in this area.

交通 Transportation

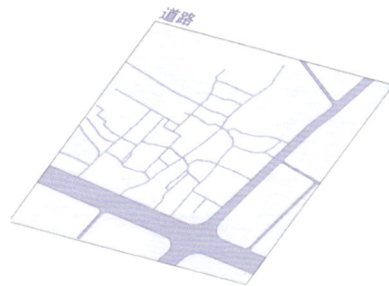

在村中有两条主要干道，道宽约 6 米，可以过车。其余道路皆为 4 米左右，仅供行人和自行车使用。片区附近则有新规划并建设的地铁枢纽茶山站，距离基地片区一路之隔。在片区东侧道路有一处公交站点，南侧有两处公交站点。

There are two main roads in the village. The road is about 6 m wide and can be used for passing. The rest of the roads are about 4 m wide and are used only for pedestrians and bicycles. Near the area there is a newly planned and constructed subway hub, Chashan Station, which is separated from the base area by a bus stop on the east side of the area and two bus stops on the south side.

场地 Place

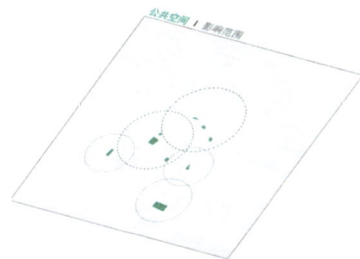

场地内的公共活动与交流空间大多数为房屋围合出的院子，数量较少，并常有被占用的情况。同时，场地周边开发强度大，房屋密度较高，没有市民的活动空间。

Most of the public activities and communication space in the venue are yards enclosed by houses, and the number is small and often there are situations that are occupied. At the same time, the development intensity around the site is large, the density of houses is high, and there is no room for public activities.

产品 + 能源 + 材料 Product+Energy+Material

片区内设有许多垃圾站点，但搭建简陋，回收不及时，没有可循环策略；片区内乱搭乱建现象严重，且都为村民的自组织行为，使用不环保的建材。

There are many garbage sites in the area, but the construction is simple. The recycling is not timely. There is no recycling strategy. The phenomenon of random construction in the area is serious, and both are self-organized behavior of the villagers, using non-green building materials.

学习环境 Learning Setting

片区附近中有一所幼儿园（茶山中心幼儿园）、一所小学（浦前中心小学）以及一所中学（常州市实验初级中学），在场地附近还有一所高中以及一所小学。

In the vicinity of the district, there is a kindergarten (Chashan Central Kindergarten), a primary school (Puqian Central Primary School) and a middle school (Changzhou Experimental Junior High School). There is also a high school and a primary school near the venue.

居民与劳动力 Resident and Labor

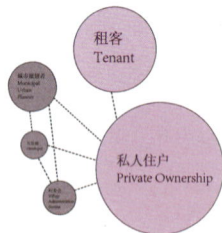

片区内的人口主要为当地居民和外来务工人员，大部分人员在城中村外进行工作。只有靠近干道路边及内部商业街附近的住户会有自家经营的商店，商住混合的模式较为常见。

The population in the area is mainly local residents and migrant workers; most of the people work outside the village. Only the residents near the main road and the nearby commercial street will have their own shops. The mixed mode of business and residence is more common.

噪声 Sound

片区内在白天噪声较多，夜晚噪音较少。由于与城市主干道间有建筑隔挡，受城市车辆影响较小。

There is more noise during the day and less noise at night. Due to the building block between the main roads of the city, it is less affected by urban vehicles.

涝水问题 Flooding Problem

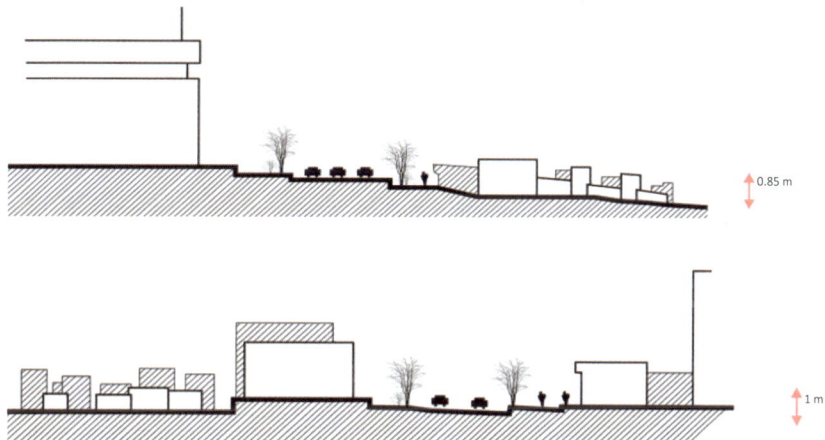

0.85 m

1 m

在梅雨季节茶山村有非常严重的涝水现象，这是由于片区的标高比城市道路低大约 800 毫米，在城市层面上是一处盆地，且片区内缺少排水措施，其积水最深处可达到 1 米深，十分影响居民的正常生活，而这也是城中村亟待解决的问题。

In the rainy season, Chashan Village has a very serious flooding phenomenon. This is because the elevation of the area is about 800 mm lower than that of the urban road. It is a basin on the city level, and there is no drainage in the area. The deepest water can reach 1 m deepth. It has a great impact on the normal life of the residents, and this is also an urgent problem to be solved in the village.

瑞典调研
Visiting Study in Sweden

自 1972 年联合国第一次环境与发展大会在瑞典斯德哥尔摩召开至今，瑞典对环境保护与可持续发展问题的研究一直走在世界前沿，近年来其研究和实践也从建筑单体尺度扩大到对城市及区域尺度可持续发展的关注。瑞典绿色建筑委员会下属的可持续发展城市实验室 CITYLAB 编制了《城市可持续发展指引》，并参与了瑞典近期的多项城市更新和开发建设项目。这些瑞典最新的城市项目很大程度上代表了人类最高的环境自觉和可持续性建设的认知与实践水平，对研究我国常州滨水地区的可持续问题具有重要的示范和参考价值。

受瑞典绿色建筑委员会和 CITYLAB 的邀请，2018 年 11 月 4 日—12 日，东南大学建筑学院院长张彤教授带领工作坊团队的 4 名教师与 17 名研究生，以瑞典可持续发展前沿为主题，深入实地开展系统性的考察与探索。期间，团队与瑞典 CITYLAB 共同举办研讨会，听取瑞典专家关于绿色建筑与可持续发展理论及多个实践案例的阐述，并在瑞典两大城市斯德哥尔摩、哥德堡实地参观了可持续发展城市建设与绿色建筑的优秀案例。案例的调研内容涵盖了可持续规划设计的理念、具体策略、实施机制等方面，调研对象涉及城市片区、工业遗产、校园、住区等多个不同类型。

Since the first United Nations Conference on Environment and Development in Stockholm, Sweden, in 1972, Sweden's research on environmental protection and sustainable development has been at the forefront of the world. In recent years, its research and practice on sustainable development have also expanded from building to urban and regional scale. CITYLAB, a sustainable urban laboratory under the Sweden Green Building Council, has developed the CITYLAB Guide and has participated in several recent urban renewal and development projects in Sweden. These latest Swedish urban projects represent, to a large extent, the highest level of cognition and practice of sustainability, and have significant reference for studying the sustainability issues in the waterfront area of Changzhou, China.

Invited by the Sweden Green Building Council and CITYLAB, from November 4th to 12th, 2018, Professor Zhang Tong, Dean of the School of Architecture of Southeast University, led the team of 4 teachers and 17 graduate students, conduct systematic investigation and exploration on the recent sustainable development in Sweden. During the period, the team and the Swedish CITYLAB jointly held seminars to listen to the Swedish experts on the theory of green building and sustainable development and a number of excellent practical cases, and visited the two major cities of Sweden, Stockholm, Gothenburg to visit cases of sustainable urban development and green buildings. The case study covers the concept, specific strategy and implementation mechanism of sustainable planning and design and the sites cover many different types including areas, industrial heritage, campus and residential areas, etc..

斯德哥尔摩皇家海港项目　是继 1994—2017 年开发的哈默比湖城后，另一个凝结整个国家意愿、智慧和科技发展水平，具有全球可持续发展示范意义的重要项目。斯德哥尔摩政府投入政策支持和强有力的实施管控，旨在将这片老工业港区更新为"一个世界级的城市发展区域"——瑞典与波罗的海各国联系的水上门户，一个新的经济、文化、休闲活动中心。

哥德堡滨水城项目　作为斯堪的纳维亚最大的可持续城市发展项目之一，将通过连接城市、水和中心，致力于创造一个向世界开放的包容、绿色和充满活力的内城。位于滨水城的林霍尔姆科学园是北欧地区工业港口可持续更新的典范，记录了一个城市衰败工业港口转变为哥德堡最具活力的知识密集型地区的历史。

斯德哥尔摩阿尔巴诺校园项目　作为欧洲可持续性共享校园典范，创造了一个极具吸引力的教育和研究环境，形成连接瑞典皇家理工学院、斯德哥尔摩大学和卡罗林斯卡学院等高校和研究机构的枢纽。同时，由位于世界上第一个国家城市公园斯德哥尔摩国家城市公园范围内，在城市的可持续发展中也发挥了重要作用。

欧盟支持的智慧发展课题　旨在通过开发城市可持续智能设计方案，实现"改造城市，实现智能、可持续发展的欧洲"的目标。基于该课题，斯德哥尔摩城市内主要研究、实践并选点示范了住区的低能耗更新改造项目（以 1960 年代的瓦拉托格社区为例）。

斯德哥尔摩瓦斯略改造项目　位于斯德哥尔摩北部快速发展地区，规划为未来的住宅区，因而需要对原区域内的基础设施进行全面系统化的可持续性改造。项目中通过政府引导建立多方合作平台，追踪并确保整个规划建设过程的实施。

除了可持续的城区建设项目以外，实地考察调研还包括了多个有代表性的绿色建筑开发项目，其中包括瑞典 Sweco 总部大楼改造项目、哥德堡里克斯比根生态正足迹住宅开发项目等。

The Royal Seaport Project in Stockholm is another important project that demonstrates the willingness, wisdom and technological development level of the whole country after the development of Hammerby Lake City in 1994–2017. The Stockholm government has invested in policy support and strong implementation control to renovate this old industrial port area into "a world-class urban development area" – a water portal connecting Sweden with the Baltic countries, a new economy, culture, leisure activity center.

As one of Scandinavia's largest sustainable urban development projects, RiverCity Gothenburg will be dedicated to creating an inclusive, green and vibrant inner city that is open to the world by connecting cities, water and centres. The Lindholmen Science Park in the waterfront is a model for the sustainable renewal of industrial ports in the Nordic region, recording the history of a city's decaying industrial port turning into the most dynamic and knowledge-intensive region of Gothenburg.

The Campus Albano Project in Stockholm, as a model for sustainable campus sharing in Europe, creates an attractive educational and research environment that connects universities such as the Royal Institute of Technology, Stockholm University and Karolinska Institute, and the hub of research institutions. At the same time, it is also played in the sustainable development of the city by the National City Park in Stockholm, the world's first national city park.

The EU-supported Smart Development Project (GrowSmarter) aims to achieve the goal of "renovating cities, achieving smart, sustainable Europe" by developing urban sustainable intelligent design solutions. Based on this topic, the main research, practice and selection of Stockholm cities demonstrate low-energy upgrading projects in residential areas (taking the Valla Torg community in the 1960s as an example).

The Väsjön Urban Development Project in Stockholm, located in the fast-growing region of northern Stockholm, is planned for future residential areas and requires a comprehensive and systematic sustainable transformation of the infrastructure in the original area. In the project, a multi-party cooperation platform is established through government guidance to track and ensure the implementation of the entire planning and construction process.

In addition to the sustainable urban development projects, field trips include a number of representative green building developments, including the Sweco Headquarters Building Renovation Project in Sweden and the residential project in Gothenburg (Brf Viva, Riksbyggen), etc..

基于现场调查、对话访谈、文献研究等研究方法获取第一手且最具时效性的资料，研究生深入研讨案例中采取了哪些可持续发展策略，如何呈现对可持续发展内涵的理解，实现可持续发展所面临的最大挑战是什么等问题，从而阐释瑞典可持续发展的理念、挑战、方法技术与实施路径等。瑞典可持续案例的研究为下一阶段开展常州滨水区规划设计工作坊提供了有价值的参考案例和技术方法，为城市与建筑的未来发展提供了可持续的重要视角，并进一步为正在承担全世界最大规模建设量的中国城市开展可持续发展的研究和实践奠定了必要基础。

Based on field research, dialogue interviews, literature research and other research methods to obtain first-hand and most timely data, graduate students deeply discussed what sustainable development strategies had been adopted in the case, how to present their understanding of the connotation of sustainable development, and what are the biggest challenges to achieve sustainable development, so as to explain the concept, challenges, methods, technology and implementation path of sustainable development in Sweden. The process of Swedish sustainable case study provides valuable reference and technical methods for the next phase of the Changzhou Waterfront Planning and Design Workshop, also providing a sustainable and important perspective for the future development of cities and buildings. Further, it has laid the necessary foundation for undertaking the research and practice of sustainable development in China's large cities.

案例研究
Case study

案例一　斯德哥尔摩皇家海港　Case 1　Stockholm Royal Seaport

皇家海港是瑞典 2008 年开始建设的重要城市更新项目，也是继哈默比湖城后又一个彰显国家意愿和可持续发展理念与技术水平的重点建设片区。该项目制定了瑞典最高标准的环境目标和具体有效的环境策略，致力于成为"世界级的可持续发展城区"。研究这一作为全球可持续发展的城市更新项目典范，为进一步在理论层面理解可持续发展的内涵，以及在实践层面实施可持续性策略都提供了重要的借鉴价值。

The Royal Seaport is one of the most important urban regeneration project in Sweden which has been started in 2008. It is another key area after the Hammarby Lake City which demonstrates the national will, the concept of sustainable development and the stage of techniques. It makes the highest environmental standards in the country and specifically effective environmental strategies. The purpose of the project is committed to becoming a world-class sustainable urban area. As a worldwide model of sustainable urban regeneration project, it provides important references both for further understanding sustainable development at the theoretical level and for implementing sustainable strategies at the practical level.

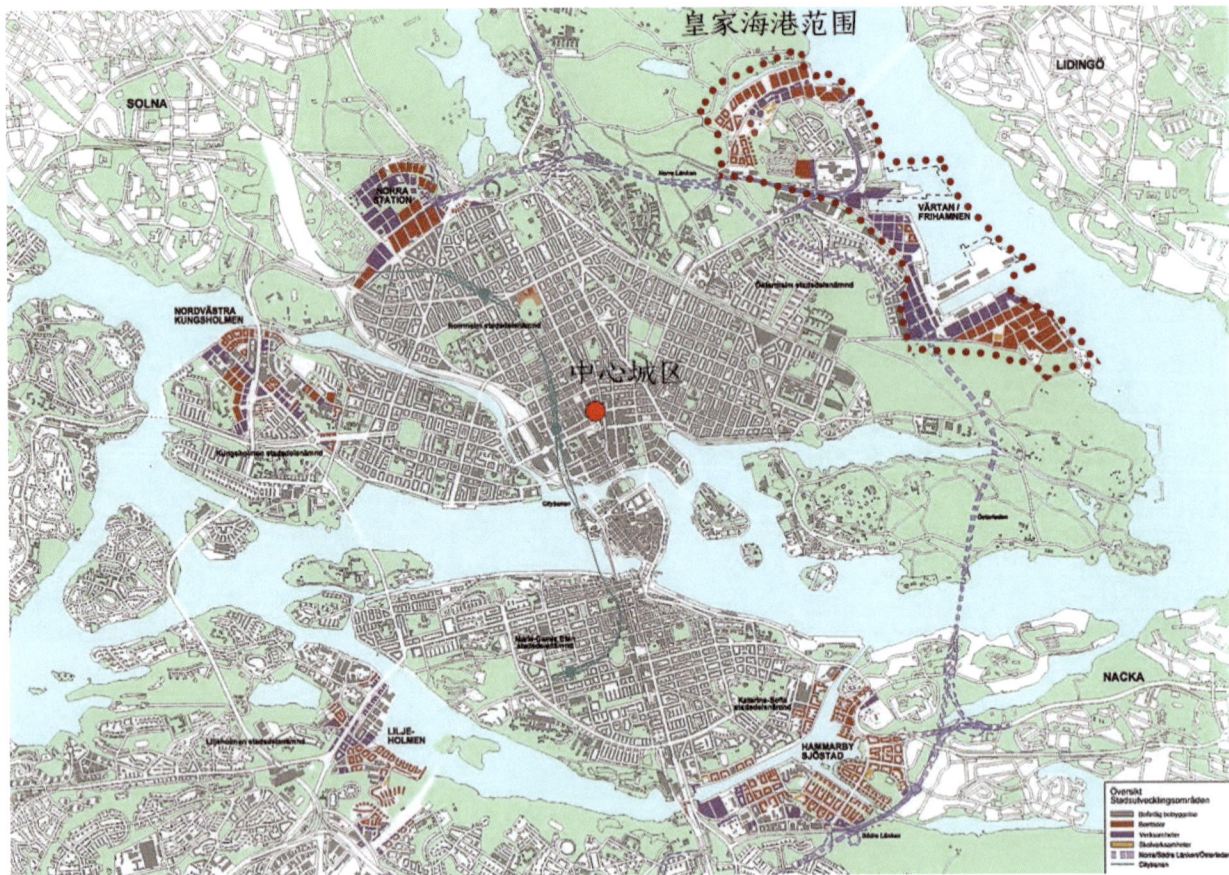

图 1 斯德哥尔摩的城市更新项目分布图

1 皇家海港概述

皇家海港位于斯德哥尔摩市区的东北区，横跨北部的鹿园地区和南部的劳登地区，距离城市中心区仅仅 3.5 公里，是整个城市发展的黄金地段。这一地区原本是斯德哥尔摩最大的工业港区，建有工业设施和居民区。作为斯德哥尔摩 2030 计划的重要组成部分，皇家海港将规划新的住宅区和商业区，工业港区将建成现代化港口码头，天然气工业区将建成博物馆、学校和图书馆、城市公共区。整个项目占地 236 公顷，预计于 2030 年完成，届时将建成住宅 12000 套，新建 60 万平方米商业面积，创造 35000 个新的工作机会。目前完工的区域是鹿园地区北部新的住宅区，第一批居民已经于 2012 年入住。

皇家海港制定了三个具体指标：

在 2020 年以前，二氧化碳排放量少于每人 1.5 吨（瑞典平均每人 4.5 吨的指标）；新建住宅建筑最大的能源使用效率不高于每平方米 55 千瓦时；在 2030 年以前，用可再生能源替代化石能源（斯德哥尔摩计划 2050 年达到这一目标）。

1 Overview of the Royal Seaport

The Royal Seaport is located in the northeastern part of Stockholm, across the Hjorthagen region in the north and the Loudden region in the south, just 3.5 kilometres from the city centre, making it a prime location for the city's development. This area was originally the largest industrial port area in Stockholm, with industrial facilities and residential areas. As an important part of the Stockholm 2030 program, the Royal Seaport will plan new residential and commercial areas, industrial ports will be built into modern port terminals, and the natural gas industrial area will be built to have museums, schools and libraries, urban public area. The entire project covers an area of 236 hectares and is expected to be completed by 2030. By then, 12,000 units will be built, 600,000 square meters of commercial space will be built, and 35,000 new jobs will be created. The currently completed area is a new residential area in the northern part of the Hjorthagen area, and the first residents have been accommodated in 2012.

The Royal Seaport has developed three specific indicators:

Carbon dioxide emissions by less than 1.5 tons per person by 2020 (the Swedish average of 4.5 tons per person); The maximum energy use of newly built residential buildings is no more than 55 kWh per square meters; Replace fossil energy with renewable energy by 2030 (Stockholm plans to achieve this goal by 2050).

图 2 皇家海港整体鸟瞰图

图 3 皇家海港总平面图

图 4 皇家海港模型

2 皇家海港的可持续发展策略

皇家海港为实现世界级可持续发展城市的目标，主要采取城市功能、交通脉络、资源能源与蓝绿体系四个方面的设计策略。

多样与多义的城市功能

作为斯德哥尔摩内城的延伸，皇家海港在城市结构上展现出强大的内聚力和灵活性来适应地区及周边的需求。街道、公园、广场与城市其他公共空间相串联，底层空间尽可能多地开放，将各种充满活力且多元的商业与活动纳入这些空间。此外，在规划中有意识注重学校、公交站点、超市、公园等设施的布局和设计，以有助于城市多元功能的复合并激活公共空间。

便捷与绿色的交通脉络

皇家海港主要通过建立便捷与绿色的交通脉络和宣传绿色出行的观念来诠释可持续的发展观。不同于其他地区以增加交通和拓宽道路来改善拥堵问题的做法，城区在规划之初就提出从根本上减少人们对于交通的需求才是重中之重。海港城密集、功能齐全且便利的城市结构为可持续交通奠定了基础。高密集型公共设施诸如零售、服务、学校被设置在公共交通节点附近，并通过人性化的设计来确保步行体验的舒适与安全。

2 Royal Seaport 's sustainable development strategies

In order to achieve the goal of a world-class sustainable city, the Royal Seaport mainly adopts four aspects of urban design, transportation, resource and energy and blue-green system design strategies.

Diverse and ambiguous city functions

As an extension of Stockholm's inner city, the Royal Seaport demonstrates strong cohesion and flexibility in the urban structure to accommodate regional and surrounding needs. Streets, parks, plazas are connected in series with other public spaces in the city, and the ground floor space is open as much as possible, incorporating a variety of dynamic and diverse businesses and activities into these spaces. In addition, in the planning, consciously pay attention to the layout and design of facilities such as schools, bus stops, supermarkets, parks, etc., to help the city's multi-functional complex and activate the public space.

Convenient and green traffic context

Royal Seaport interprets a sustainable development concept by establishing a convenient and green transportation context and promoting green travel. Different from other regions to increase traffic and widen the road to improve congestion, the city proposed at the beginning of the plan to fundamentally reduce people's demand for transportation is the top priority. The dense, functional and convenient urban structure of the Royal Seaport laid the foundation for sustainable transport. Highly intensive public facilities such as retail, services, and schools are placed near public transportation nodes and are designed humanly to ensure the comfort and security of the walking experience.

图 5 多功能滨水街区

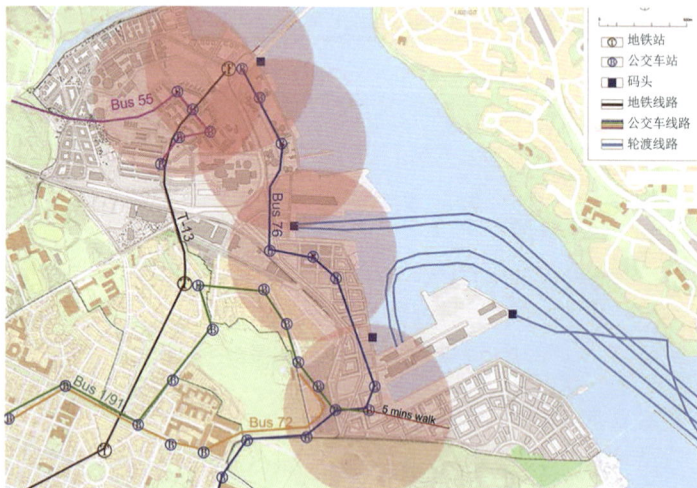

图 6 便捷的交通脉络

循环与高效的资源利用

皇家海港一系列闭合的环路系统不仅减少了资源的浪费，还有效控制了废物在本地区的产生。污水处理系统通过尽可能多的闭环系统，使营养物质返回耕地，从而减少对湖泊和海洋的影响。雨水就地处理而不经排水管网和污水处理厂，通过雨水花园、地漏、过滤装置等对其进行过滤，以有效缓解系统运作压力与负荷。垃圾处理延续了哈默比湖城的技术，通过真空抽吸系统来实现垃圾的回收利用。

生态与环保的蓝绿体系

皇家海港通过发挥生态系统的主动性来建立一个健康和弹性的城市环境。由于毗邻里拉凡登湖，通过建设可持续的雨水管理体系，有效降低雨水中的污染物并改善水资源状况。同时在气候适应性方面做出了回应措施，每个地区的植被和土壤兼具景观与生态功能，它们将被用于渗透与滞留雨水。

皇家海港拥有最高标准的环境目标，致力于成为世界级可持续发展城区的典范。从 2008 年启动到 2030 年预计建设完成，是一个漫长的历程，同时也是瑞典通过这一城市更新实践向全世界诠释其对可持续发展理念最深刻理解的过程。至今已落成的皇家海港新住宅区很好地贯彻了可持续发展的理念，也为将来整体的区域更新奠定了良好的开端，提供了示范性的经验。

Cycle and efficient resource utilization

The Royal Seaport 's series of closed loop systems not only reduces waste of resources, but also effectively controls the generation of waste in the region. The sewage treatment system returns nutrients to the cultivated land through as many closed-loop systems as possible, thereby reducing the impact on lakes and oceans. The rainwater is treated on site without passing through the drainage network and the sewage treatment plant, and is filtered by rainwater gardens, floor drains, filtration devices, etc., to effectively alleviate the system operation pressure and load. Garbage disposal continues the technology of Hammerby Lake City, which uses a vacuum pumping system to recycle waste.

Ecological and environmentally friendly blue-green system

The Royal Seaport creates a healthy and resilient urban environment by harnessing the initiative of the ecosystem. Adjacent to LillaVartan Lake, through the construction of a sustainable rainwater management system, effectively reduce pollutants in the rainwater and improve water resources. At the same time, in response to climate adaptation, vegetation and soil in each region have both landscape and ecological functions, which will be used to infiltrate and retain rainwater.

The Royal Seaport has the highest standards of environmental goals and is committed to being a model of a world-class sustainable urban development. It is a long journey from the start of 2008 to the completion of construction in 2030. It is also a process in which Sweden has explained the most profound understanding of the concept of sustainable development to the world through this urban renewal practice. The new residential area of the Royal Seaport, which has been completed to date, has implemented the concept of sustainable development and laid a good start for the overall regional renewal in the future, providing exemplary experience.

[1] STAD S. Sustainable Urban-development Program[M]. Stockholm: Edita Bobergs, 2017
[2] Executive Office of Stockholm. Vision Stockholm Royal Seaport 2030[M]. EO Grafiska AB, 2010
[3] STAD S. Stockholm Royal Seaport Sustainability Report 2015[M]. Stockholm: Edita Bobergs, 2015
[4] STAD S. Stockholm Royal Seaport Sustainability Report 2017[M]. Stockholm: Edita Bobergs, 2017
[5] STAD S. Vision 2040: A Stockholm for Everyone[M]. Stockholm, 2015
[6] Louise H, Nils B, Karl H R. Can Stockholm Royal Seaport be part of the puzzle towards global sustainability?-From local to global sustainability using the same set of criteria[J]. Journal of Cleaner Production, 2017(140): 72-80

图 7 产能建筑

图 8 垃圾回收点

图 9 雨水过滤系统

图 10 雨水池塘

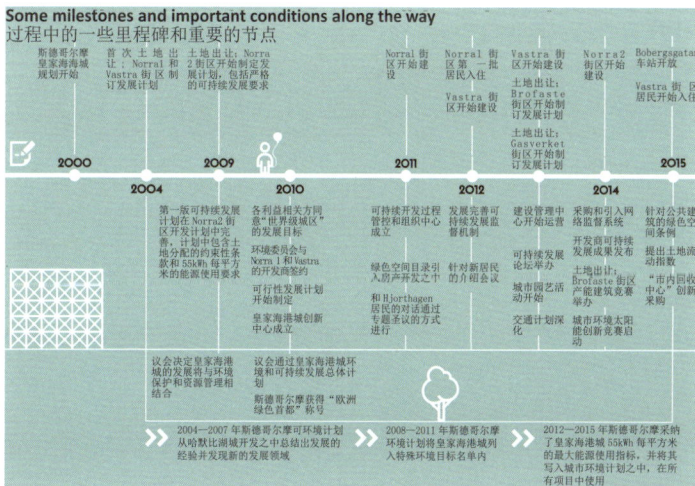
Some milestones and important conditions along the way
过程中的一些里程碑和重要的节点
图 11 项目进程管理

案例二　哥德堡滨水城林德霍姆科学园　Case 2　Lindholmen Science Park, RiverCity Gothenburg

图 例
1　南河岸
2　内城
3　林德霍姆
4　拉姆山
5　基维尔镇
6　巴克布朗
7　自由港
8　灵岛
9　中心车站区
10　吉贝里芦苇丛
11　的塔运河
12　滨河区 2021 年规划

图 12 瑞典哥德堡滨河区城市地图

哥德堡是仅次于瑞典首都斯德哥尔摩的第二大城市，具有瑞典最大的港口，辐射范围覆盖北欧三国工业最发达的地区，是当之无愧的北欧工业中心。随着瑞典近代工业化发展逐步完成，工业的衰退为城市留下了丰富的工业遗产。哥德堡政府及公众积极探索产业转型和城市发展的新策略，逐步实现了工业港口城市的新时代转变。通过研究全面阐释哥德堡滨水城的历史性转变，并重点以哥德堡林德霍姆科学园更新项目为例，分析其历史演变、发展策略、环境评估、建筑立面与基础设施改造等方面内容。

Gothenburg is the second largest city after Stockholm, Sweden. It has the largest port in Sweden and covers the most developed industries in the three Nordic countries. It is a well-deserved Nordic industrial center. With the gradual completion of modern industrialization in Sweden, the industrial recession has left a rich industrial heritage for the city. The Gothenburg government and the public actively explore new strategies for industrial transformation and urban development, and gradually realize the new era of industrial port cities. Through the study, the historical transformation of Gothenburg RiverCity Project is comprehensively explained, and the historical project of the Lindholmen Science Park in Gothenburg is taken as an example to analyze its historical evolution, development strategy, environmental assessment, building facade and infrastructure renovation.

图 13 哥德堡滨水城整体鸟瞰图

图 14 哥德堡滨水城总平面图

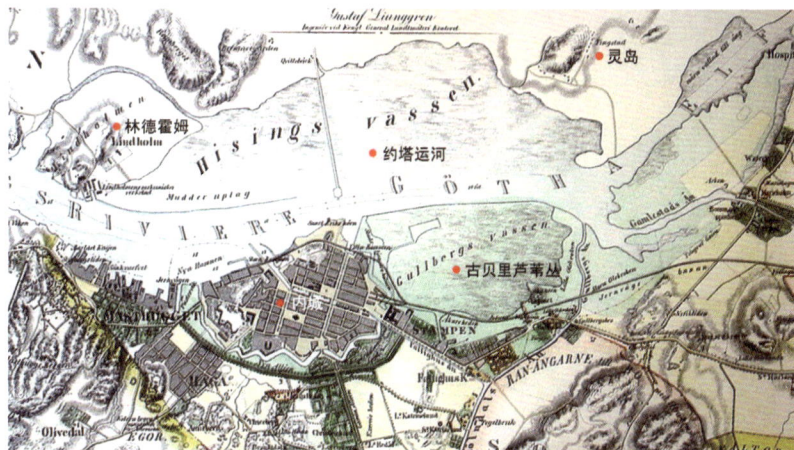

图 15 哥德堡滨水城历史地图

哥德堡滨水城项目涵盖了 19 世纪最为重要的两个港口的更新——林德霍姆和自由港。其中，林德霍姆是林德霍姆港的遗址。在战争期间，港口被改建为一个大型码头仓库，近 50 年来它一直是远洋船只的港口，可以运载普通货物和汽车。在后来的几年里，林德霍姆已经转变为一个领先的科学和教育中心，专注于数字通信。在哥德堡 2021 年滨河区城市规划中，林德霍姆片区将发展成为一个知识经济中心，在现有集群的基础上加强与媒体、艺术和学术界合作，从而对城市发挥巨大影响。

The Gothenburg RiverCity Project covers the renewal of the two most important ports of the 19th century - Lindholm and Frihamnen Freeport. Among them, Lindholm is the site of Lindholmshamnen. During the war, the port was converted into a large dock warehouse. For nearly 50 years, it has been the port of ocean-going vessels, which can carry ordinary cargo and cars. In the years that followed, Lindholmen has transformed into a leading science and education center focused on digital communications. In Gothenburg's 2021 riverfront urban planning, the Lindholm area will develop into a knowledge-based economic center, strengthening cooperation with the media, art and academia on the basis of existing clusters, thus exerting a huge impact on the city.

1 概况：历史与现状

林德霍姆位于桑内加德港和自由贸易区（自由港）之间，是希辛延岛的第一个工业区。早在 1850 年代中期，林德霍姆就建立了一个造船厂，用于建造钢制船舶，随后又因增设了一个专门用于蒸汽船的工程而迅速扩建。

如今，林德霍姆科学园是一个致力于移动通信、智能车辆和运输系统以及现代传媒等产业的典范型科技园区。园区的历史记录了一个衰败的城市旧工业区如何成为哥德堡最具活力的知识密集型地区的故事。园区的重点产业是互联网技术、远程信息以及媒体业，大约全国 75% 的影视制造都在该园区。科学园解决了一连串的决策危机，营造了典范般的滨水环境，可以为国内具有类似特征的城市区域的发展提供参考。

2 工业遗产的可持续再生策略
多产业互动合作，协同发展

林德霍姆科学园从创立以来就致力于为哥德堡建立一个更美好的未来。它将前造船厂区变成一个有吸引力的新社区和现代生态系统。它完美地融合了教育和科技，通过协同作用让其能够持续吸引投资并且促进创新。许多科技园区是纯粹的物业项目，而林德霍姆中的组织既可以负责房地产开发，又能够开展联合研究项目，鼓励互动并建立共享品牌。

1 Overview: History and Current Situation

Located between Sannegårdshamnen and the Free Trade Zone (Frihamnen), Lindholm is the first industrial area of Hisingen. As early as the mid-1950s, Lindholm established a shipyard for the construction of steel ships, which was subsequently rapidly expanded by the addition of a special project for steamships.

Today, Lindholmen Science Park is a model-based technology park dedicated to mobile communications, smart vehicles and transportation systems, and modern media. The history of the park documents how a declining urban old industrial district became the story of Gothenburg's most dynamic, knowledge-intensive region. The key industries of the park are internet technology, telematics and the media industry. About 75% of the country's film and television manufacturing is in the park. The Science Park has solved a series of decision-making crises and created a model-like rivercity environment that can provide reference for the development of urban areas with similar characteristics in China.

2 Sustainable regeneration strategy for industrial heritage
Multi-industry interaction and co-operation

Since its inception, the Lindholmen Science Park has been dedicated to building a better future for Gothenburg. It transforms the former shipyard area into an attractive new community and modern ecosystem. It is a perfect blend of education and technology, and through synergy it continues to attract investment and promote innovation. Many technology parks are purely property projects, and organizations in Lindholm can be responsible for both real estate development and joint research projects, encouraging interaction and building shared brands.

1. 林德霍姆科学园
2. Swedband AB 办公楼
3. Ericsson AB 办公楼
4. Kuggen 办公楼
5. SEB 办公楼
6. 查尔姆斯林德霍尔姆大学教学楼
7. 林德霍姆技术高中
8. Ester Mosessons 高中
9. Hasselblad 办公楼演艺剧场
10. Polhensgymnasiet 高中

图 16 林德霍姆科学园平面图

图 17 林德霍姆科学园

加速城市生产和创新

林德霍姆是一个生产加速器——园区的运转促使公众参与并做出贡献，引入专业知识人才，发挥规模集聚效应。并且林德霍姆中新的 AI 竞技场和未来移动计划会集了瑞典乃至国际的专业知识；因此，林德霍姆同时也是创新的加速器。为了让哥德堡地区继续发展并吸引有才能的人才促进地区成长，还需要诸多不同要素集聚，如住房、教育条件良好的学校、工作、丰富的文化等。政府和市民需有效利用科学园对城市发展的带动作用，参与并促进可持续发展，创造无穷无尽的可能性。

瑞典哥德堡的工业遗产保护更新拥有更为丰富的内容。在城市层面，工业遗产政府将保护视为和发展一体化的要素，保留下的遗产形成不同时期的历史叠加，从而形成城市整体的文脉。在工业区层面，倡导不同产业分时序入驻：前期吸引培训类产业和教学科研机构入驻，为地区带来知识活力；此后政府及基金会等机构共同合作吸引新企业入驻，多产业协同发展，并提供混合功能的新社区。在建筑遗产层面，根据声、光、降水量等条件进行环境可持续评估，判断建筑的改造和保留价值，尽可能地保留下重要的工业建筑遗产和构筑物遗产等，并将新的技术应用到具体建筑改造中。

Accelerate urban production and innovation

Lindholm is a production accelerator – the operation of the park promotes public participation and contribution, the introduction of specialized knowledge talents, and the use of scale agglomeration effects. Lindholmens new AI Arena and Future Mobility program brings together Swedish and international expertise; therefore, Lindholm is also an accelerator of innovation. In order to continue the development of the Gothenburg region and attract talented talents to promote regional growth, many different factors need to be gathered: housing, schools with good educational conditions, work, and rich culture. The government and citizens need to make effective use of the Science Park's role in urban development, participate in and promote sustainable development, and create endless possibilities.

The industrial heritage protection update in Gothenburg, Sweden, has a richer content. At the urban level, the industrial heritage government regards protection as an element of integration with development, and the preserved heritage forms a historical superposition of different periods, thus forming the context of the city as a whole. At the industrial zone level, it advocates the different industries to participate in the time series: in early stage it attracts in the training industry and the teaching and research institutions to settle in, bringing the knowledge vitality to the region; since then, the government and foundations have cooperated to attract new enterprises to settle in, making multi-industry coordinated development, and offering a new community with mixed functionality. At the level of architectural heritage, environmental sustainability assessments are carried out based on conditions such as sound, light, precipitation, etc., to judge the transformation and preservation value of the building, to preserve important industrial building heritage and structure heritage as much as possible, and to apply new technologies to concrete building renovation.

[1] Lagerqvist B. Heritage and Peacebuilding[M]. Britain：Boydell & Brewer, 2017: 221-234

[2] Zhang Yifan. Shorelines: Re-thinking and learning from the industrial heritage in Gothenburg [D]. Gothenburg: Chalmers University of Technology, 2014

[3] Lindholmen Science Park. From shipbuilding industry to Science Park［EB/OL］.(2019).https://www.lindholmen.se/en/about-us/history

[4] Gothenburg. Lindholmen – History, Vision and Role as an Accelerator［EB/OL］.(2019).https://www.investingothenburg.com/news/lindholmen-history-vision-and-role-accelerator

[5] City of Gothenburg.Rivercity Gothenburg Vision[EB/OL].(2012).http://alvstaden.goteborg.se/

图 18 集装箱式住房外立面

图 19 林德霍姆城市模型展览

案例三　斯德哥尔摩阿尔巴诺校园　Case 3 Campus Albano, Stockholm

图 20　瑞典阿尔巴诺校园总平面图

斯德哥尔摩阿尔巴诺校园是基于全新可持续理念的城市更新项目，建成后将成为由 20 世纪老工业区蜕变而成的三大教育机构共享的城市核心科学城。随着可持续理念在校园规划中越来越被重视，阿尔巴诺校园规划设计采取可持续发展理念——社会生态城市主义，整合诸多生态理论并结合城市化现状，以求在理论和实施层面指导阿尔巴诺校园的建设。阿尔巴诺校区于 2019 年获得 CITYLAB 认证。作为可持续校园的典范，该项目提供了一个可供参考的全新理念，其可持续策略和具体实施手法对校园规划具有重要的借鉴意义。

阿尔巴诺校园项目位于瑞典斯德哥尔摩市中心以北的三角地带，是重要的城市发展地段，也是斯德哥尔摩三所主要大学——斯德哥尔摩大学（abbr. SU）、卡罗林斯卡学院（abbr. KI）和瑞典皇家理工学院（abbr. KTH）的相交地带，同时更位于世界上第一个国家城市公园斯德哥尔摩国家城市公园的边界内。

The Stockholm Albano Campus is an urban renewal project based on a new sustainability concept. Upon completion, it will become the city's core science city shared by the three educational institutions transformed from the twentieth century old industrial area. As the concept of sustainability is increasingly valued in campus planning, Albano Campus Planning and Design adopts the concept of sustainable development - social ecological urbanism, integrates many ecological theories and combines the status quo of urbanization, in order to guide the construction of the Albano campus in theory and implementation. The Albano Campus became received the CITYLAB certification in 2019. As a model of sustainable campus, the project provides a new concept for reference, and its sustainable strategy and implementation methods have important implications for campus planning.

The Albano Campus Project is located in the triangle north of central Stockholm, Sweden. It is an important urban development and is also contains the main universities in Stockholm - Stockholm University (abbr. SU), Karolinska Institute (abbr. KI). It intersects with the Royal Institute of Technology (abbr. KTH) and is located within the border of Stockholm's National City Park, the world's first national city park.

图 21 阿尔巴诺校园整体鸟瞰图

基地原本作为工业用地，是一片由铁路穿过的废弃砾石场，在未来几年建成后将成为拥有 15000 名学生和科研人员的学习研究中心。该项目于 2015 年 11 月动工，以改善斯德哥尔摩现有高等教育机构之间的联系为目标，同三所大学共同组成中心科学城——从北部的 SU 到 KTH，再到 KI 的哈加斯塔登校区，总共建造约 100000 平方米的大学校舍和 1000 所学生公寓，以及餐厅、咖啡馆等其他配套服务设施。将来这里会成为三校师生共享资源和相互交流的重要场所，也是低能耗生态可持续校园的典范。

Originally used as an industrial land, the base is a desert gravel field that passes through the railway. It will become a learning and research center with 15,000 students and researchers after it is completed in the next few years. The project started in November 2015 with the goal of improving the links between the existing higher education institutions in Stockholm. Together with the three universities, it forms the Central Science City – from SU to KTH in the north to Hagasta in KI. In the boarding area, a total of about 100,000 square meters of large school buildings and 1,000 student apartments, as well as restaurants, cafes and other ancillary facilities were built. In the future, it will become an important place for teachers and students of the three schools to share resources and communicate with each other. It is also a model for a low-energy, ecologically sustainable campus.

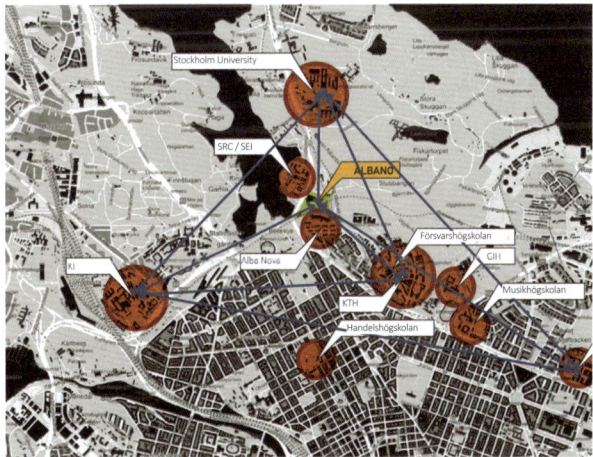

图 22 基地位于几个重要教育组团的中心位置

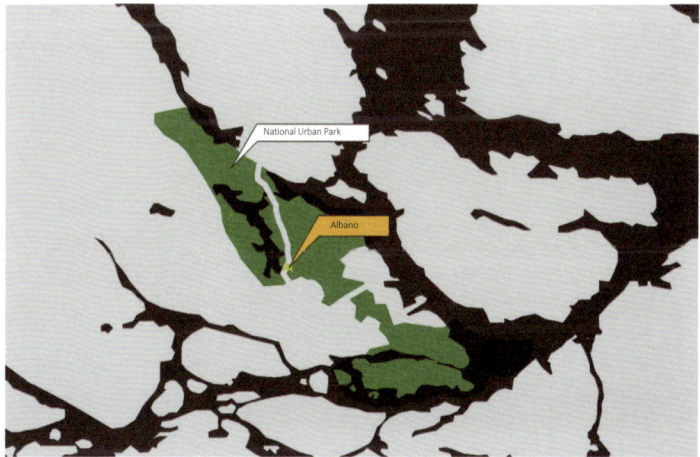

图 23 基地位于斯德哥尔摩国家城市公园范围内

1 项目愿景

阿尔巴诺校园项目旨在真正实施社会生态校园综合型规划设计，实现环境和社会可持续发展的双重目标。

（1）在环境可持续方面，从项目规划到实施全阶段各个方面，必须考虑环境的长期影响来指导项目开发，并涉及从材料选择到自行车道设计的一切内容。例如，项目的实施要能够增加该地区物种多样性，建立完善的用于灰水处理的水系统，改善当地微气候，加强城市国家公园已知的生态传播路径等。

（2）在社会可持续方面，该项目旨在创造一个有吸引力的知识交流环境，形成斯德哥尔摩中心科学城的重要战略地位。规划者试图通过将阿尔巴诺纳入更加持续的城市结构，改善阿尔巴诺与周围城市和环境要素的关联，从而实现促进公共交流空间的建立、加强与周边机构和城市环境的连接、促进高品质多元文化的发展、建立动态持续弹性灵活机制的目标。

1 The visions

The Albano Campus Project aims to truly implement the comprehensive planning and design of social ecological campus and achieve the dual goals of environmental and social sustainable development.

(1) In terms of environmental sustainability, from the project planning to the implementation of all aspects of the implementation, the long-term impact of the environment must be considered to guide project development, and everything from material selection to bicycle lane design. For example, the implementation of the project should be able to increase species diversity in the region, establish a sound water system for grey water treatment, improve local microclimate, and strengthen the known ecological transmission routes of urban national parks.

(2) In terms of social sustainability, the project aims to create an attractive environment for knowledge exchange and form an important strategic position in the Central Science City of Stockholm. Planners attempt to improve the connection of Albano with surrounding cities and environmental factors by integrating Albano into a more sustainable urban structure, thereby achieving promoting the establishment of public communication spaces, strengthening connections with surrounding institutions and urban environments, promoting the development of high quality multi culture and establishing a dynamic, sustainable and flexible mechanism.

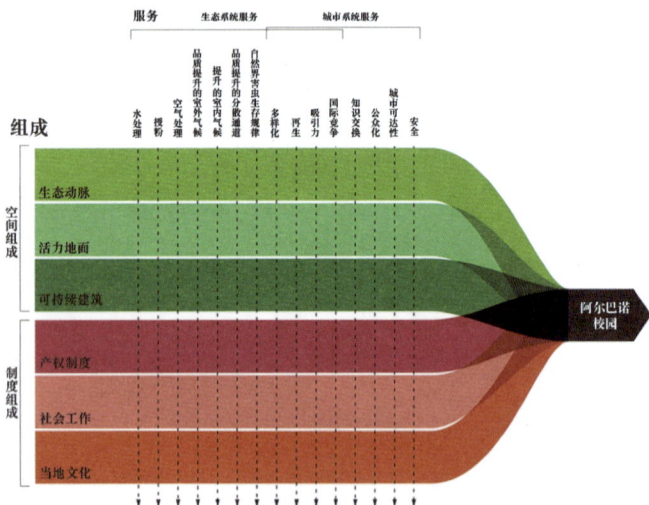

图 24 阿尔巴诺校园规划设计中的社会生态城市主义实施过程

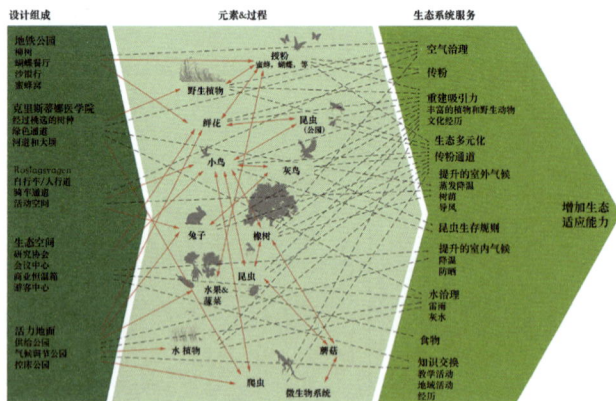

图 25 阿尔巴诺校园的生态可持续发展过程

2 可持续理念——社会生态城市主义

为了实现阿尔巴诺可持续共享校园的愿景，在规划设计过程中，由生态学家、城市规划师和建筑师共同组成的跨学科团队——拼贴小组，开创了一种城市可持续发展的新范式：社会生态城市主义。它强调城市化和生态功能的整合，以及众多利益相关者共同参与规划和设计过程，以促进社会和生态变化方面不断适应和转变的能力。该团队的思想核心是，每个人都应该尽可能地支持社会价值和生态服务功能的实现。因此他们整合了弹性思维、制度理论、城市形态和社会生态系统的相关研究，提出了另一种结合生态和社会诸多要素的可持续策略，即社会生态城市主义，并将其运用于阿尔巴诺校园规划设计。

目前，越来越多的校园正试图引入可持续发展的理念，但研究重点更多地在建筑单体、景观设计或单纯生态学层面，一个真正结合社会学、生态学与城市化发展中校园现状的可持续性策略还非常缺乏。阿尔巴诺校园项目则提供了一个独特的机会，将城市化与生态可持续发展的概念相融合，以其独有的社会生态城市主义的新模式成为可持续发展的大型校园区域的领先典范。同时，生态策略自始至终贯穿至整个前期规划、设计、施工环节。

2 Sustainability concept - social ecology urbanism

In order to realize the vision of Albano's sustainable shared campus, in the planning and design process, the interdisciplinary team composed of ecologists, urban planners and architects, the Patchwork team, created a new urban sustainable development paradigm: social ecological urbanism. It emphasizes the integration of urbanization and ecological functions, as well as the involvement of many stakeholders in the planning and design process to promote the ability to adapt and transform socially and ecologically. At the core of the team's thinking is that everyone should support social value and ecological service functions as much as possible. Therefore, they integrated elastic thinking, institutional theory, urban morphology and social ecosystem research, and proposed another sustainable strategy that combines ecological and social factors, namely social ecological urbanism, and applied it to Albano campus planning and design.

At present, more and more campuses are trying to introduce the concept of sustainable development, but the research focus is more on the construction unit, landscape design or pure ecology, a sustainability strategy with a true combination of sociology, ecology and urbanization is still very scarce. The Albano Campus Project offers a unique opportunity to combine the concepts of urbanization and ecological sustainability with its unique social eco-urbanism model as a leading example of a sustainable large campus area. At the same time, the ecological strategy can be carried through to the entire pre-planning, design and construction process from beginning to end.

————————————————————————————————————

[1] Hoque A, Clarke A, Sultana T. Environmental sustainability practices in South Asian university campuses: an exploratory study on Bangladeshi universities[J]. Environment, Development and Sustainability, 2017, 19(6).

[2] Barthel S, Colding J, Ernstson H, et al. Albano Resilient Campus: A case-based exploration of urban social-ecological design (Q-book Albano)[S], 2010: 10.13140/RG.2.2.12457.85608

[3] Rawaf R. Social-Ecological Urbanism: Lessons in Design from the Albano Resilient Campus[R], 2017

[4] Colding J, Barthel S, Bendt P, et al. Urban green commons: Insights on urban common property systems[J]. Global Environmental Change, 2013(23): 1039-1051

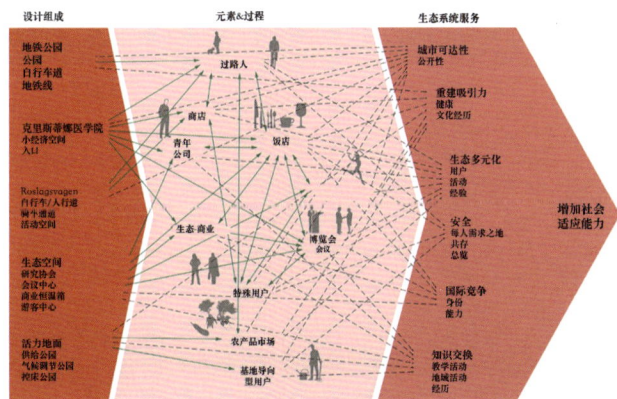

图 26 阿尔巴诺校园的社会可持续发展过程

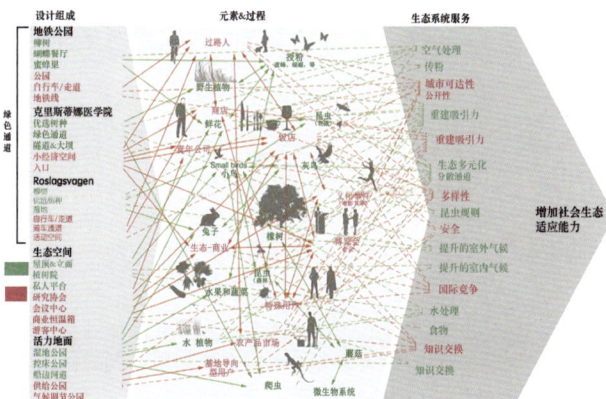

图 27 阿尔巴诺校园的社会—生态可持续发展过程

案例四　欧盟智慧发展课题　Case 4　The GrowSmarter Project

智慧城市和社区引领项目

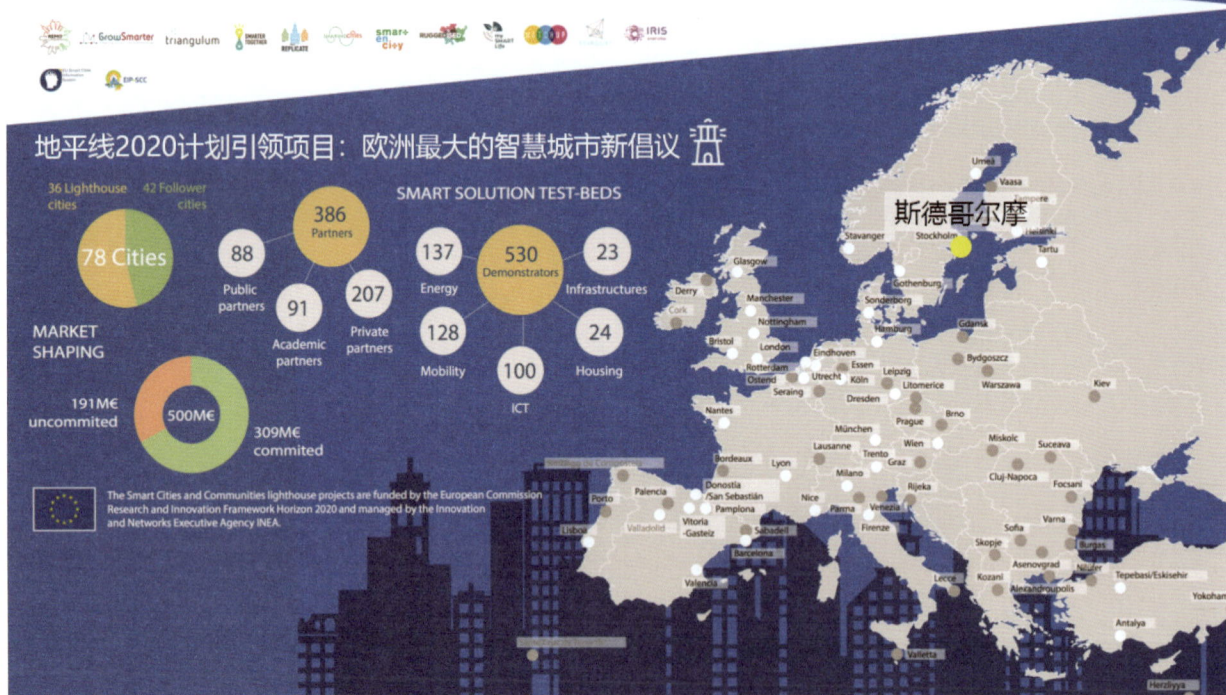

图 28 欧洲智慧城市新倡议

瑞典作为最早关注城市可持续发展及社区更新的国家之一，已开展了数十年的城市可持续规划建设与社区低能耗改造，积累了先进的可持续发展策略和技术。其中，基于欧盟支持的智慧发展课题，瑞典三大可持续发展引领城市之一的斯德哥尔摩为城市社区的可持续更新提供了完整的借鉴方案。以斯德哥尔摩瓦拉托格社区更新项目为例，重点关注社区低能耗改造与管理、基础设施集成等方面的实践策略与技术方案，为低能耗社区的可持续改造与管理提供了参考。

As one of the first countries to pay attention to urban sustainable development and community renewal, Sweden has carried out decades of urban sustainable planning and construction and low-energy transformation of the community, and accumulated advanced sustainable development strategies and technologies. Among them, based on the EU-supported GrowSmarter, Stockholm, one of Sweden's three, leading sustainable development cities, provides a complete reference for sustainable urban renewal. Taking the Valla Torg community renewal project in Stockholm as an example, the focus is on practical strategies and technical solutions for low-energy transformation and management, infrastructure integration, etc., which provide a reference for sustainable transformation and management of low-energy communities.

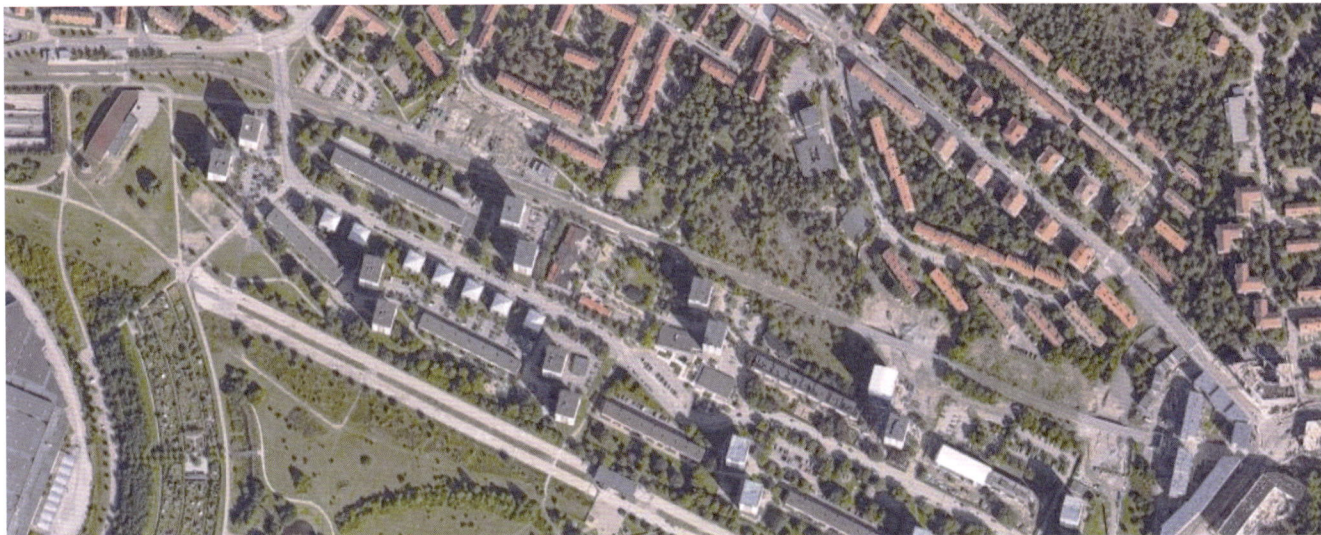

图 29 瓦拉托格社区更新后平面图

图 30 瓦拉托格社区更新后照片

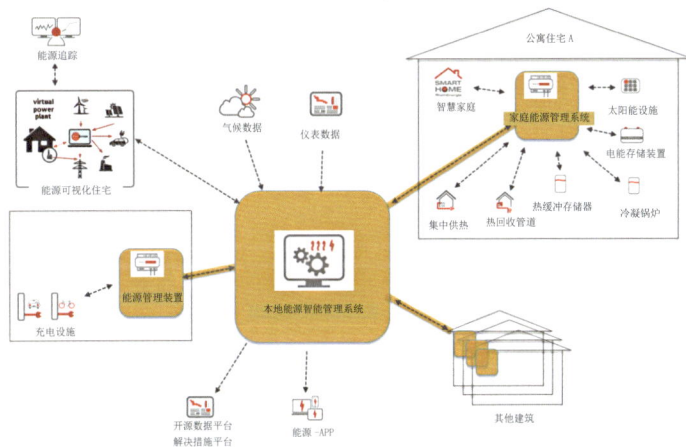

图 31 社区本地能源智能管理系统

1 欧盟智慧发展课题

智慧发展课题是欧盟最大的研究和创新计划地平线 2020 计划所资助的三大课题之一，并且是该计划下首次呼吁智慧城市和社区可持续建设的课题。该课题通过城市政府与环境技术公司协同合作，为城市的智慧可持续发展提供了解决思路。同时，它会集了城市和产业，从建设低能耗社区、集成基础设施架构、建设可持续的城市交通体系三大方面整合和展示了 12 个智能城市解决方案，为其他城市提供在实践中如何运作和借鉴的经验。

1 GrowSmarter

The GrowSmarter is one of the three major projects funded by the Horizon 2020, the largest research and innovation program in the European Union, and is the first project under the program to call for the sustainable construction of smart cities and communities. The project, through collaboration between the city government and environmental technology companies, provides solutions to the city's smart and sustainable development. At the same time, it brings together cities and industries to integrate and display 12 smart city solutions from the three aspects of building low-energy communities, integrating infrastructure and building a sustainable urban transport system, providing other cities with how to operate in practice and learn from the experience.

瑞典斯德哥尔摩作为该项目的三大引领城市之一，参与了智慧可持续城市的建设，其中，瓦拉托格是 1960 年代建设的公寓社区，亟待低能耗更新与可持续发展。该课题运用三大方面的 12 个智能解决方案来提高能源效率，减少气候影响，并创造更多就业机会。同时，以解决方案为基础，该项目正努力将城市和产业融合，创造一个完整成熟的市场体系，从而支持城市向智能及可持续发展的方向过渡发展。

2 智慧发展课题中的低能耗社区改造措施

欧洲有 1/3 的住区建设于 1950—1970 年之间，这些住区因为当时技术与材料的局限，面临着居住环境恶化、建筑耗能过高的问题，迫切地需要改造。同时，社区改造成为转型时期的城市更新的重要组成部分，且智慧发展课题将开发低能耗社区放在行动领域中的首位，由此可见低能耗社区改造的迫切性与必要性，

在低能耗社区解决方案中，从局部设施、系统管理，从家庭层面到社区层面，智慧发展课题提出了四大方向：
（1）节能建筑翻新；
（2）构建低碳建筑材料物流系统；
（3）打造家庭智能节能管理系统；
（4）建设社区本地能源智能管理系统。

As one of the three leading cities in the project, Stockholm, Sweden, participated in the construction of smart sustainable cities. Among them, Valla Torg was an apartment community built in the 1960s, which needed to be updated with low energy consumption and sustainable development. The project uses 12 smart solutions in three areas to improve energy efficiency, reduce climate impact, and create more jobs. At the same time, based on the solution, the project is trying to integrate the city and industry to create a complete and mature market system, thus supporting the city's transition to smart and sustainable development.

2 Regeneration measures of low-energy community in GrowSmarter

One-third of the settlements in Europe were built between 1950 and 1970. Due to the limitations of technology and materials at the time, these settlements faced the problem of deteriorating living environment and excessive energy consumption of buildings, and is urgently needed to be transformed. At the same time, community transformation is an important part of urban renewal in the transition period, and the GrowSmarter project will be the first in the field of action to develop low-energy communities. This shows the urgency and necessity of low-energy community transformation.

In the low-energy community solution, from the local facilities, system management, from the family level to the community level, the GrowSmater project proposes four major directions:
(1) Energy-efficient building renovation;
(2) Building a low-carbon building material logistics system ;
(3) Creating home smart energy saving management system ;
(4) Building a community local energy intelligent management system.

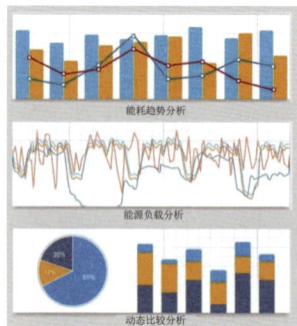
图 32 家庭能源管理系统

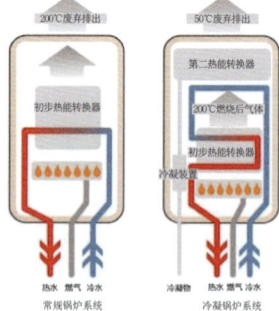
图 33 新旧锅炉系统原理对比图

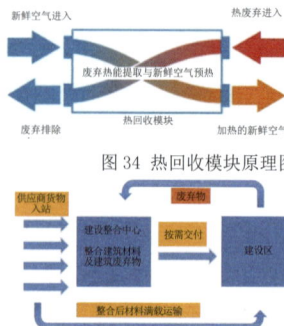
图 34 热回收模块原理图

图 35 低碳建筑材料物流运输系统图

图 36 瓦拉托格社区区位图

3 瓦拉托格社区更新项目

瓦拉托格社区处于斯德哥尔摩南部，是斯德哥尔摩最早的现代化郊区之一，紧邻城市核心。瓦拉托格社区更新项目包含了 300 多间建于 1961 年的公寓，与大多数老旧建筑的问题相同，这些公寓存在着热桥、密封性较差、隔热不佳的问题，同时缺乏能源回收及智能化系统管理的措施。这些问题使建筑在使用过程中会消耗大量不必要的能量。如今在智慧发展课题的解决方案下，这一社区已完成智慧、低能耗的改造。项目采用从节能化改造到智能化能源管理的系统方案，将能源总体消耗减少了 60％以上。

面对城市旧住区的改善需求持续增长的现状，我们不应该只是简单地进行外立面改造与绿化种植，而应该更加关注住区改造后的智慧社区的营造和建筑的可持续使用。以瓦拉托格旧社区的改造更新为案例借鉴，从建筑细节到城市系统都体现着可持续、智慧化的思想。智慧发展从局部到整体的低能耗改造经验、从家庭到社区的智慧化系统，是值得被深入学习和借鉴的。

3 Valla Torg Regeneration Project

The Valla Torg community is located in the south of Stockholm and is one of the first modern suburbs in Stockholm, close to the core of the city. The Valla Torg Community Regeneration Project contains more than 300 apartments built in 1961, the same as most older buildings, which have thermal bridge problems, poor sealing, poor insulation, and lack of energy recycling and intelligent system management measures. These problems cause the building to consume a lot of unnecessary energy during use. Nowadays, under the solution of the GrowSmarter Project, this community has completed the transformation of smart and low-energy. The project adopts a system plan from energy-saving transformation to intelligent energy management, which reduces the overall energy consumption by more than 60%.

In the face of the continuous improvement of the demand for improvement in the old residential areas of the city, we should not only be a simple façade renovation and green planting, but should pay more attention to the creation of smart communities after the renovation of the residential area and the sustainable use of the building. Taking the renovation of the old community of Valla Torg as a case study, from the architectural details to the urban system, the idea of sustainable and intelligent is reflected. The GrowSmarter's low-energy transformation experience from local to overall, from the family to the community's intelligent system, is worthy of further study and reference.

[1] European commission. What is Horizon 2020[EB/OL], 2014
[2] GrowSmarter. GrowSmarter: Bringing together cities & industry to stimulate uptake of smart city solutions[EB/OL], 2015
[3] GrowSmarter. Technical factsheets: low energy districts[EB/OL], 2015
[4] GrowSmarter. Technical factsheets: integrated infrastructures[EB/OL], 2015
[5] GrowSmarter. Technical factsheets: sustainable urban mobility[EB/OL], 2015

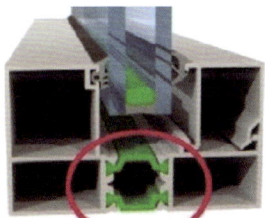

图 37 隔热玻璃及装置

图 38 垃圾光学分拣回收桶

图 39 1960 年代瓦拉托格社区老照片

图 40 社区终端回收站

案例五　斯德哥尔摩瓦斯略改造项目　Case 5　Urban Development Project, Väsjön, Stockholm

图 41 瓦斯略中心现状航拍图

近年来，在国内外城市发展中虽然在规划设计阶段越来越重视可持续发展的理念，但在实施层面关注较少。瑞典除了积累了先进的可持续发展策略和技术，其全过程的实施机制也为实现可持续发展提供了关键保障。其中，位于斯德哥尔摩的瓦斯略改造项目是瑞典最新的可持续发展规划项目之一，通过政府引导建立多方合作平台，追踪并确保可持续规划的实施推进。

1 瓦斯略改造项目的愿景与可持续策略

瓦斯略改造项目位于瑞典首都斯德哥尔摩的北部，是一个处于快速发展的地区——索伦蒂娜区。瓦斯略区域被定位为未来的住宅区，同时需要对原区域内的供水等基础设施进行大规模改造，因

In recent years, although domestic and international urban development has paid more and more attention to the concept of sustainable development in the planning and design stage, it has paid less attention at the implementation level. In addition to accumulating advanced sustainable development strategies and technologies, Sweden's implementation mechanism throughout the process provides a key guarantee for achieving sustainable development. Among them, the Väsjön Urban Development Project in Stockholm is one of Sweden's latest sustainable development projects, through the government to guide the establishment of a multi-party cooperation platform to track and ensure the implementation of sustainable planning.

1 The vision and sustainability strategy of the Väsjön Urban Development Project
The Väsjön Urban Development Project is located in the northern part of Stockholm, Sweden, in a rapidly growing area, the Sollentuna District. The Väsjön area is positioned as a future residential area and requires extensive renovation

图 42 瓦斯略中心城市意象图

图 43 交通模式分区图

图 44 现状调研

而该区域需要更为全面的具有可持续性的规划设计。基于调研及访谈确定了未来瓦斯略地区的愿景：一个小规模、多元化且以自然为导向的区域，并营造出具有活力和生活氛围的场所感。

具体包括三方面规划目标：

（1）改变市民原有的生活方式，引导人们开展活跃的日常活动。

（2）一个多元、外向的区域。在这里，以城市和大自然互动交融，社区配备有具有吸引力的设施，游客和居民都会自发来到室外的开放空间。

（3）既是生活环境，又是聚会场所。每个人都有运动和训练机会，都能享受具有创造性的环境，体验丰富的步行道，靠近并享受大自然。

of infrastructure such as water supply in the original area, which requires a more comprehensive and sustainable planning. Based on research and interviews, the vision of the future Väsjön region is determined: a small, diverse, and nature-oriented area that creates a sense of vibrancy and a sense of living.

Specifically, it includes three aspects of planning goals:

(1) Change the original lifestyle of the citizens and guide people to carry out active daily activities.

(2) A multi-faceted, extroverted area. Here, the city and nature interact and the community is equipped with attractive facilities, visitors and residents will spontaneously come to the open space outside.

(3) It is both a living environment and a meeting place. Everyone has the opportunity to exercise and train, to enjoy a creative environment, to experience the rich walking trails, to get close to and enjoy nature.

通过长期和周密的规划，政府制定了详细的目标和策略。陶斯科根和若索科根自然保护区之间的瓦斯略地区为活跃的生活提供了独特的条件。步行距离内有四个美丽的湖泊，其中法特仑湖、苏根湖和若索湖大部分都处于未受破坏的大自然中，第四个湖泊——瓦斯略湖，将成为新建筑集中的中心点，连接广场、公园小径和长廊。瓦斯略区和艾德伯格区之间是一个运动区，设有网球厅、足球场和瓦萨博肯滑雪场。 另外，政府全面分析了整个索伦蒂娜的蓝绿结构，以此为基础规划了瓦斯略的蓝绿线，创造了一个连接北部的陶斯科根自然保护区和南部的若索森林的自然走廊，沿途为不同的人群提供良好的游乐环境与生活空间。

2 基于合作平台的实施过程

在瓦斯略改造项目中，市政府为了形成利益互诉的机制，确保规划的有效实施，创建了交流合作平台——瓦斯略共识平台，为各个利益相关方提供会面交涉、协调利益的平台，推动项目发展。合作平台参与方包括瓦斯略、索伦蒂娜市和建筑商，参与形式包括联系沟通和各种活动。对于这个平台许多利益相关者参与了开发，除了市政当局，还有建筑商、业主、瓦斯略拜肯、体育协会以及该地区的其他协会和用户。合作包括协调、活动项目管理

Through long-term and thorough planning, the government has set detailed goals and strategies. The Väsjön region between the Törnskogen and Rösjöskogen Nature Reserves offers unique conditions for an active life. Within walking distance there are four beautiful lakes, of which Fjäturen, Snuggan and Rösjön are mostly in unspoiled nature, and the fourth lake, Lake Väsjön, will be the central point of the new building, connecting the square, park trails and promenades. Between the Väsjön and Edsberg Districts is a sports area with a tennis hall, a football field and the Väsjöbacken ski area. In addition, the government comprehensively analyzed the blue-green structure of the entire Sollentuna, based on which the blue-green line of Väsjön was planned, creating a natural corridor connecting the northern Törnskogen Nature Reserve and the southern Rösjö Forest. Different people provide a good play environment and living space.

2 Implementation process based on cooperation platform

In the Väsjön project, in order to form the mechanism of mutual benefit litigation and ensure the effective implementation of the plan, the municipal government has established a platform for communication and cooperation, the GassynVäsjön platform, to provide a platform for mutual negotiation and coordination of interests and promote project development. Participants in the cooperation platform include Väsjön, Sollentuna and builders, and participation forms include communication and various activities. For this platform many stakeholders have participated in the development, in addition to municipalities, as well as builders, owners, Väsjöbacken, sports associations, other

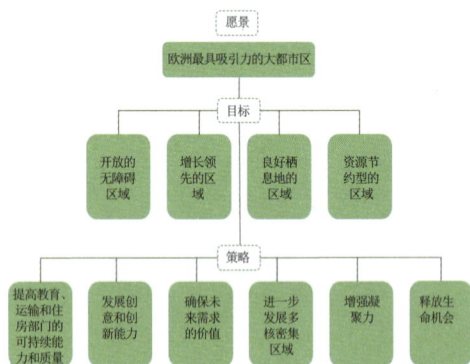

图 45 目标策略图

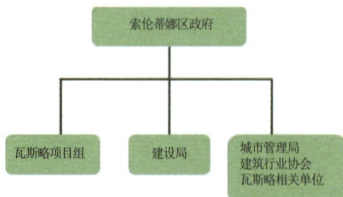

图 46 组织结构图

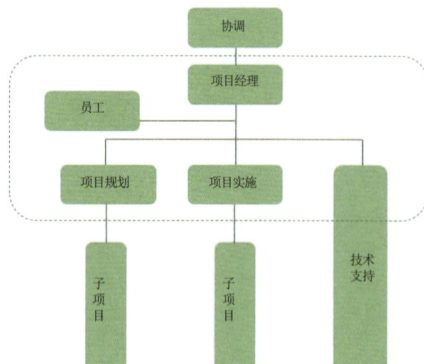

和联合调节，每年约八次。在方案生命全周期的过程中，这样的沟通合作平台为设计后续的实施和反馈过程提供了强有力的保障。

在索伦蒂娜区政府眼中，瓦斯略不是一个项目，而将其更深刻地理解为一个促进城市可持续发展的交流平台。他们基于规划地段的土地所有权，与开发商共同协商交流，制定土地政策，以便把出让条件和节能减排要求捆绑，再配合严密监管，基本保证了开发满足愿景要求。此外，规划建设的利益相关方众多，诸如技术提供商、能源供应商、施工单位等，这无疑提升了博弈过程的复杂程度，也给合作加大了难度。这种情况下，索伦蒂娜区政府积极发挥协调者、牵线人角色，促进不同企业之间的有效沟通交流，进而保障合作效率与合作质量。因而，政府不仅应充分发挥约束监督的责任，也应具备足够的领导力，积极搭建项目的合作平台，协调各个利益相关方的利益，建立公开透明的利益交换与沟通的平台机制。

associations and users in the region. Cooperation includes coordination, activity project management and joint adjustment, approximately eight times a year. In the process of the whole life cycle of the program, such a communication and cooperation platform provides a strong guarantee for the design of the follow-up implementation and feedback process.

In the eyes of the Sollentuna District Government, Väsjön is not a project, but a deeper understanding of it as a communication platform to promote sustainable urban development. Based on the land ownership in the planned area, they negotiated and exchanged with the developers to formulate a land policy, so as to bundle the conditions for transfer and energy conservation and emission reduction, and then closely cooperate with the supervision to ensure that the development meets the vision requirements. In addition, there are many stakeholders in planning and construction, such as technology providers, energy suppliers, construction units, etc., which undoubtedly increase the complexity of the game process and increase the difficulty of cooperation. Under this circumstance, the Sollentuna District Government actively plays the role of coordinator and matchmaker to promote effective communication between different enterprises, thereby ensuring the efficiency and quality of the cooperation. Therefore, the government should not only give full play to the responsibility of binding supervision, but also have sufficient leadership, actively build a cooperation platform for projects, coordinate the interests of various stakeholders, and establish an open and transparent platform for interest exchange and communication.

[1] Holmstedt M, Cunningham A. Väsjö trafikanalys Sweco[R]. Sweden. SWECO, 2013-04-16
[2] Johansson M, Wiklund E,Hanson S. Trafikutredning Väsjön[R]. Sweden. SWECO, 2011

图 47　建设流

AQUA URBANISM CHANGZHOU

GENERAL VISIONS

Changzhou Tianning: a Liveable and Sustainable Aqua-city

常州天宁：一座可持续发展的宜居水城

RECONNECT THE NETWORKS

RECYCLE THE RESOURCES

REVITALIZE THE WATERFRONT

RECONDENSE THE CITYLIFE

共建多样互联

循环资源利用

复兴水岸空间

凝聚城市活力

RECONNECT THE NETWORKS

Through diverse transportation modes and connecting blue and green areas.

共建多样互联

- 多样便捷交通　Transportation of Diverse Convenience
- 遍布互联水网　Water of Fabricated Networks
- 连续开放绿地　Green of Open Continuity

依循常州内城原有致密的河道和街巷，恢复被填埋的水道，接通断阻道路，再构多网耦合的结构系统。依托系统构建的网络化基础设施，发展包括地铁、BRT、新能源公交、自行车、水上巴士、步行在内的多样、便捷的公共交通系统。依托河道、街巷营建点线面结合的生态景观环境和连续开放的公共空间，将城市蓝绿网络和公共开放空间相叠合，修复生态质量，激发城市活力。

Following the original dense fabric of rivers and streets in the inner city of Changzhou, the buried waterways will be restored, the blocked roads will be re-connected, and a multi-network coupling structure will be constructed. Relying on the systematic networks of infrastructure, the diversified and convenient public transportation system including subway, BRT, bio-energy bus, water bus, bicycle and pedestrian will be developed. The ecological environment combined with the point, line and surface and continuous public space will be constructed based on waterways and streets, overlapping the urban blue-green networks and public space to restore the ecological quality and stimulate the vitality of the city.

RECYCLE THE RESOURCES
Through reducing consumption and smart energy systems.

循环资源利用

- 节约资源耗费　Reduce the Resource Consumptions
- 更新再生能源　Renew the Renewable Energies
- 构建循环模型　Construct the Cycle Model

构建密集、紧凑、功能混合的街区，大力发展公共交通，节约城市各种设施的运营能耗。发展包括太阳能、生物质能、地热能在内的可再生能源，逐步淘汰矿物质燃料和高能耗设施。在一定规模的区域内，建立热、水、垃圾互联的区域资源循环再生网络，创设城市资源可持续发展的常州模式。

Dense, compact and mix-use city blocks are to be built. Public transportation is to be developed, and the energy consumption of various urban facilities can be lowered. Renewable energy sources, including solar, biomass and geothermal, will be developed, phasing out fossil fuels and energy-intensive facilities step by step. Within a certain scale, a local recycling network for the interconnection of heat, water and waste will be built, and a Changzhou model of sustainable urban resources will be developed.

REVITALIZE THE WATERFRONT

By opening it to the public and improving the ecological situation.

复兴水岸空间

- 改善生态环境　Improve the Ecological Environment
- 开放便捷可达　Open, convenient and Accessible
- 多样链接水网　Multi-linked Water Fabric

京杭大运河沿线，常州是唯一一个运河主河道穿过内城的城市。从春秋淹城以降，常州是江南最具代表性的水网城市之一，曾经拥有迷人的水城肌理和高效的水网基础设施。重构在快速城市化过程中被撕裂的水网，恢复并提升水道的行洪、通行、景观和生态机能，是建设宜居水城的必由之路。在此基础上，将河道水体从被遗忘的背面转向城市生活的正面，打通主要河道沿岸空间，复兴水岸公共生活，构建连续开放、富有吸引力的亲水公共空间系统。

Along the Grand Canal, Changzhou is the only city where the canal runs through the inner city. Since Yancheng in Spring and Autumn Dynasty, Changzhou has been one of the most representative water towns in Yangtze Delta. It once possessed charming water-town fabric and efficient water-network infrastructure. The only way to build a contemporary livable aqua-city is to reconstruct the water-network fractured by the brutal process of urbanization, and to restore and improve the multi-functions of the rivers with flood discharge, passage, landscape and ecology. Based on this, the water body of the river will be transformed from the forgotten back side to the front side of urban life, the river bank area will be opened up, the public life will be revived, and the continuous open and attractive aqua-urban space will be built.

RECONDENSE THE CITYLIFE
By mixing use and vital local economy and combining with connected to the aqua-urban culture.

凝聚城市活力
- 混合城市功能　Mix the Urban Use
- 构建当地经济　Build the Local Economy
- 再造河城文化　Rebuild the Aqua-urban Culture

摒弃机械分离的功能规划，倡导功能混合的"马赛克模型"。城市发展的业态定位不仅要树立标志性，吸引外来游客，也要注重针对本地居民的日常生活服务，提供更多自主就业机会，构建自给自足的当地经济和社会系统。在城市化发展的"下半场"，重新认识存在于包括"城中村"在内的传统社区弹性、灵活、易变的组织结构和自下而上的社会活力，探索自组织、渐进式的更新改造路径。从传统河城文化中汲取营养，激发和凝聚城市日常生活的活力，树立城市更新、活力再造的常州模式。

The functional planning of mechanical separation should be abandoned and the "Mosaic model" of mix-use city should be advocated. Urban development should not only set up icons and attract tourists, but also focus on the daily life of local residents, by offering more jobs and building a self-sufficient local economic and social system. In the coming "second half" of urbanization, the traditional community, including "urban village", should be re-valued for its resilient, flexible and variable organizational structure and bottom-up social vitality, so as to explore the self-organizing and progressive approach of renewal and regeneration. Nutrition from the traditional water town culture should be absorbed, stimulating and condensing the vitality of the daily life, setting up the Changzhou model of urban renewal and regeneration.

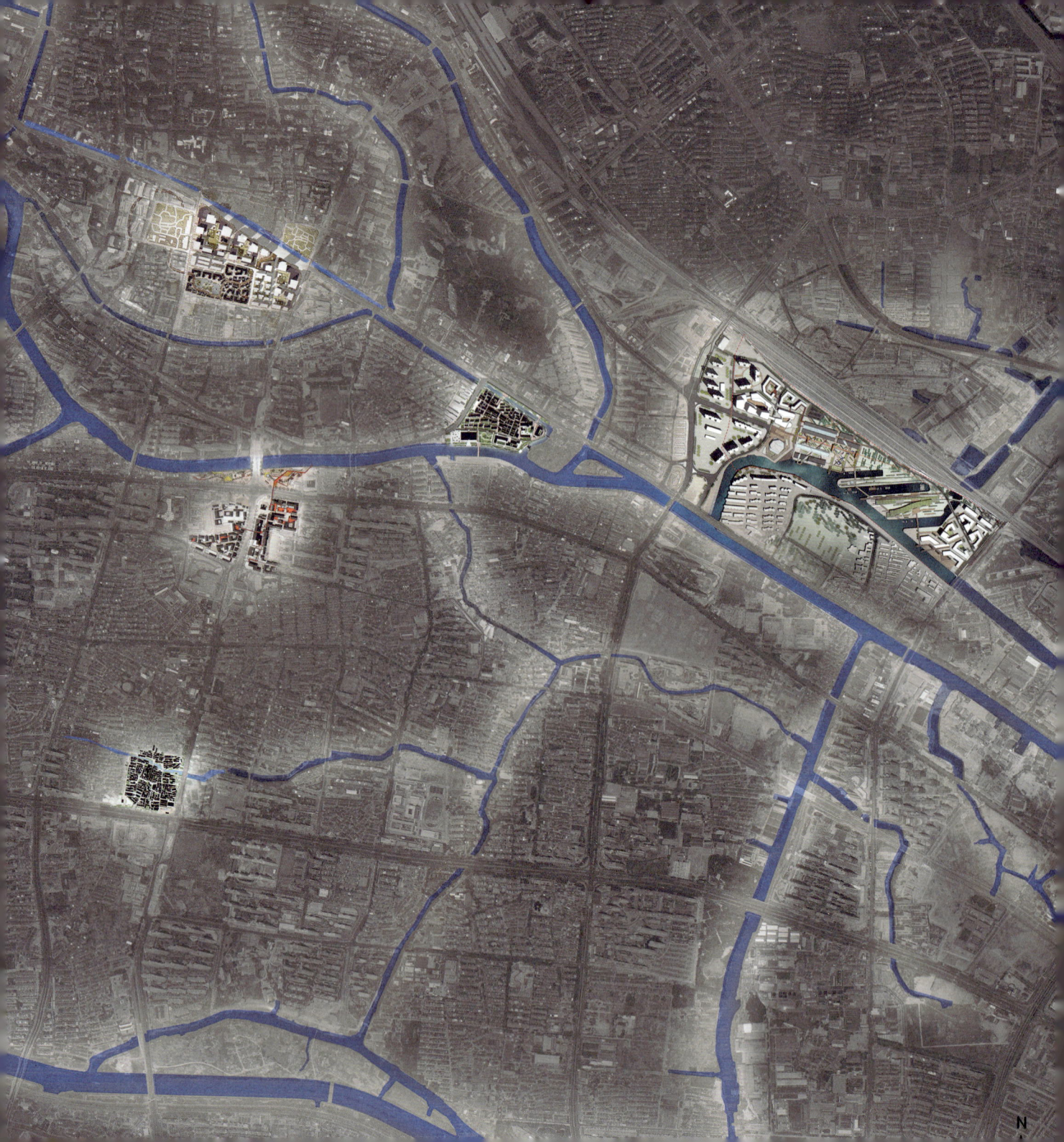

N

1. 水 + 历史文化
WATER + HISTORY AND
CULTURE

2. 水 + 混合社区 + 工业遗产
WATER + MIXED COMMUNITY
+ INDUSTRIAL HERITAGE

3. 水 + 铁路设施
WATER + RAILWAY
FACILITY

4. 水 + 公共服务
WATER + PUBLIC SERVICE

5. 水 + 城中村
WATER + URBAN VILLAGE

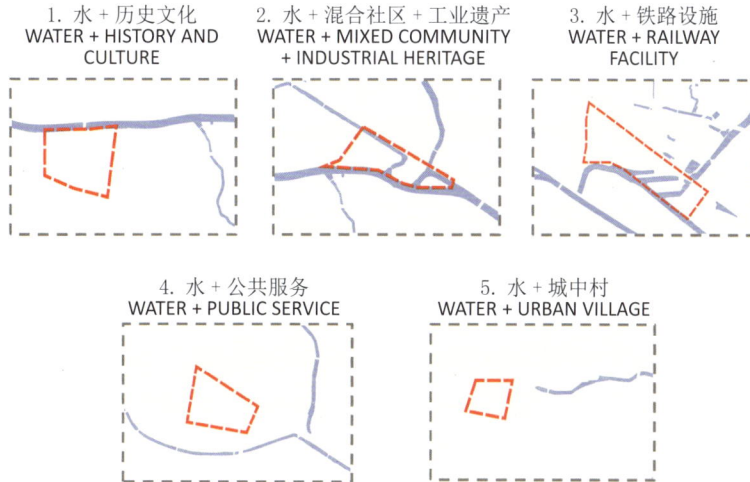

本课题对天宁区城市空间环境与基础设施系统的可持续性更新和发展进行研究和设计，提出环境可持续发展更新策略与规划导则，选择五块不同特点的典型滨水公共空间节点进行示范性设计。

This topic carries out researches and designs on the sustainable renewal and development of the urban space environment and infrastructure system in Tianning District, puts forward the renewal strategy and planning guidelines for the sustainable development of the environment, and selects five typical waterfront public space nodes with different characteristics for demonstration design.

水 + 历史文化
Water + History Culture
场地：同济桥 Site: Tongji Bridge

方案一 老城新径
Project 1   New Trace, Old Town

CITYLAB 重点关注领域分析 Focus Area of CITYLAB

重点关注领域 Focus Area		现状评价 Assessment	问题总结 Problem	协同因素 Synergy	冲突因素 Conflict	解决方案 Solution
空间与整体城市品质	[1] 功能 Function	[10] 功能混合 Mixed Use 现状街区有少量混合，如居住街区沿街商业的设置，但总体比较低端。各功能区之间的混合并不紧密，如清凉禅寺旁有与相对的商业位置。 [11] 经济适用房 Affordable Housing 现状基地内的住房主要是一片城中村，生活质量差	1. 功能混合比较单一，不是居住、服务、娱乐、文化、工作的整体混合。 2. 城中村如何改造提升现有的生活质量（房屋权属、套型、价格水平）使得居住在城中村内的人也能负担得起，和周围高档郊区的居住分异应该如何解决	[2][6][15]	[11]	1. 居住、服务、娱乐、文化、工作的整体混合。 2. 改造提高城中村现有的生活质量
	[2] 开发结构 Development Structure	[12] 整体开发结构 Integrated Development Structure 大运河人文展示带的重要节点，道路交通与周围连通顺畅	1. 蓝绿体系断裂，不能串联整个结构。 2. 街坊的分异与隔离。城中村与附近小区界线分明，围墙相隔。 3. 城中村建筑建设密度过密，公共活动空间不足，生活质量如隐私性等均没有办法很好的保证	[3][6][7][10][11]	[5]	位于运河文化节点和城市形成整体
	[3] 场地 Place	[13] 公共空间 Public Space 现状公共空间主要集中在北边绿地、道路交叉口附近的广场	公共空间分布不均，在城中村内部几乎没有可供本地人使用的公共空间	[1][2]		增加城中村内部安全可达的公共、半公共空间和走廊
	[4] 学习环境 Learning Setting	教育资源较为丰富，现状基地内有三所学校（两所初中、一所职高的某个学院）基地外也分布有幼儿园与小学	1. 中小学与周围相当于一个独立的个体，围墙相隔。 2. 学习设施没有很明显地体现在公共服务系统和蓝绿体系中。 3. 与交通的关系处理，没有很好的步行或者自行车系统。 4. 学校没有很好地与周边社区的设施共享（周末的操场）	[7][12]	[9][10][11]	
	[5] 文化遗产 Culture Heritage	一个国家级文物保护单位张太雷故居，一个省级文物保护单位清凉禅寺	建筑物在某种程度上建成，但缺乏整体历史环境			首先进行综合建设，下一步文化插入。将有价值的拆迁废料作为新建筑的原材料
	[6] 本地服务和就业 Local Supplier and Labor	[14] 社会协议 Social Clause 在城市更新改造中不会考虑雇佣本地或其他人。一般是建筑公司招投标，雇佣的也往往是农民工等劳动力。 [15] 循环经济 Circular Economy 服务于附近居民和学生的服务业，共享经济没有体现	1. 原有的花鸟虫鱼市场业态的维持。 2. 城中村居民在新的城市更新背景下获得就业的机会（商业、服务业）。 3. 学校和宗教主要靠依靠拨款，寺庙可以通过法会等方式获得一定的收入	[1][5][8]		
基础设施	[7] 交通 Transportation	[16] 绿色出行 Sustainable Travel Mode 公共交通较为便利，地块位于两个轨道交通站点之间，公交可达性较好，但是选择绿色出行的居民并不多	1. 现状主要考虑非机动车出行，地块被城市两条主干路隔开，步行流线被打断。 2. 现状有自行车专用道，使用情况不佳。 3. 地块内的步行并不连续，各功能块之间联系不强	[1][2]	[5]	1. 与整个城市的联系，构建体系。 2. 创建连续的步行系统与自行车系统，整个地块的可达性要提升。 3. 合适停车设施的容量与布局。 4. 增加不同方式的公共交通换乘，保证连续性
	[8] 信息通信技术 Information and Communication Technology	保障了人民基本通信安全和通信权力，但是没有将通信技术管理运用到地块的运营中	不够智能和整体的通信网	[1][2]	[5]	将智慧交互运用到地块的运营中
优良的空气声光环境	[9] 空气 Air	空气质量尚可，中国的大部分地区有时会出现雾霾天气	空气质量尚可提高	[12][13][17]	[7]	改进当前的空气质量，减少对空气的影响，甚至能促进空气的改善
	[10] 照明 Lighting					
	[11] 声音 Sound	较差：由于城市主干道的存在，且沿街未形成有效的绿化屏障，建筑物建造时未充分考虑隔音，因此沿街建筑均会受到较大噪音干扰；缺少积极的声音体验	1. 噪音干扰较大。 2. 缺少积极的声音体验	[12][14]		1. 增加沿街绿带作为绿化隔音屏障。 2. 创造更多积极的声音体验，如水声、鸟叫声
多功能的绿地系统和气候适应性	[12] 蓝绿结构 Blue and Green Structure	[17] 生物多样性 Biodiversity 较差，动植物种类十分有限（关于动植物的数量和种类有待进一步调研）。 [18] 生态系统服务 Ecosystem Service 一般，供给服务几乎为零，调节服务目前未知，文化服务有所提现但仍需进一步加强，能够提供基本的支持服务。 [19] 绿地要素 Green Area Factor 一般，基地总面积22.2公顷，基地内现有绿地面积2.4公顷，其中不可利用的绿地有0.35公顷	1. 绿色空间总量不足，生物多样性差。 2. 公园绿地、绿道等公共空间网络难以有效串联，存在较多断点。 3. 开放性，感知度不强，人与水的互动性较弱。 4. 绿地系统孤立，与水系、道路、其他公共空间联系较弱	[2][5][7][16][17][9][11][13]	[6]	1. 增加地块总体绿化面积和动植物种类。 2. 缩小南北地块之间汽车道路的宽度，增加城市道路与水系间腹地面积。 3. 弱化道路边界，增加滨水步道和亲水平台，去除滨水区域的栏杆，水绿更好地渗透入建筑，与居民形成一定的有效互动。 4. 将别的功能（如展览）融入滨河绿地区，形成混合的功能，增加一些公共性的广场，使该公共空间成为最有活力的区域
	[13] 气候适应性 Climate Adaption	较差：现状并未考虑到任何对环境变化的抗压能力，以及对减少极端暴雨、洪水、海平面上升的贡献措施	面对气候变化的抗压力不够，场地环境的弹性和灵活性不够	[2][12]	[6]	增强环境抗压力，将建筑、基础设施和自然文化价值融入长远变化的气候中
自然资源循环	[14] 物质流动 Material Flow	资源利用率低，没有任何可再生资源				太阳能照明设计。用地下管道运输废物，而不是用船和汽车
	[15] 产品 Product	现状使用材料符合国家环保标准，中国建设现状未过多地考虑此问题		[6][9][13][17]		使用绿色的、无公害的材料
	[16] 水 Water	一般，基本能够保证居民饮用水的安全供应，但是缺乏有效管理的废水循环（黑水和灰水的排放渠道有待考证）	缺乏有效管理的废水循环	[17]		建立有效的废水排放系统，将雨水和生活污水排放渠道分离
	[17] 能源 Energy	[20] 低碳能源系统 Energy System with Low Carbon Footprint 差，没有整体有效的能源系统，未使用可再生能源，没有垃圾分类系统，废弃垃圾和污水的能量得不到回收和再利用。总体碳排放量较高且大多来源于交通和住宅，现有绿地消化的二氧化碳十分有限	1. 总体碳排放量较大。 2. 缺乏能源回收系统和可再生能源的使用	[12][16][7]	[8][10][6]	1. 降低总体碳排放量。 2. 建立垃圾和污水能源回收再利用。 3. 使用可再生能源

水 + 历史文化

根据 CITYLAB 的 17 个重点关注领域的分析中，选取其中 9 个对场地有关键性影响的要素，通过叠图的方法进行现状问题分析，最后总结成四个核心问题，并根据其拟定愿景目标和策略。

According to the analysis of the seventeen key focus areas proposed by CITYLAB, select nine key factors that have a key impact on the site, conduct status quo analysis through mapping, and finally summarize into four core issues, and formulate vision goals and strategies according to them.

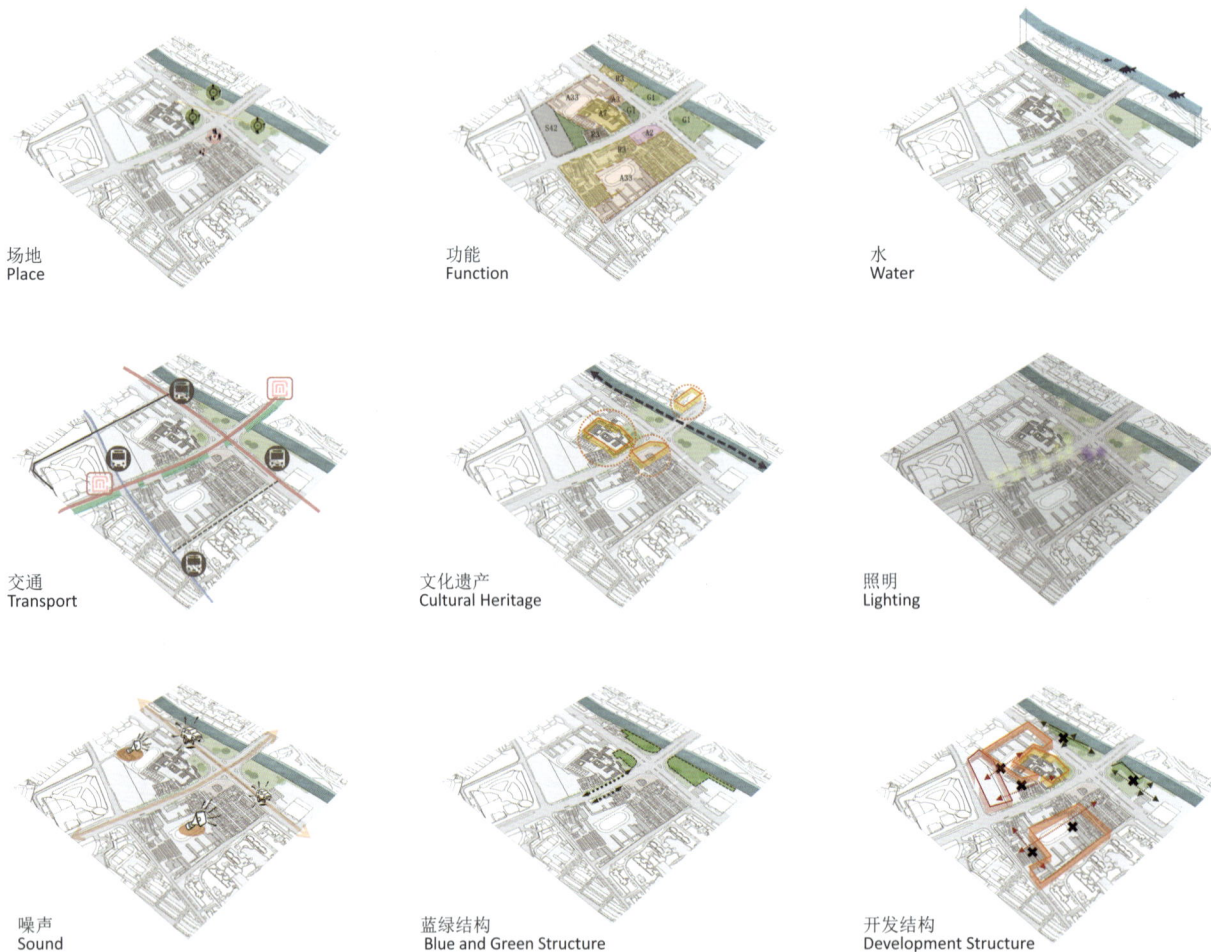

场地
Place

功能
Function

水
Water

交通
Transport

文化遗产
Cultural Heritage

照明
Lighting

噪声
Sound

蓝绿结构
Blue and Green Structure

开发结构
Development Structure

解决方案 Solutions

在对选取的重点领域逐一进行基地现状调研后，通过 9 个对场地有关键性影响要素的分析，依据 CITYLAB 提出的指导意见，分别提出应对的策略，并且用叠图的方法表示在图中。

After the survey of the selected key areas on the base status one by one, through the analysis of nine key factors affecting the site, and according to the guiding opinions put forward in CITYLAB, the corresponding strategies were proposed, and the mapping method was also used to express the strategies in the figure.

场地
Place

功能
Function

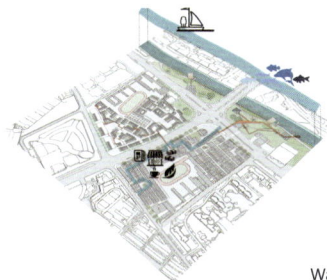

水
Water

交通
Transport

文化遗产
Cultural Heritage

照明
Lighting

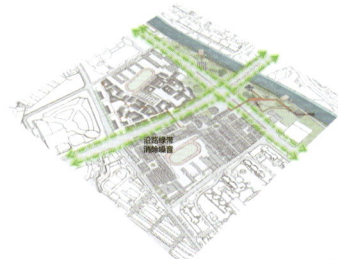

噪声
Sound

蓝绿结构
Blue and Green Structure

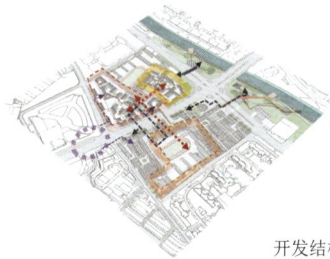

开发结构
Development Structure

地块被割裂
步行难到达

运河空间弱
滨水无渗透

公共空间少
地块活力低

遗产价值高
发挥效果弱

目标定位 Visions and Goals

Vision：A vibrant waterfront space connected to history and culture

新旧共生，文化相合的滨水活力区

Connecting functions
交通串联整体

Utilizing of waterfront space
滨水空间利用

Rebuilding public space
公共空间重塑

Setting up a main tone on history and culture
历史文化传承

交通串联整体

滨水空间利用

公共空间重塑

历史文化传承

以交通为首要设计，以步行立体交通为主。

Target transportation as the primary design, prioritize pedestrian three-dimensional transportation.

加强渗透，建立生态叙事线。

Strengthen infiltration, and establish ecological narrative line.

充考虑三种人群，连接学校和文物保护单位。

Take full consideration of three types of users and connect schools and heritage units.

以一条叙事线串联历史民俗三个功能区。

Using a narrative line to connect three functional areas of history and folk custom.

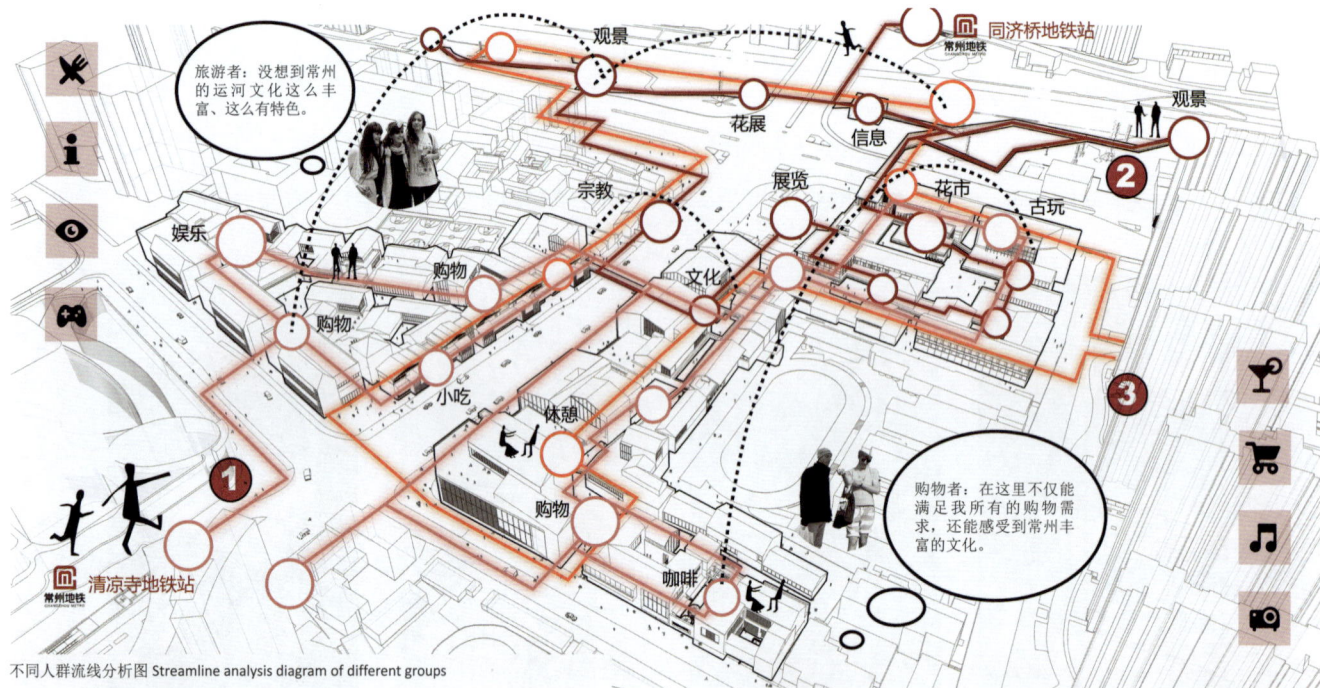

旅游者：没想到常州的运河文化这么丰富、这么有特色。

观景

花展

信息

同济桥地铁站
常州地铁

观景

宗教

展览

花市

古玩

娱乐

购物

文化

购物

小吃

休憩

购物者：在这里不仅能满足我所有的购物需求，还能感受到常州丰富的文化。

购物

清凉寺地铁站
常州地铁

咖啡

不同人群流线分析图 Streamline analysis diagram of different groups

1. 购物者流线

购物者在此可以体验到休闲、文化、民俗、饮食等多种不同的购物体验，并且提供了丰富的节点广场、二层休息平台，水街的串联引导及二层文化连廊起到骨架作用，从而形成有活力的商业街区。

2. 旅游者流线

结合运河文化和独特花鸟鱼虫以及清凉寺、张太雷特色文化，复兴德安门以及德安老街的重要激活作用，加之商业的带动，形成复兴老南门的重要契机和纽带，以文化的角度从片区带动整体。

3. 居民流线

对于日常生活在此的居民而言，通过花鸟同济桥原址花鸟虫鱼市场的复兴来唤起城市记忆，包含了鲜花、古玩、二手市场、跳蚤市场以及室外的集市，打造沿大运河风光带，为居民提供丰富而高质量的公共活动空间。

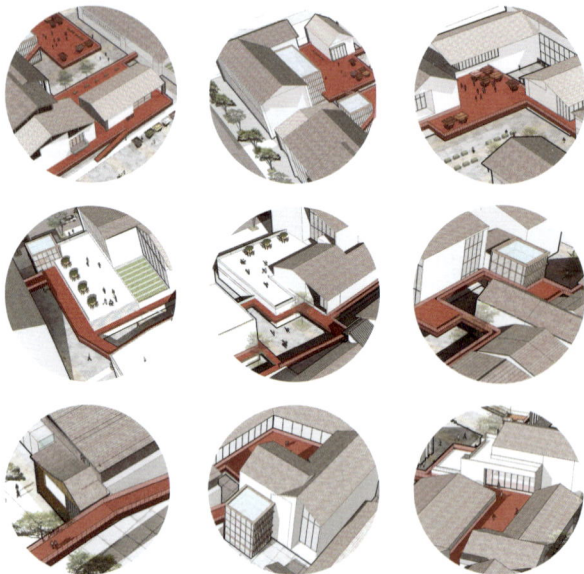

立体连廊
地上地下的互望，创造多样性的空间

水上巴士
便捷换乘水路联运的公共交通

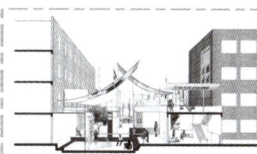

创意集市
灵活有趣的多样性街道空间

景观小品
树形结构的垂直花园，创造另人惊叹的景观

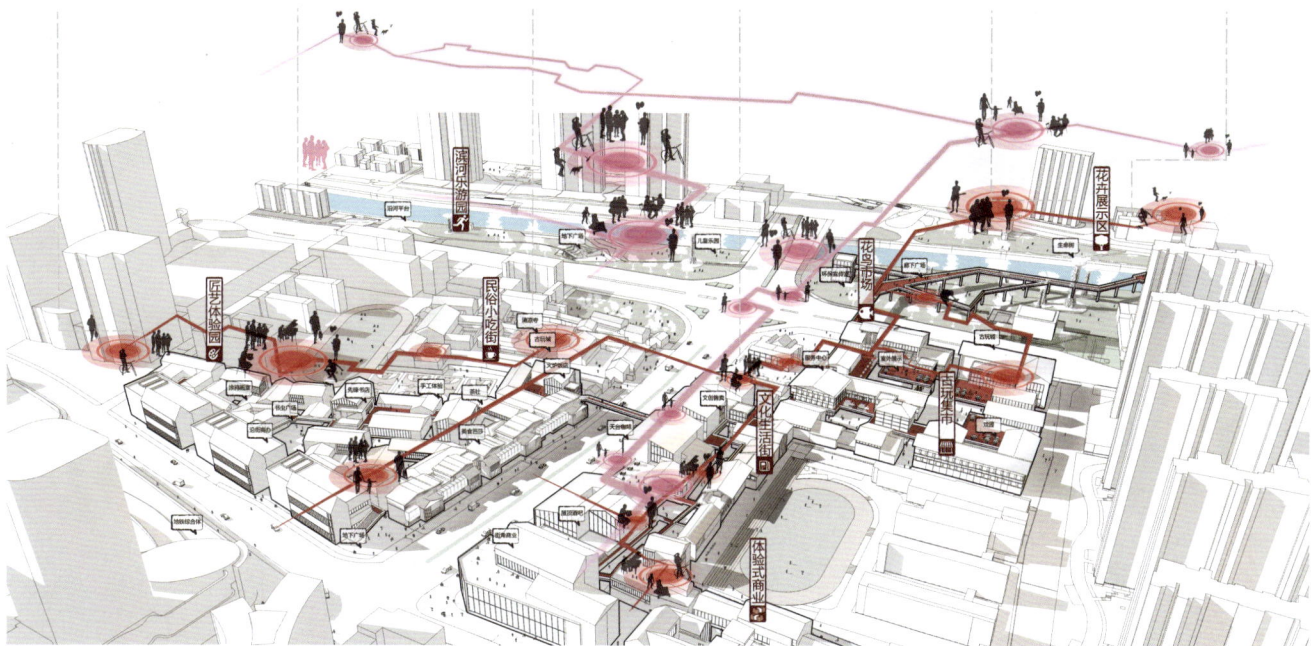

文化塑造策略:

1 文化序列的延续与演绎　　**2 集散和娱乐空间的塑造**　　**3 标志场所的丰富与演变**

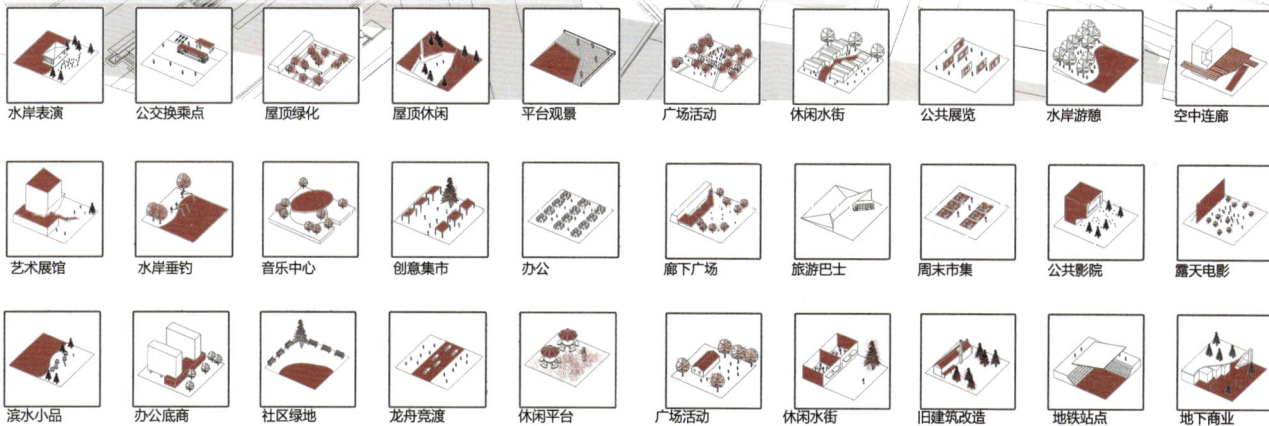

水岸表演	公交换乘点	屋顶绿化	屋顶休闲	平台观景	广场活动	休闲水街	公共展览	水岸游憩	空中连廊
艺术展馆	水岸垂钓	音乐中心	创意集市	办公	廊下广场	旅游巴士	周末市集	公共影院	露天电影
滨水小品	办公底商	社区绿地	龙舟竞渡	休闲平台	广场活动	休闲水街	旧建筑改造	地铁站点	地下商业

核心设计策略——文化叙事游线的建立：
充分挖掘基地文化，在实现对文化融入、传承、复兴的基础上，与多种模式的商业结合，通过空间廊道将二者串联成一个整体，进而集聚人群，激活场地，带动整体片区的发展。整个地块主要建筑分为民俗、文化和休闲商业三个分区，具体的业态有文化、民俗和休闲商业，并且通过路径将商业与清凉寺、张太雷故居等文化点和运河绿地景观相串联贯通。

Core design strategy - establishment of cultural narrative tour line:
We aim to fully excavate the base culture on the basis of realizing the integration, inheritance and revival of the culture. We would combine the cultural and commercial areas with various business models and connect them into a whole through the space corridor; hence we can gather people, activate the site and drive the development of the whole area. The main buildings are divided into three zones: folk custom, cultural and leisure business. The commercial area is connected with the Qingliang Temple, Zhang Tailei's Former Residence, and other cultural spots as well as the green landscapes of canal through the path.

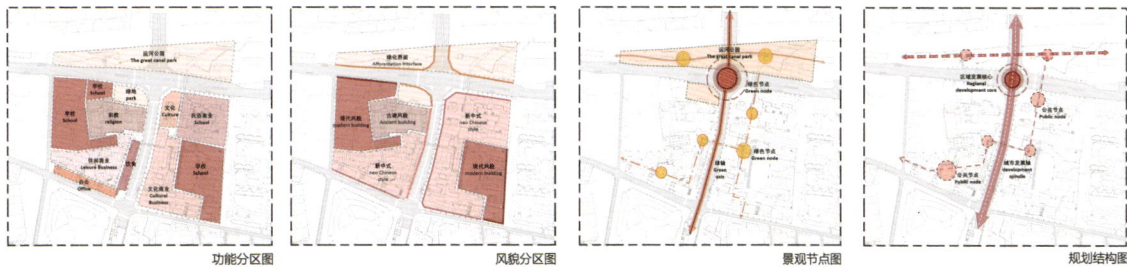

功能分区图   风貌分区图   景观节点图   规划结构图

廊道分析

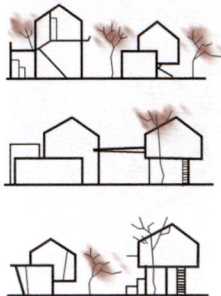

功能重组

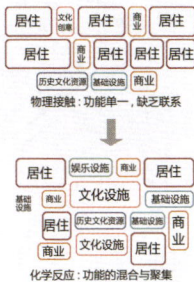

物理接触：功能单一，缺乏联系

化学反应：功能的混合与聚集

1. 水平空间复合模式分析

合水平模式：
由功能分区
到功能混合

2. 垂直空间混合模式分析

合垂直模式：
由单一功能
到复合功能

3. 建筑场地融合模式分析

合内外模式：
由室内外空间分离
到灰空间整合联动

运河公园生态分析

生态体验系统

生物安全格局

水生态安全格局

城市风热安全格局

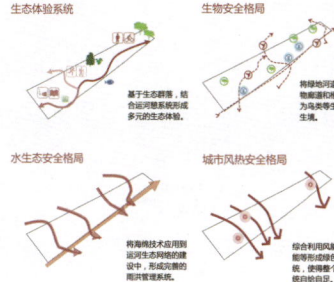

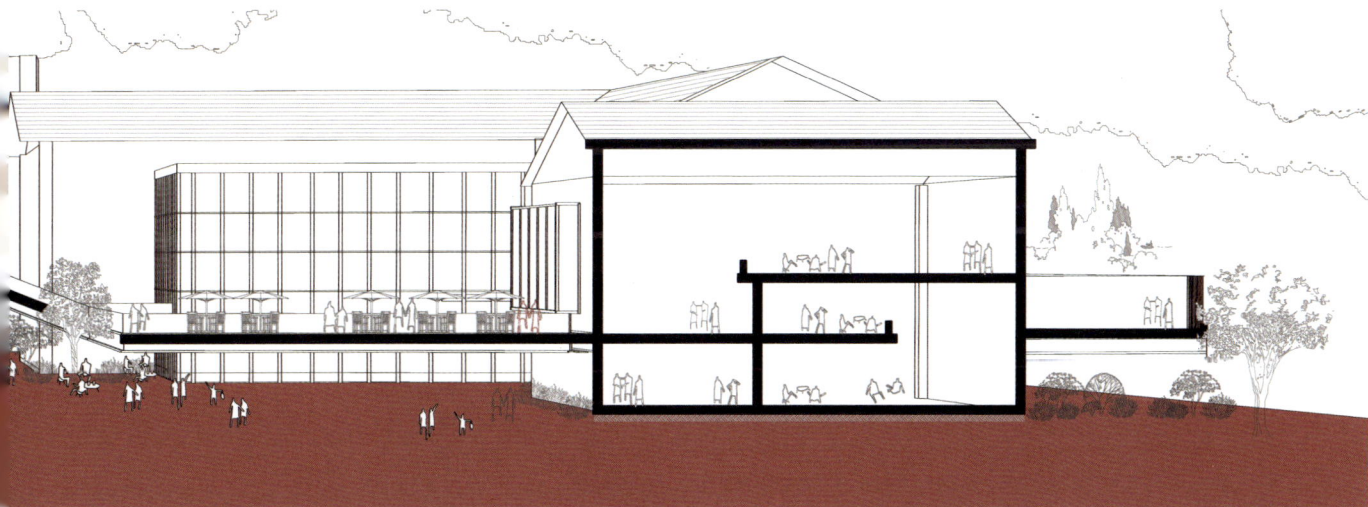

建筑分析 Building Analysis

立体交通分析 Three-dimensional Traffic Analysis

文化价值 Cultural value

可利用价值 Utilization value

建筑处置方式 The proposal

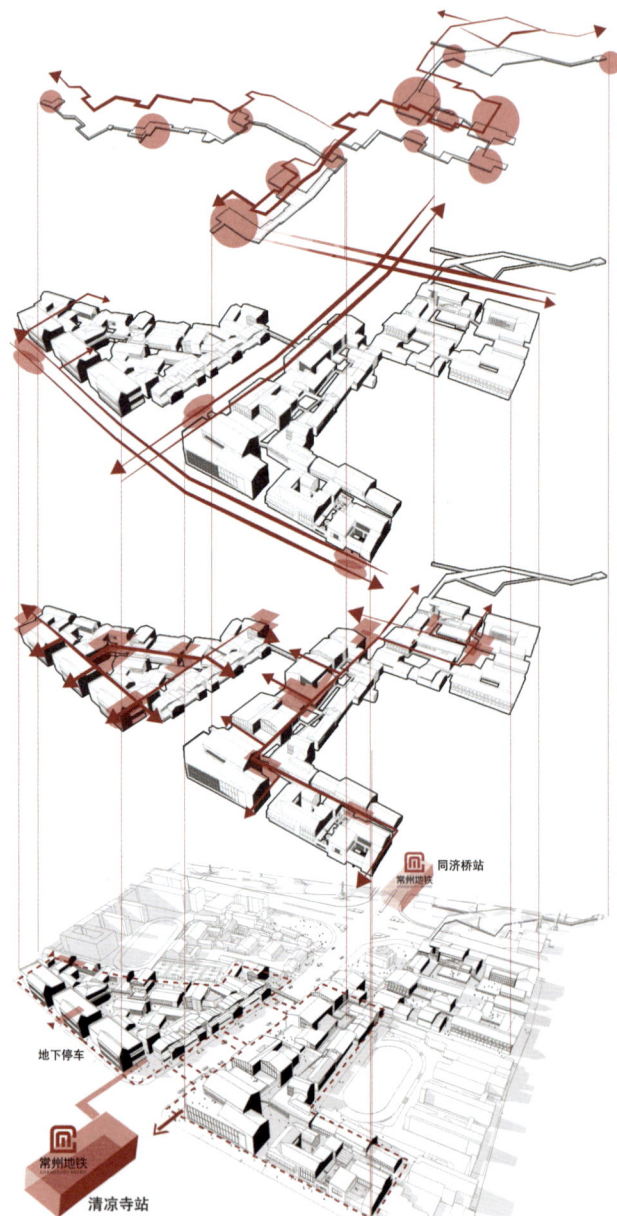

同济桥站
常州地铁

地下停车

常州地铁

清凉寺站

廊下空间 Corridor space

平台转换 Platform conversion

二层平台 The second floor platform

水 + 历 史 文 化

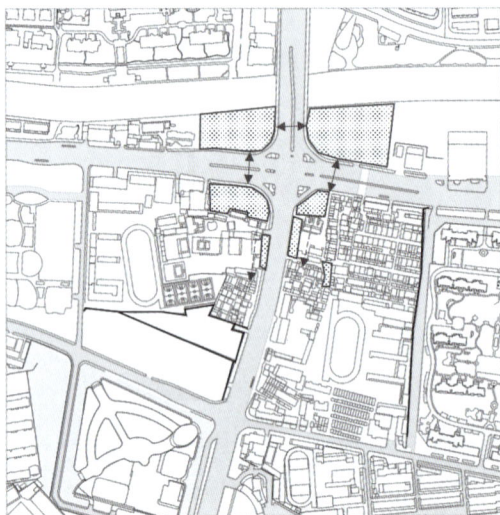

公共空间
围墙

基地原本公共空间状况

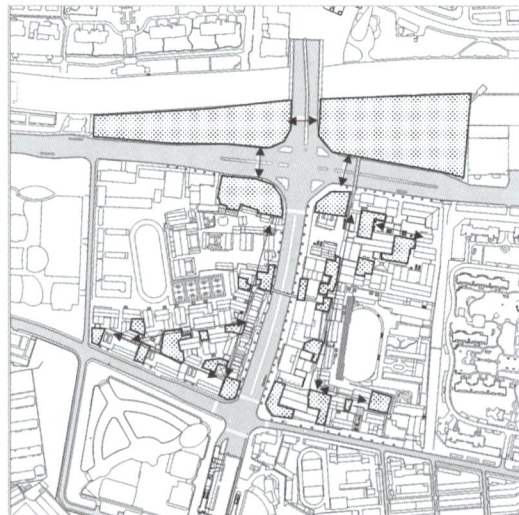

公共空间

设计后公共空间状况

公共空间
行道树

基地蓝绿系统现状

公共空间
行道树
水街

设计后蓝绿系统状况

运用海绵城市的生态雨洪系统，运河绿地最大化地实现滞留渗透、传输引导、资源利用的雨水管理过程，使雨水在下渗过程中逐层净化，最终排入运河。

Using the ecological rainwater and flood system of sponge City, so that the canal green space maximizes the rainwater management process of detention infiltration, transmission guidance and resource utilization, so that the rainwater can be purified layer by layer in the infiltration process and finally discharged into the canal.

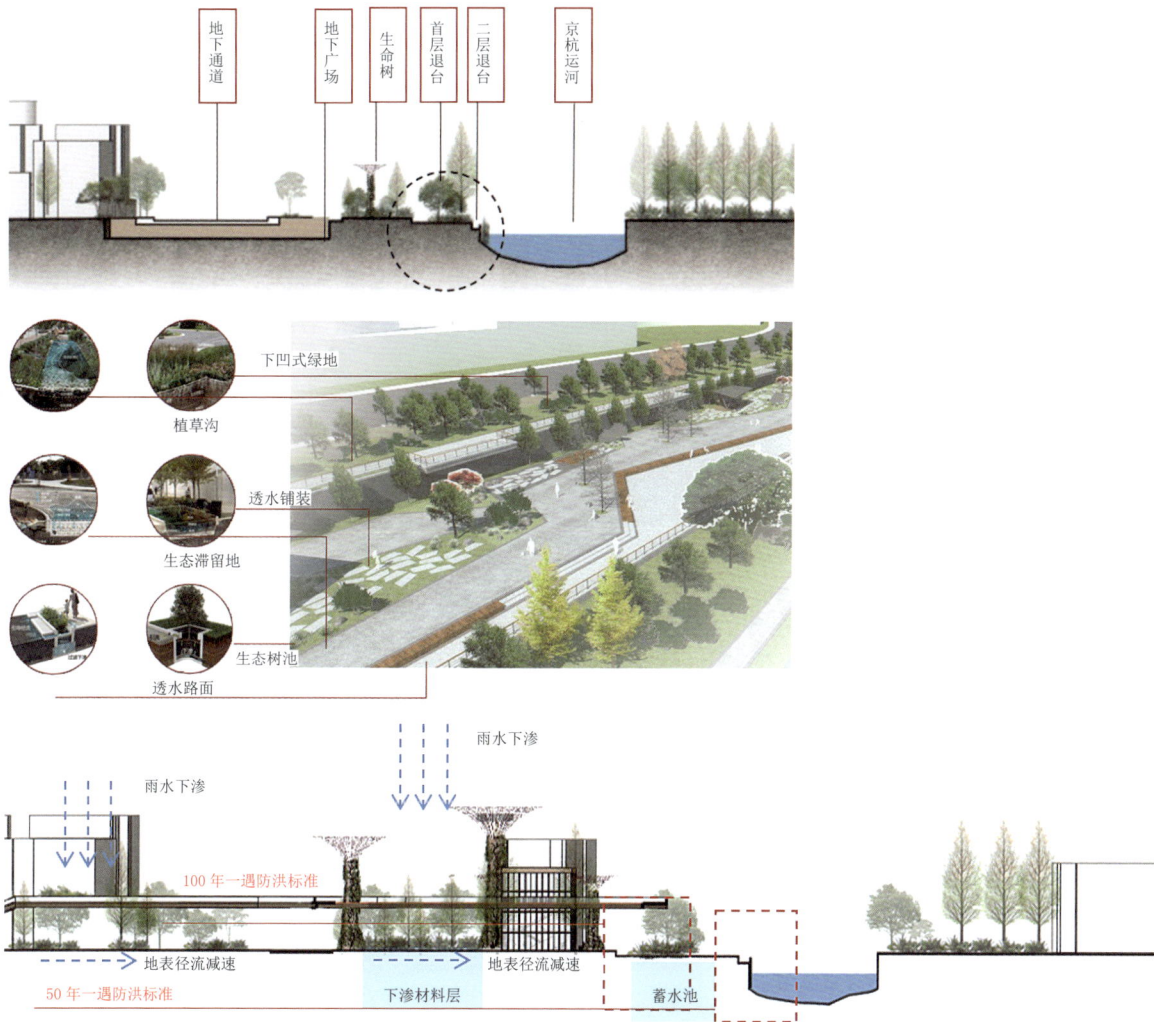

地下通道　地下广场　生命树　首层退台　二层退台　京杭运河

下凹式绿地

植草沟

透水铺装

生态滞留地

生态树池

透水路面

雨水下渗

雨水下渗

100年一遇防洪标准

地表径流减速

地表径流减速

50年一遇防洪标准

下渗材料层

蓄水池

鸟瞰效果图　Aerial view

总平面图　Master Plan

水 + 混合社区 + 工业遗产
Water + Mixed Community + Industrial Heritage
场地：舣舟亭社区 Site: Yizhouting Community

方案二　活力社区的连续"有机质"
Project 2　Continuous Organic Matter in Vibrant Community

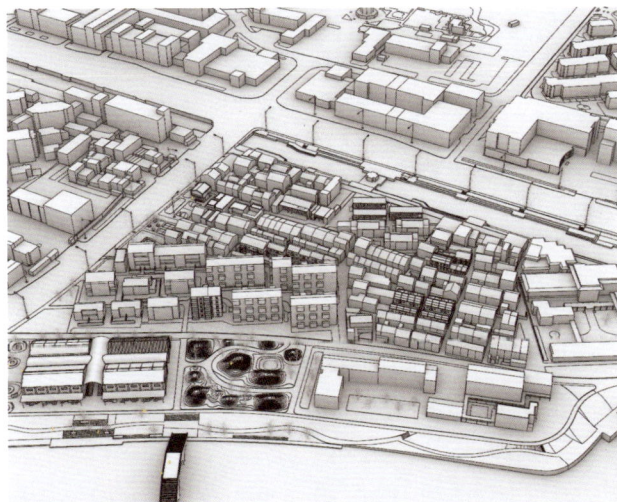

策略一：梳理街巷，创造联系，织补网络

愿景 Visions

（1）改造工厂建筑和学校为当地居民提供更多的工作机会，形成循环经济模式。
（2）改善运河河岸和社区内部环境，打造一个生态友好区域。
（3）新建基础设施和公共场所，改善当地居民的生活条件。
（4）改造民居作为更新样本，引导居民进行自我更新。

(1) Renovate the industrial factory buildings and teaching facilities to create more jobs for the local people and to build a circular economy.
(2) Improve the environment along the canal and in the communities to make it a more ecologically friendly area.
(3) Newly built infrastructure and public spaces to improve the living condition for the local people.
(4) Refurbish some of the dwellings in the communities to set up a model for the villagers on how to develop their own houses.

策略二：共享活力，柔化边界，共同富裕

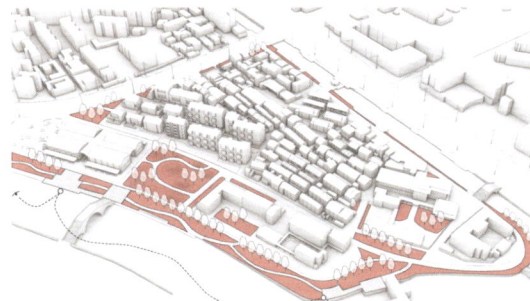

策略三：修复生态，构建绿网，水岸复兴

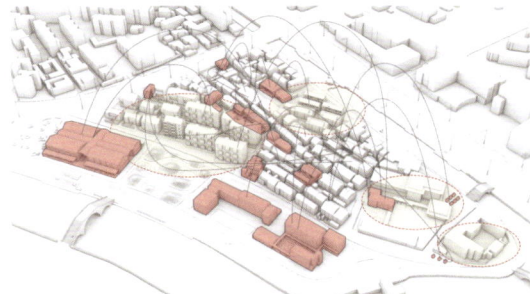

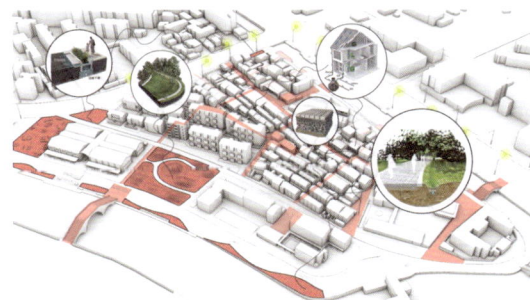

策略四：物质循环，节约能源，海绵社区

105

图例 Legend

绿地
Greenland
教育
Education
商业
Commercial
改建建筑
Updating Building
增加绿地
Adding Greenland
游船码头
Dock
活力广场
Vigor Square
水上游线
Pleasure Boat Route

Ⅰ 功能 Function

1. 丰富运河沿岸功能，植入公共服务及文化功能，增加城市联系。
2. 植入社区活动中心、早餐店、茶室、卫生站、棋牌功能。
1. Enrich the functions along the canal, embed public services and cultural functions, and increase urban links. 2. Implant the functions of community activity center, breakfast shop, tea room, health station, chess and cards.

活动场地

图例 Legend

绿化场地
Green Public Space
广场
Public Square
运动场地
Sport Space
室内活动场所
Indoor Public Space
围墙
Wall

Ⅲ 场地 Place

1. 打破部分围墙，共享活动场地。
W2. 新建广场、茶室、棋牌室等公共场所。
1. Break parts of the fence and share the venue. 2. Built new public places such as plaza, teahouse, chess and card room.

图例 Legend

网络
Network
室内节点
Indoor Node
室外节点
Outdoor Node
边界
Boundary

Ⅱ 开发结构 Development Structure

1. 打破或者柔化内部不同发展结构之间的边界。
2. 顺应场地自身发展结构。
1. Break or soften the boundaries between different internal development structures. 2. Combined with the development structure of the site itself.

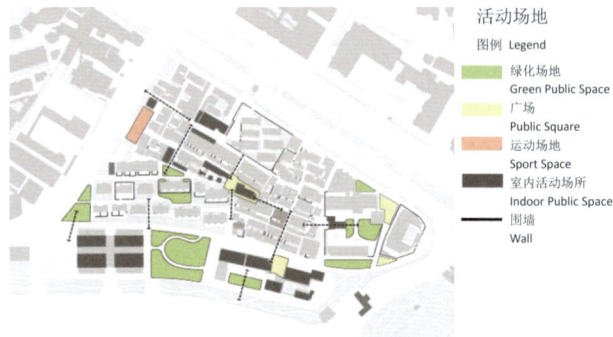

滨水绿廊

图例 Legend

滨水绿廊
Greenland
滨水广场
Water Front Square
游船码头
Marina
茶室
Teahouse
步道
Footpath
自行车道
Cycle Path
围墙
Wall

Ⅲ 场地 Place

3. 增加滨水空间节点与层次，提供多元滨水体验。
3. Increase the spatial nodes and levels of waterfront, and provide multiple waterfront experiences.

街巷空间

| 拆除部分围墙 | 拆除部分建筑 | 拆除部分辅房 | 拆除部分违建 | 拆除部分建筑 |

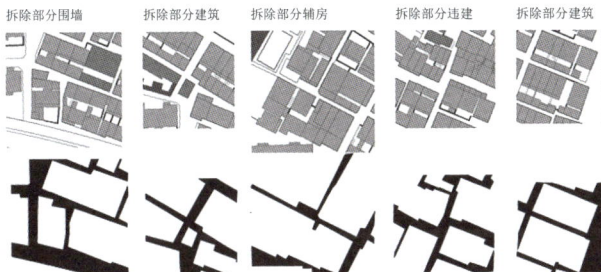

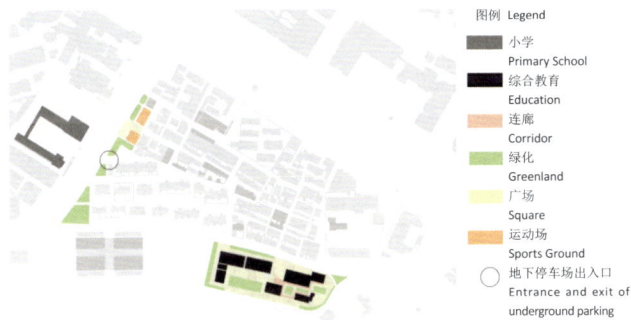

图例 Legend

车行道路
Road
步行通道
Walk
地下停车场
Parking

III 场地 Place

4. 重新构建公共场所和场地的关系。拆除部分违建及质量较差的建筑，打通基地内部与滨水空间的联系，串联活力节点。

4. Rebuild the relationship between public places and venues. Remove some illegal and poor quality buildings, connect the base with the waterfront space, and connect the dynamic nodes in series.

V 交通 Transportation

1. 点状空间（场地）：分散，封闭，缺乏联系，使用较少。

1. Node space : Dispersion, closure, lack of contact, low vitality, less use.

图例 Legend

小学
Primary School
综合教育
Education
连廊
Corridor
绿化
Greenland
广场
Square
运动场
Sports Ground
地下停车场出入口
Entrance and exit of
underground parking

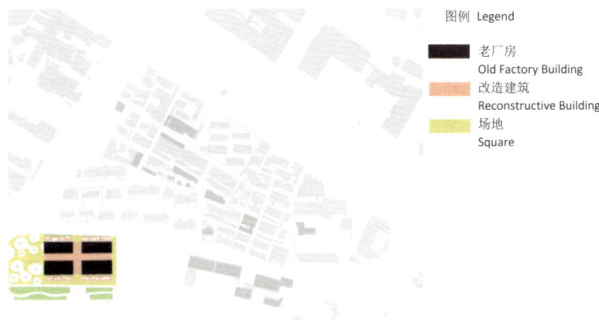

图例 Legend

老厂房
Old Factory Building
改造建筑
Reconstructive Building
场地
Square

IV 学习环境 Learning Setting

1. 重新利用工会干部学校的教学建筑，发展新的功能，结合场地进行设计。 2. 基地西侧设置绿地广场，满足集散需求。

1. Reuse the teaching buildings of trade union cadre schools, develop new functions, and design them in combination with the venues. 2. Greenbelt plaza is set on the west side of the base to meet the demand of distribution.

VI 文化遗产 Cultural Heritage

1. 重新对工业厂房进行改造利用，突出厂房原本的文化功能，解决本地居民就业问题。 2. 统一设计厂房及周边景观环境，丰富室内及室外空间。

1. Reconstruct and utilize the industrial plant again, highlight the original cultural function of the plant, and solve the employment problem of local residents. 2. Unified design of plant and surrounding landscape environment, enrich indoor and outdoor space .

水 + 混合社区 + 工业遗产

図例 Legend
kWh/m²
2000
1805
1610
1415
1220
1025
830
635
440
245
<50

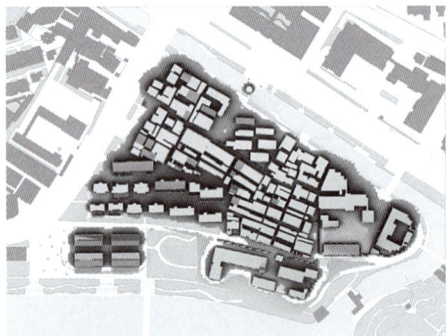

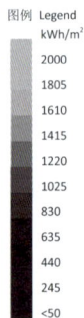

Ⅶ 照明 Lighting

1. 通过改造民居改善民居的采光。
2. 拆除居民的私搭乱建，扩宽街道宽度。
1. Improve the lighting of residential houses by transforming residential houses. 2. Demolish the private buildings of residents and widen the street width .

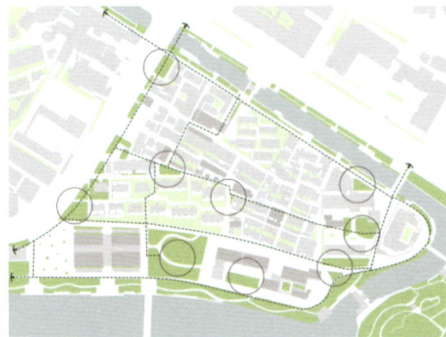

図例 Legend
绿廊
Green Corridor
其他绿地
Other Greenland
运河
Canal
绿化节点
Green Node

Ⅸ 蓝绿结构 Blue and Green Structure

1. 打通绿廊。
1. Connecting green space

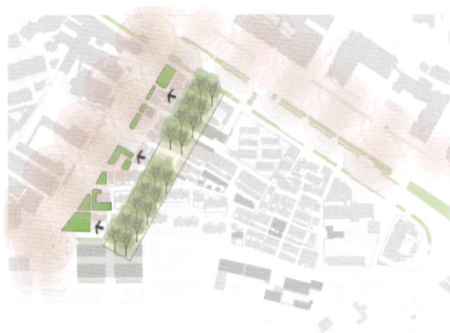

図例 Legend
噪音
Sound
隔离绿带
Greenland

Ⅷ 噪声 Sound

1. 设置绿化带，种植高大树木降低噪音污染。
1. Set up green belts and plant tall trees to reduce noise pollution.

図例 Legend
渗水绿地
Seepage Green Space
排水路径
Drainage Path

Ⅹ 气候适应性 Climate Adaptation

1. 滨河景观带与地面可渗透，雨水不会集中在地表。
1. The riverfront landscape belt is permeable to the ground, and the rainwater is not concentrated on the surface..

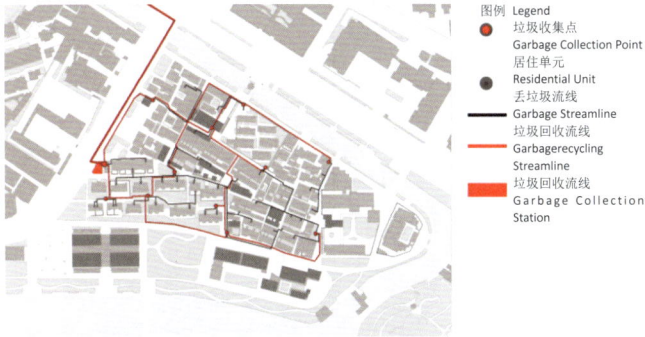

图例 Legend
- 垃圾收集点 Garbage Collection Point
- 居住单元 Residential Unit
- 丢垃圾流线 Garbage Streamline
- 垃圾回收流线 Garbagerecycling Streamline
- 垃圾回收流线 Garbage Collection Station

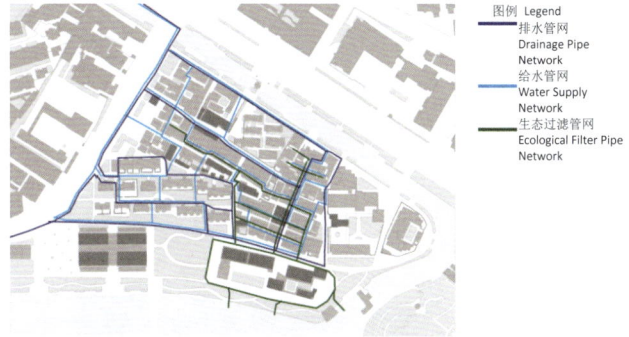

图例 Legend
- 排水管网 Drainage Pipe Network
- 给水管网 Water Supply Network
- 生态过滤管网 Ecological Filter Pipe Network

XI 物质流动 Material Flow

1. 提高绿地生态功能。
2. 建立垃圾分类和能源回收中心。

1. Improve the ecological function of green space. 2. Create a waste sorting and energy recycling center.

XII 水 Water

1. 改善绿地生态功能，提高容纳雨洪的能力。2. 场地内部水的供应同时需要考虑消防的问题，可以在局部节点配合水景设置消防水池。3. 鼓励对雨水的回收利用和对生活废水的净化处理。4. 更换水管设施，拆除私搭乱建。

1. Improve the ecological function of green space and the ability to accommodate rainwater. 2. The water supply in the site needs to consider the problem of fire protection at the same time. The fire pool can be set up at the local node in cooperation with the water feature. 3. Encourage the recycling of rainwater and the purification of domestic wastewater. 4. Replace the water pipe facilities and dismantle the private buildings.

XIII 信息通信技术
Information and Communication Tecnology

1. 通过改造住宅建立一个智慧化的社区系统。
1. Build an intelligent community system by transforming the house.

XIV 当地服务和就业
Local Supplier and Labor

1. 改造民居、学校用房和工业厂房提供就业机会。
2. 创造循环经济模式，提供可持续的就业岗位。

1. Renovate of residential, school buildings and industrial plants to provide employment opportunities. 2. Create a circular economy model that provides sustainable jobs.

延 陵

南

桃

园

路

古 运 河

雨水沉淀池
Rainwater
Sedimentation Tank

雨水花园
Rain Garden

信息交流咖啡店
Information Center
/Cafe

篮球场
Basketball Court

Square

羽毛球场
Badminton Court

雨水花园
Rain Garden

垃圾站
Dump

小学
Primary School

托儿所
Child-care Centre

饺子店
Dumpling
Store

儿童活动
Children Land

桃园二村
Residential

雨水沉淀池
Rainwater
Sedimentation Tank

棋牌
Chess and Mahjong
Room

棋牌
Chess and Mahjong
Room

早餐店
Breakfast Bars

住宅
Houses

小卖部
Retails

社区中心
Community Center

干休所
Cadre Recuperation

潘家村
Urban Village

民宿
Homestay

花鸟店
Flower Shop

社区休闲
Community Leisure

社区休闲
Community Leisure

喷泉广场
Fountain Square

食品市场
Food Market

滨水休闲
Waterfront Leisuret

滨水休闲
Waterfront Leisuret

地下停车出入口
Parking Entrance

雨水花园
Rain Garden

老年活动中心
Senior Activity Center

入口广场
Square

儿童教育
Children Education

亲水平台
Hydrophilic Platform

总平面图　Master Plan

方案拆改建示意图 Schematic Diagram Demolition and Reconstruction

基地现状 Current Situation

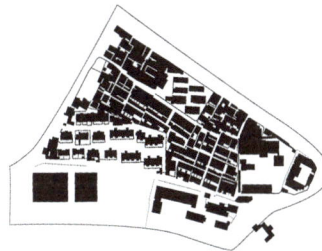

拆除部分建筑 Removed Buildings

拆除部分围墙 Removed Walls

打通街巷 Connect the Streets

保留建筑 Remained the Buildings

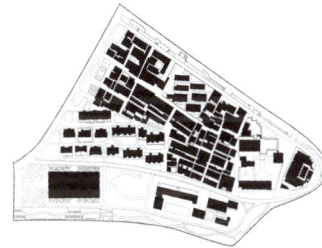

改造建筑 Renovated Buildings

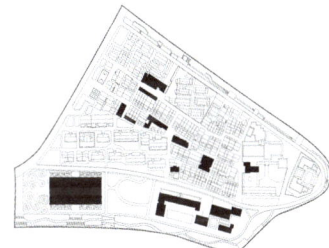

新建建筑 New Buildings

设计方案 Comprehensive Plan

路

河

院
nium

香火街
Incense Street

寺庙
Temple

香火街
Incense Street

茶室
Tea House

东坡公园
Dongpo Park

N

1:800

水
+
混
合
社
区
+
工
业
遗
产

通过对场地高程的竖向分析，我们可以清晰地看到场地呈现出一种东高西低的趋势，在三个点处出现了谷底。设计希望通过一套整合的雨水收集系统来有效处理直接排水的现象，同时丰富街巷景观。

Through the vertical analysis of the site elevation, we can clearly see that the site presents a trend of high east and low west and begins a bottom at three points. The design aims to effectively handle direct drainage through an integrated rainwater harvesting system, and the same time, enrich the street landscape.

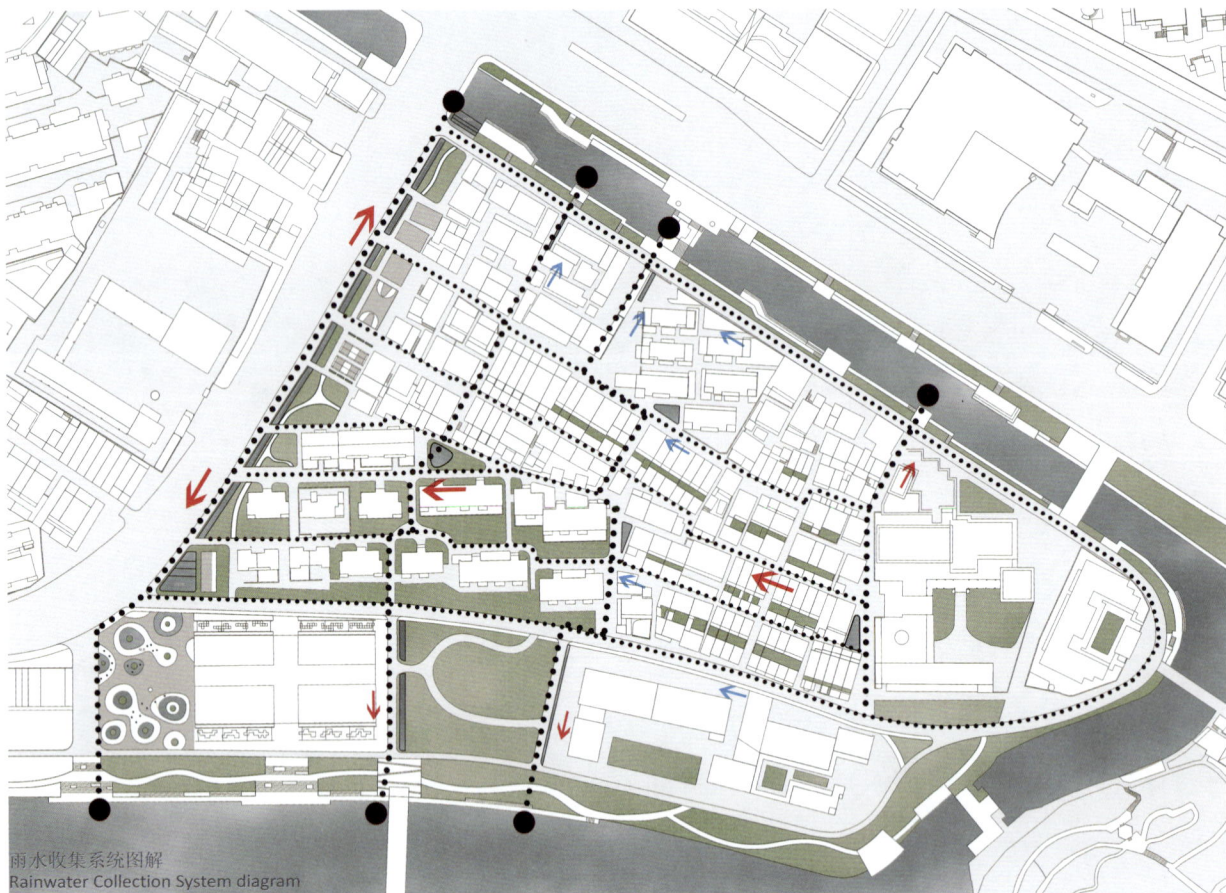

雨水收集系统图解
Rainwater Collection System diagram

市河断面 City River Section

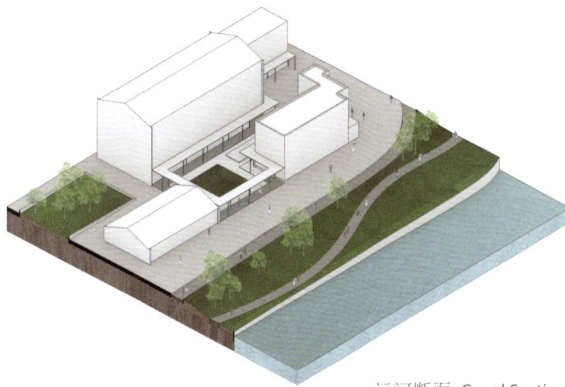

运河断面 Canal Section

落水管

落水管

排水沟　植草沟

地漏
庭院

植草沟　排水沟

市政管道　排水管

市政管道

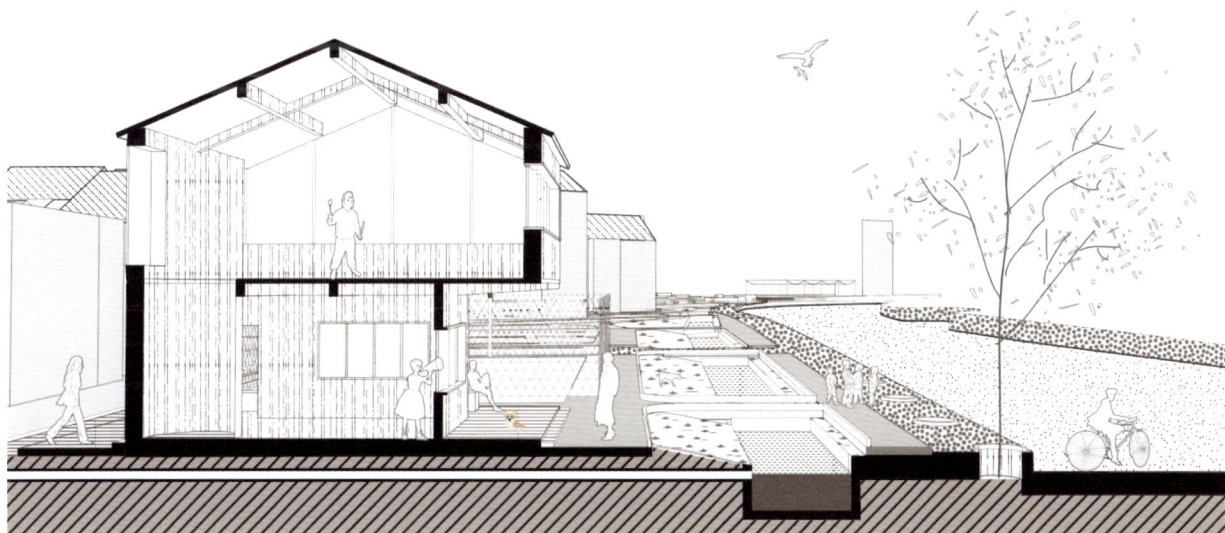

方案场景图 Scenario Map

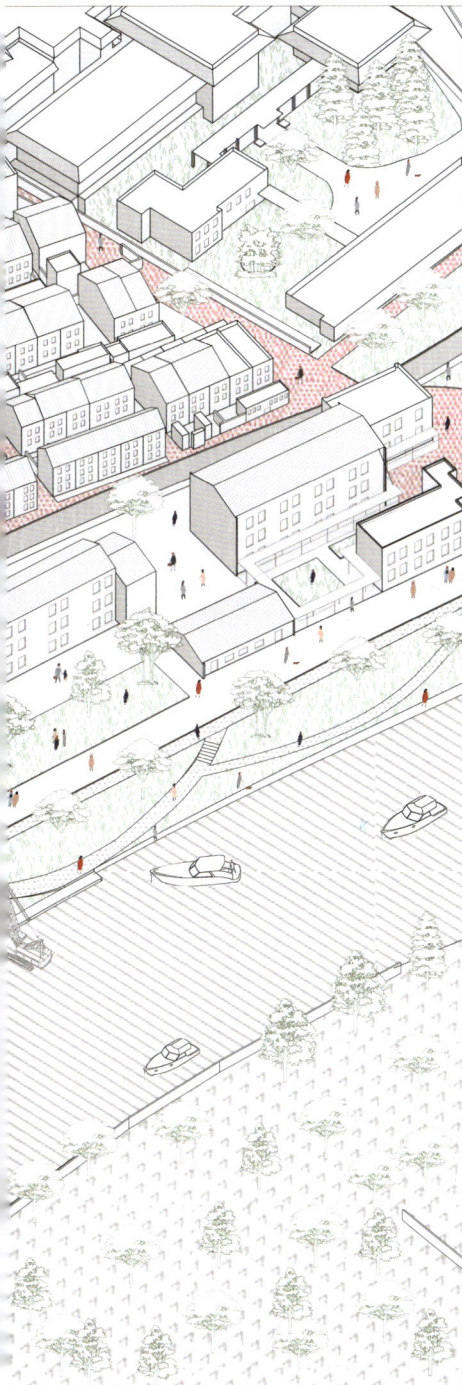

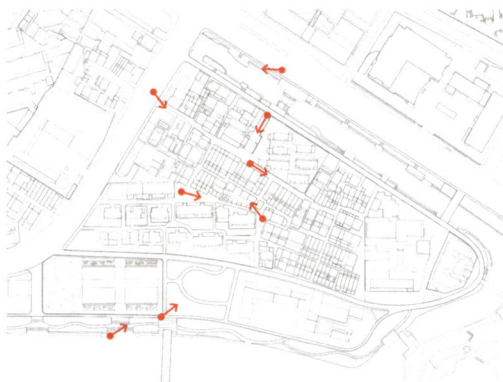

我们对设计之后的街道空间进行了采样，在不同的地点不同的角度拍摄了8张节点场景，主要围绕在滨水空间及改造之后的公共场所。

We sampled the street space after design and took 8 node scenes at different angles from different locations; these photos are taken mainly around the waterfront space and public places after the renovation.

地点与角度

Scene 01
工厂沿河界面
Factory along the river interface

Scene 02
临街售卖廊改造
Street-side sales gallery renovation

Scene 03
雨水收集景观坡地
Rainwater collecting landscape slope

Scene 04
城中村界面改造
Urban village interface update

Scene 05
街区咖啡厅兼宣传口
Street cafe and propaganda

Scene 06
早餐店改造
Breakfast shop renovation

Scene 07
市河滨水空间更新
City river water space update

Scene 08
城中村街巷改造
City village street lane update

工厂遗迹及周边广场改造：
场地面积 7000 平方米；建筑面积 3200 平方米。
设计通过将原本分离的四栋厂房单体连接成整体，来植入共享的社区功能，不仅兼顾了社区内部的需求同时也给游客提供了特色的餐饮与休憩空间。利用城中村拆建所产生的废砖设计的广场，唤起了人们对历史的感知。

Reconstruction of factory ruins and surrounding squares:
Site area 7000 square meters;
Building area 3200 square meters.
The design incorporates the shared community functions by connecting the originally separated four buildings into a single unit, which not only takes into account the needs of the community but also provides visitors with a special dining and rest space. The use of the waste brick design of the square created by the demolition of the village in the city has aroused people's perception of history.

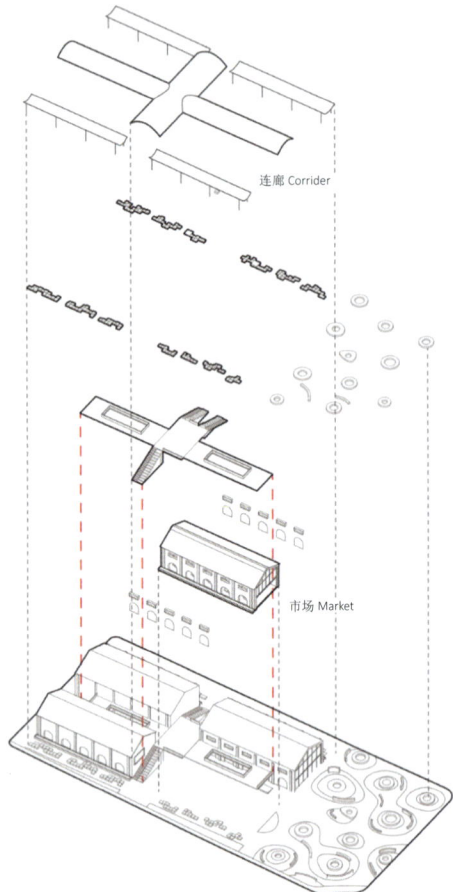

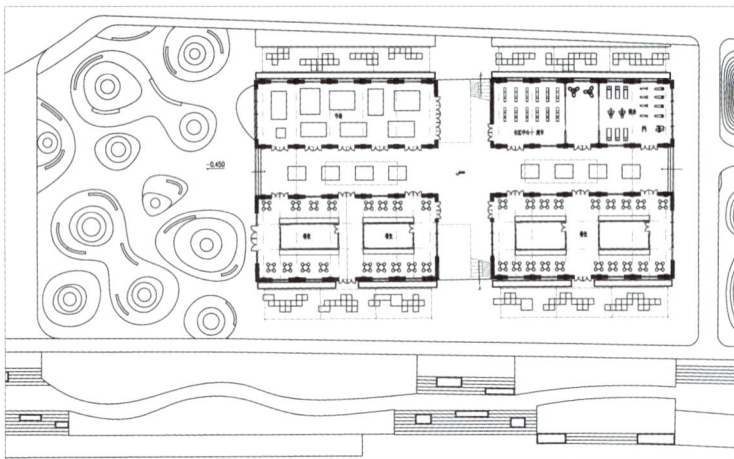

连廊 Corridor

市场 Market

厂房设计平面图

沿着桃园路布置的雨水回收系统将整个场地的雨水通过层层渗透汇集到景观水池中，再通过专门的净化处理系统将过滤后的雨水净化，用于工厂广场上的互动喷泉。人们不仅可以与水进行互动，促进相互之间的沟通，还可以通过这个生态循环模型来学习到关于可持续的先进理念。

The rainwater recovery system along Taoyuan Road integrates the rainwater from the entire site into the landscape pool through layer-by-layer infiltration, and then purifies the filtered rainwater through a special purification treatment system for the interactive fountain on the factory square. People can not only interact with water, promote mutual communication, but also learn advanced concepts about sustainability through this ecological cycle model.

社区入口节点设计：
场地面积 714 平方米；建筑面积 136 平方米。
社区入口拆除了部分的破旧建筑，将空地重新归还给市民活动。新建了一个篮球场和两个羽毛球场。此外还有一栋节点建筑，一层为临售，二层为咖啡屋，为市民提供服务，同时兼顾社区的宣传功能。其底层开放的灰空间也为等候延陵小学放学的学生家长提供了沟通与休息的场所。

Community entrance node design：
Site area 714 square meters;
building area 136 square meters.
Some of the dilapidated buildings are demolished and the open space is returned to the public. A new basketball court and two badminton courts have been built. In addition, there is a node building. The first floor is for temporary sale and the second floor is for coffee shop. It provides services for the public and takes into account the publicity function of the community. The open gray space at the bottom of the building also provides a place for communication and rest for parents of students waiting for Yanling Primary School to leave school.

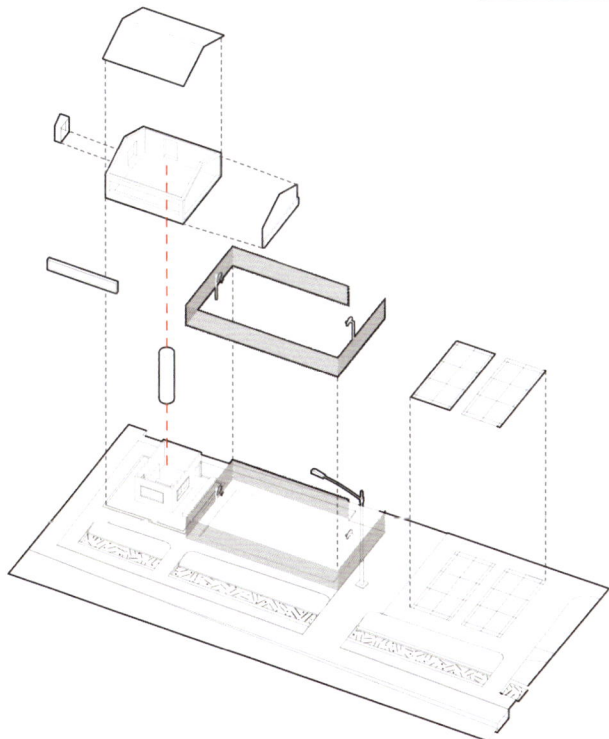

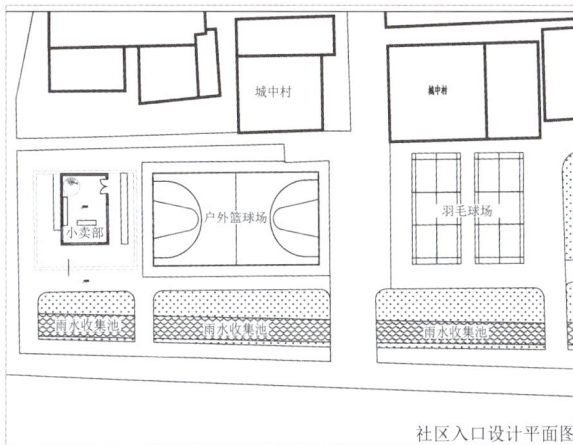

社区入口设计平面图

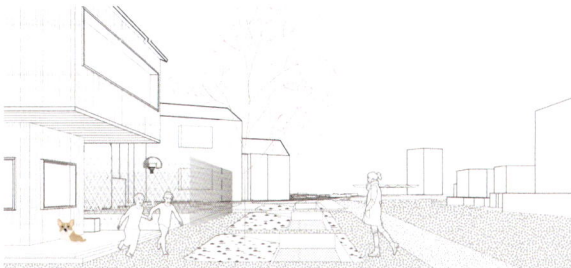

水 + 混合社区 + 工业遗产

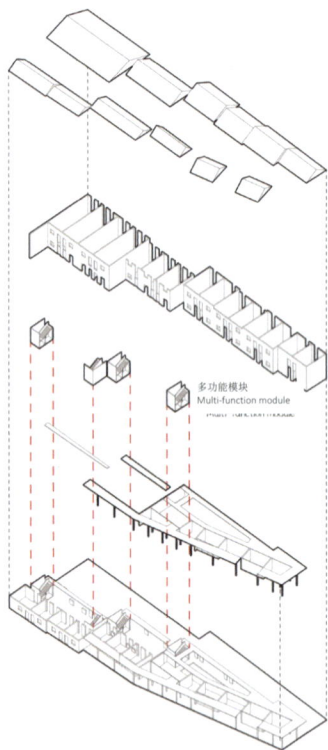

模块化设计单体 Modular Design Unit

城中村与工人小区边界设计：
建筑面积 1000 平方米。
拆除原有的墙体边界，重新用连廊联系，但
是共享的功能让两边的居民互相沟通起来。

Boundary between urban village and the
workers' community :
Site area 1000 square meters.
The original wall boundary is removed and the
corridor is used to form a visual demarcation,
the shared function allows the residents on
both sides to communicate with each other.

边界设计平面图

Module 01
卫生间 + 储藏　面积 6 平方米
Toilet + storage area 6 square meters

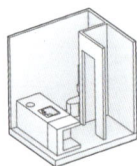

Module 02
晾晒 + 厨房　面积 6 平方米
Drying+ kitchen area 6 square meters

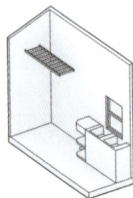

Module 03
卫生间 + 淋浴　面积 6 平方米
Toilet + shower area 6 square
meters

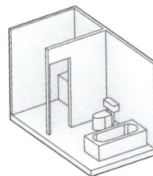

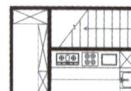

Module 04
厨房 + 卫生间 + 储藏　面积 14 平方米
Kitchen + toilet + storage area 14 square meters

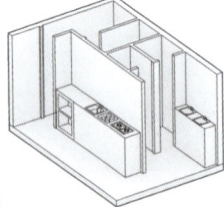

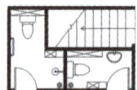

Module 05
楼梯 + 卫生间 ×2　面积 14 平方米
Stairs + bathroom × 2 area 14 square
meters

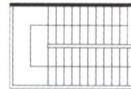

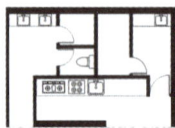

Module 06
楼梯 + 厨房 + 储藏　面积 14 平方米
Stairs +kitchen+ storage area 14
square meters

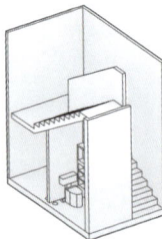

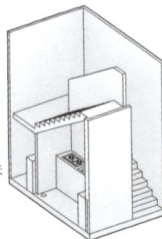

城中村组团改造：建筑面积 520 平方米。
城中村的改造主要是有效改善居住环境。通过置入一些模块，将厨卫、楼梯储藏等功能一体化，以影响最小的方式改造城中村。

Group transformation of villages in the city :
Site area 520 square meters.
The rehabilitation of the village is mainly to improve the living environment. Through the installation of some modules, the functions of kitchen and bathroom storage, stair storage and other functions will be integrated to transform the village in the least affected way.

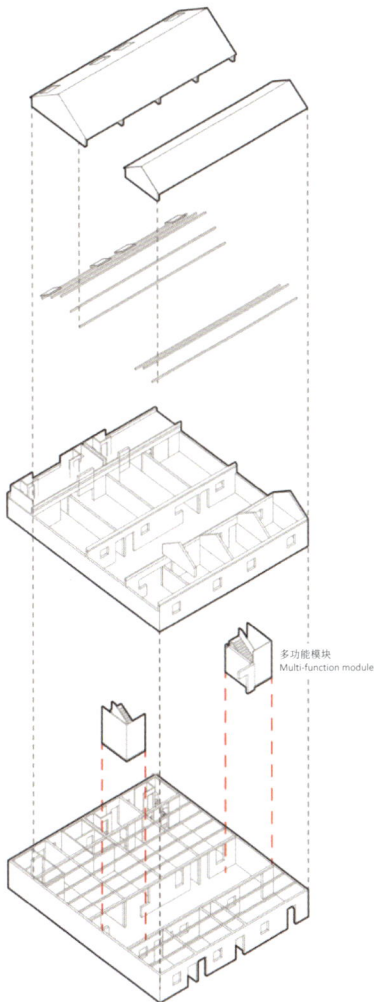

多功能模块
Multi-function module

城中村组团平面图

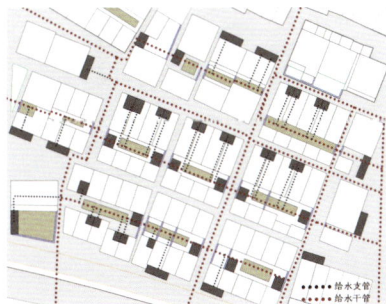

城中村给水图解 Water Supply Diagram

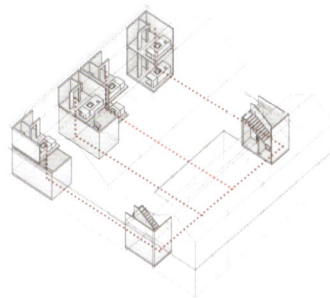

模块置入图解 Module Placement

方案三　水网城市中的创意乐园
Project 3　Park of LOHAS

场地 / 背景介绍 Site / Background

区位 Location

基地距离常州旧城中心 2.5 公里，老运河支流从基地南部通过。

The site is 2.5 km from old city center and has the branch of canal flow passing its southern area.

在常州市总体规划和控制性详细规划中，暂时保留了东货场和青龙港的货运功能。其余部分主要置换为居住用地，基地东部为公园。

In Changzhou's master plan and regulatory detailed plan, the freight functions of the East Freight Yard and the Qinglong Port are temporarily reserved. The rest is mainly replaced by residential land, and the eastern part of the base is a park.

历史沿革 History

1958 年地形图

1978 年地形图

1991 年地形图

沪宁铁路于 1908 年通车，长久以来是我国最繁忙的铁路区段。

The Shanghai-Nanjing Railway was built in 1908 and has long been the busiest railway section in China.

青龙港古已有之，太平天国时期被毁。

The Qinglong Port was existed in ancient time. It was destroyed during the Taiping Heavenly Kingdom.

东货场已经投入使用，初见雏形。

The East Freight Yard has been put into use and is in its infancy.

东货场和青龙港贴近现在的肌理。

The East Freight Yard and the Qinglong Port are close to the present texture.

水 + 铁路设施

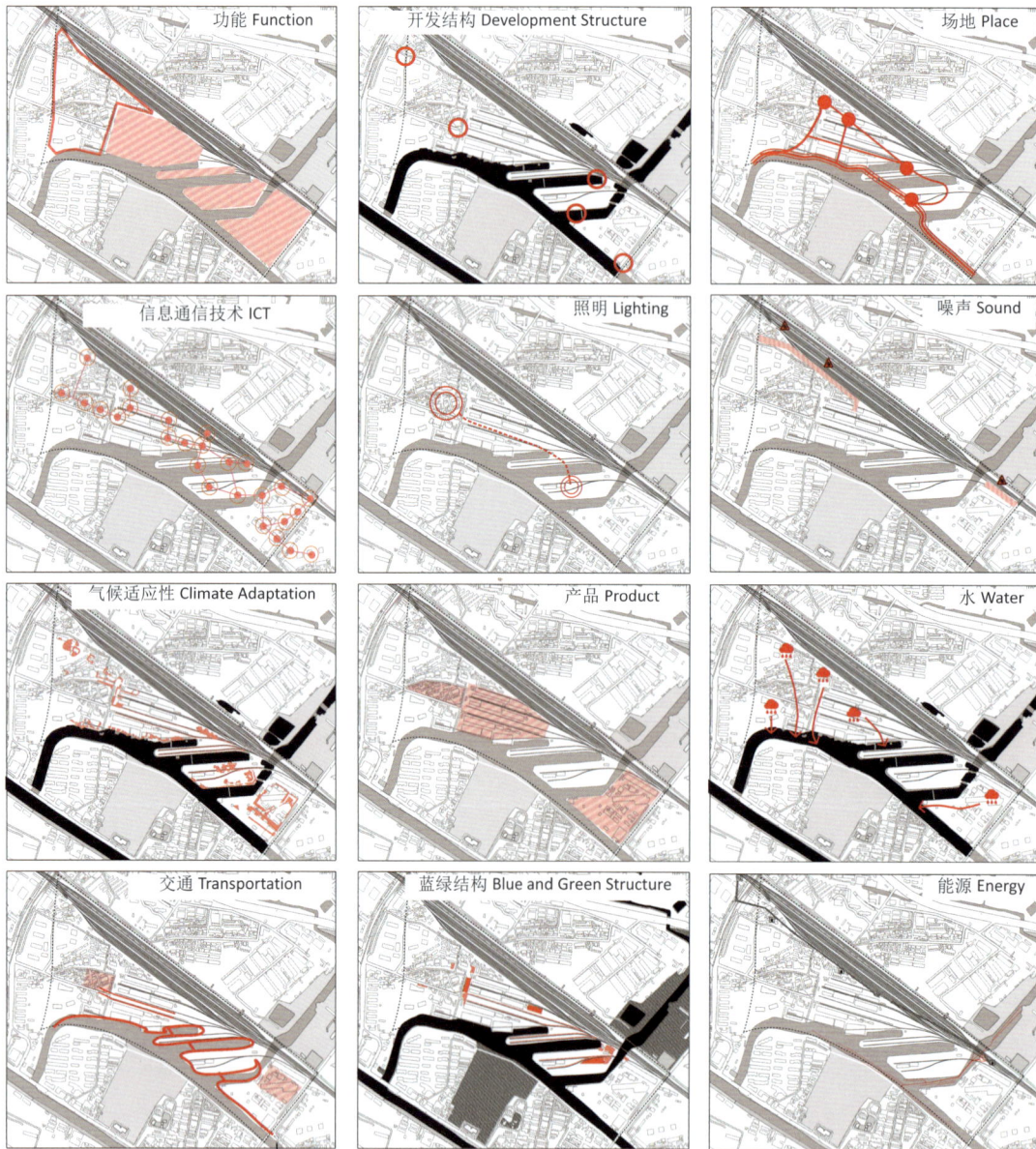

功能 Function

开发结构 Development Structure

场地 Place

信息通信技术 ICT

照明 Lighting

噪声 Sound

气候适应性 Climate Adaptation

产品 Product

水 Water

交通 Transportation

蓝绿结构 Blue and Green Structure

能源 Energy

CITYLAB 重点领域叠图 Focus Area Overlay of CITYLAB

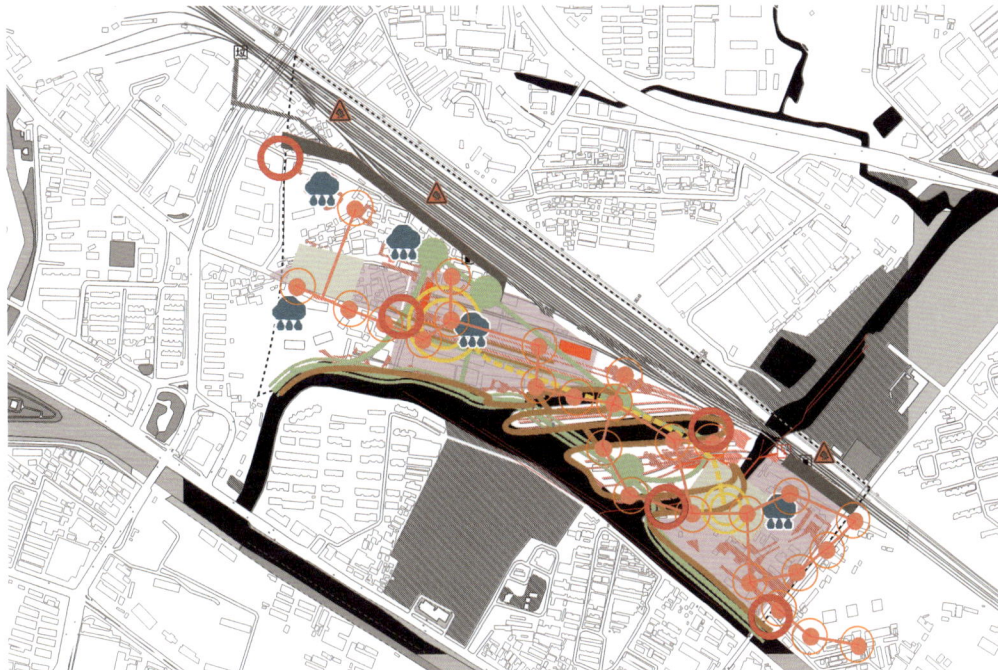

基地空间结构 Space Structure

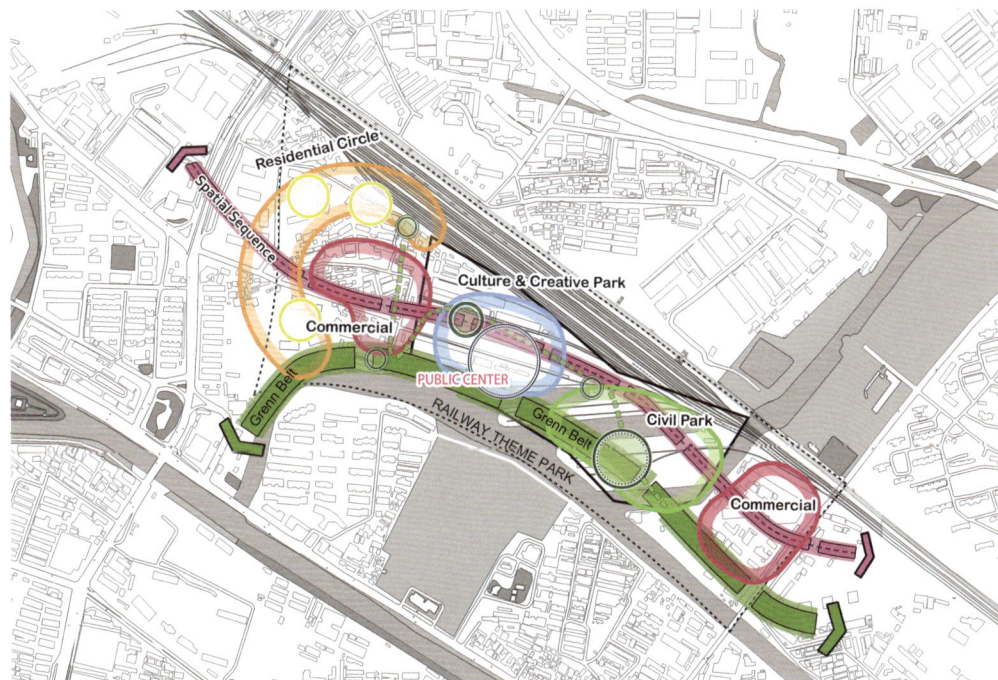

水
+
铁
路
设
施

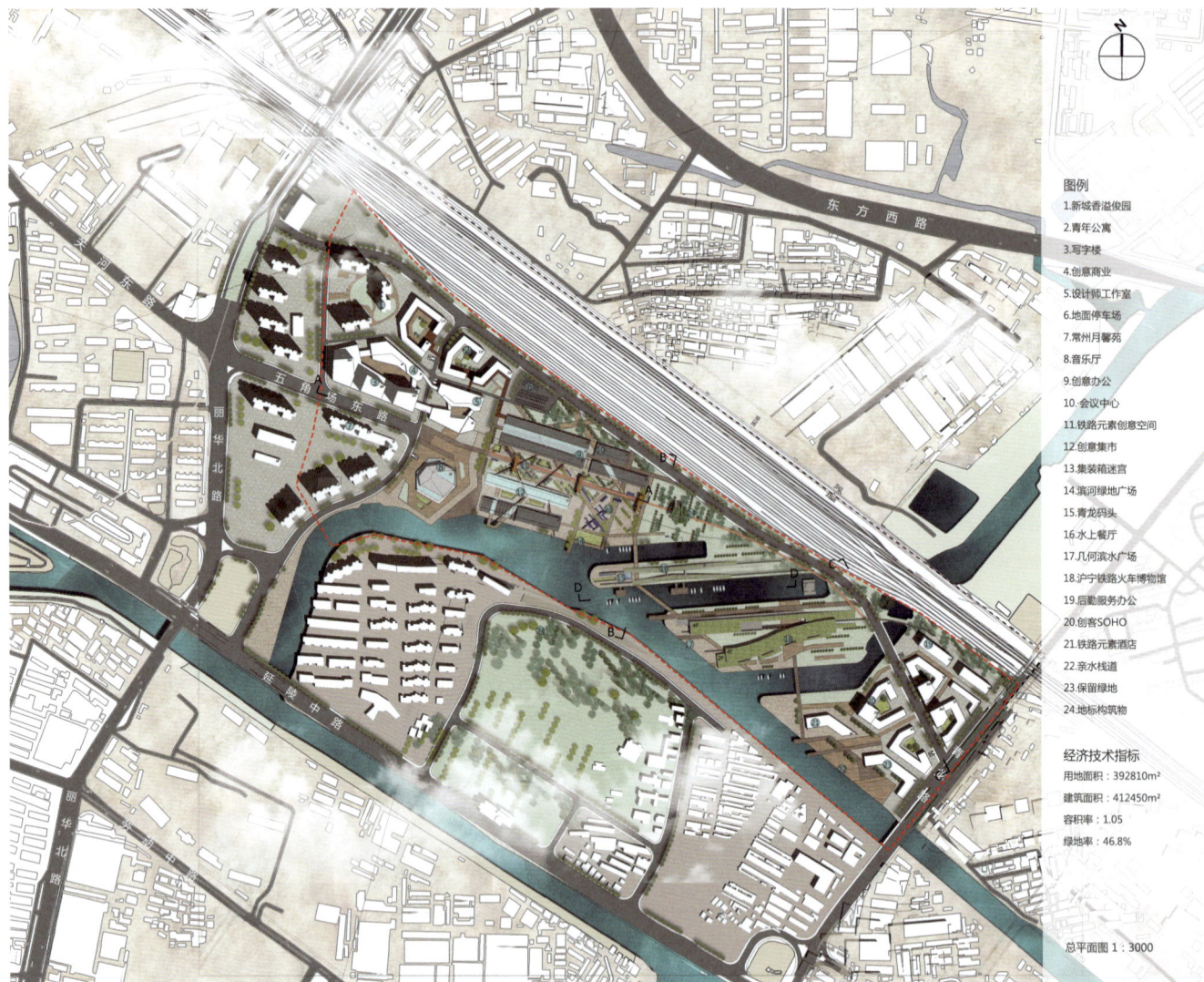

图例
1.新城香溢俊园
2.青年公寓
3.写字楼
4.创意商业
5.设计师工作室
6.地面停车场
7.常州月馨苑
8.音乐厅
9.创意办公
10.会议中心
11.铁路元素创意空间
12.创意集市
13.集装箱迷宫
14.滨河绿地广场
15.青龙码头
16.水上餐厅
17.几何滨水广场
18.沪宁铁路火车博物馆
19.后勤服务办公
20.创客SOHO
21.铁路元素酒店
22.亲水栈道
23.保留绿地
24.地标构筑物

经济技术指标
用地面积：392810m²
建筑面积：412450m²
容积率：1.05
绿地率：46.8%

总平面图 1：3000

设计策略 Design Strategies

串联滨水空间：延续城市脉络，构建生态网络
Linkage of Waterfront Space: Continueing the Urban Context, Building the Ecological Networks

可到达道路及积极节点
Accessible road and positive nodes

水上游线与登陆点
Water line and landing point

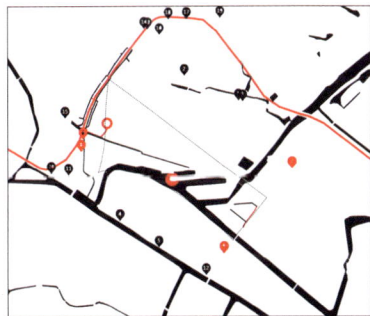

可到达性最终结果叠图
The mapping result of the accessible boundaries

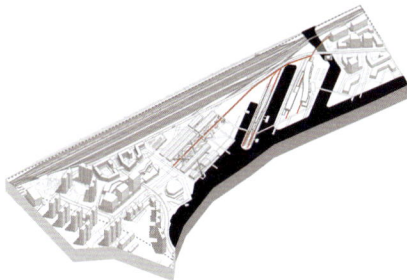

轨道系统 Rail system

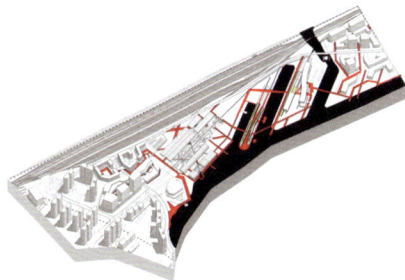

空中步廊 Overhead corridor

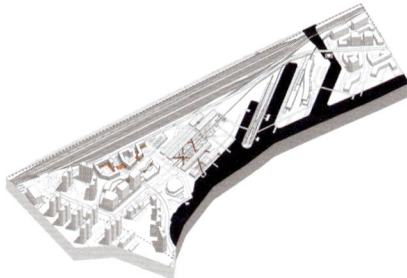

滨水步廊 Waterfront corridor

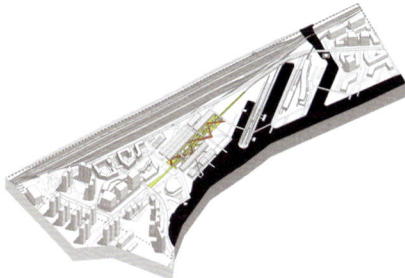

车行系统 Motor-system

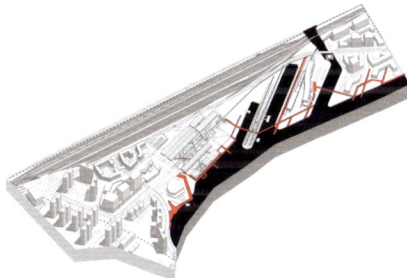

步行道 Pavement

核心轴线 Main axis

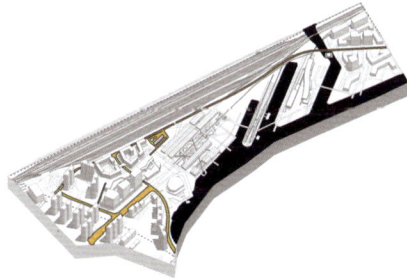

滨水空间 Waterfront

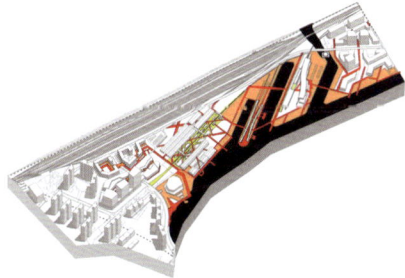

慢行系统 Slow traffic system

置换老弱功能：引入新型产业，激发地块活力
Replace the Urban Functions: Introduce New Industries and Stimulate the Vitality of the Land

保留建筑继承与铁轨关系，
功能上置入文创办公和展览，
空间上营造中轴公共空间，
成为场地历史遗迹的核心。

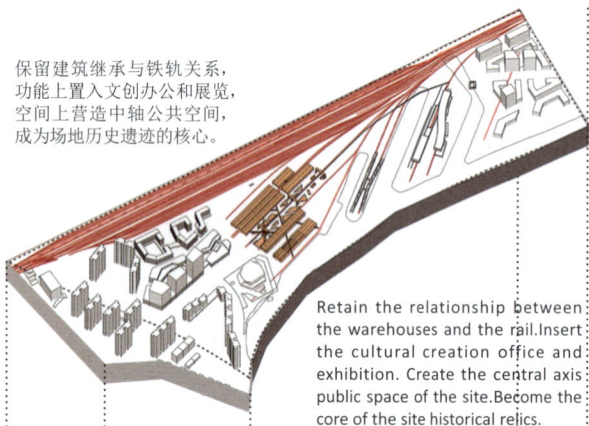

Retain the relationship between the warehouses and the rail.Insert the cultural creation office and exhibition. Create the central axis public space of the site.Become the core of the site historical relics.

新建建筑顺应铁轨形态肌理，功能上置入码头餐厅和铁路博物馆，空间上融入码头与河岸间之势态，仰望场地未来之意景。

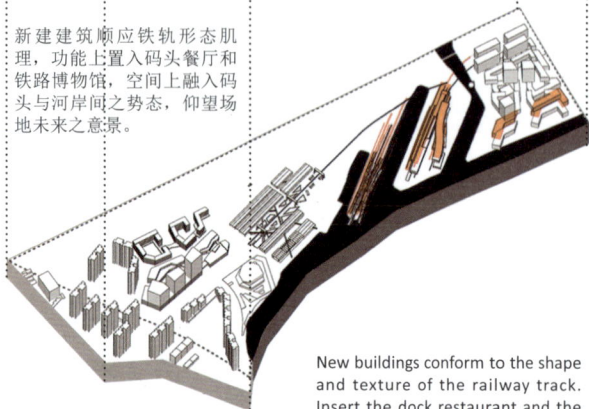

New buildings conform to the shape and texture of the railway track. Insert the dock restaurant and the railway museum. Integrate the tendency between the wharf and the riverbank. And look up to the future view of the site.

可保留建筑和地块建筑肌理
Texture of retaining buildings comparing with buildings of the plots

可保留建筑和地块铁路、运河关系
Relationship between retaining buildings and the historical railway & canal

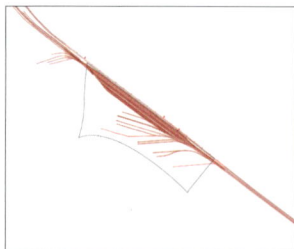

铁路肌理与基地
Texture of the railway in the basement

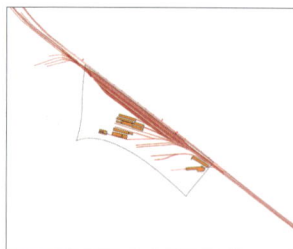

铁路与可保留建筑关系
Relationship between the railway and the retaining buildings

运河系统肌理与基地边界
Texture of the canal system at the base boundary

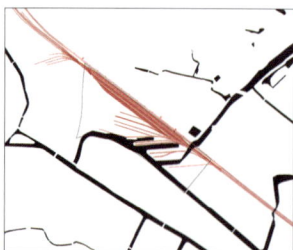

运河与铁路关系
Relationship between the canal system and the railway

置换老弱功能：引入新型产业，激发地块活力
Replace Old and Weak Functions: Introduce New Industries and Stimulate the Vitality of the Land

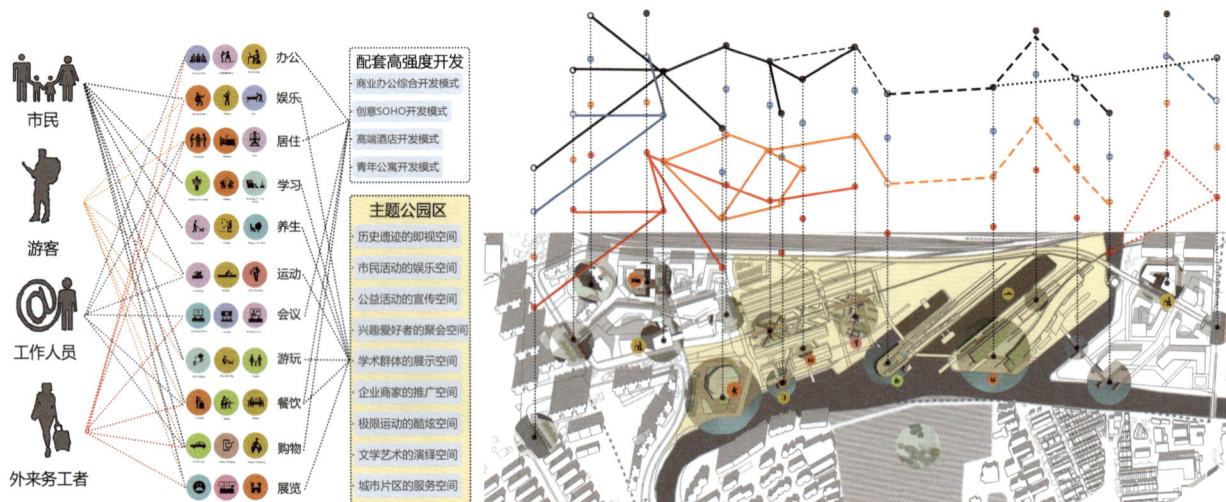

构建共享价值：完善服务体系，引导增量市场
Build Co-Shared Value: Improve the Service System, Guide the Incremental Market

利用场地集装箱的单元可变性及龙门架的可操作性，对集装箱以共享单元的形式在线上供人们预约使用，以满足商家销售活动、艺术家展览、企业团建、兴趣爱好者聚会等对不同空间的需求。集装箱单元组合的可变性演绎城市广场在时间维度上的丰富多彩。

Using the site container unit variability, and the gantry frame's maneuverability, the containers are available online in the form of shared units to meet the demand for different spaces such as merchant sales events, artists' exhibitions, enterprise team building, get-together and so on. The variability of container unit combination deduces the richness and variety of city square in time dimension.

文化遗产保护 Cultural Heritage Preservation

成果分析 The Results

业态分析 Analysis of the Programs

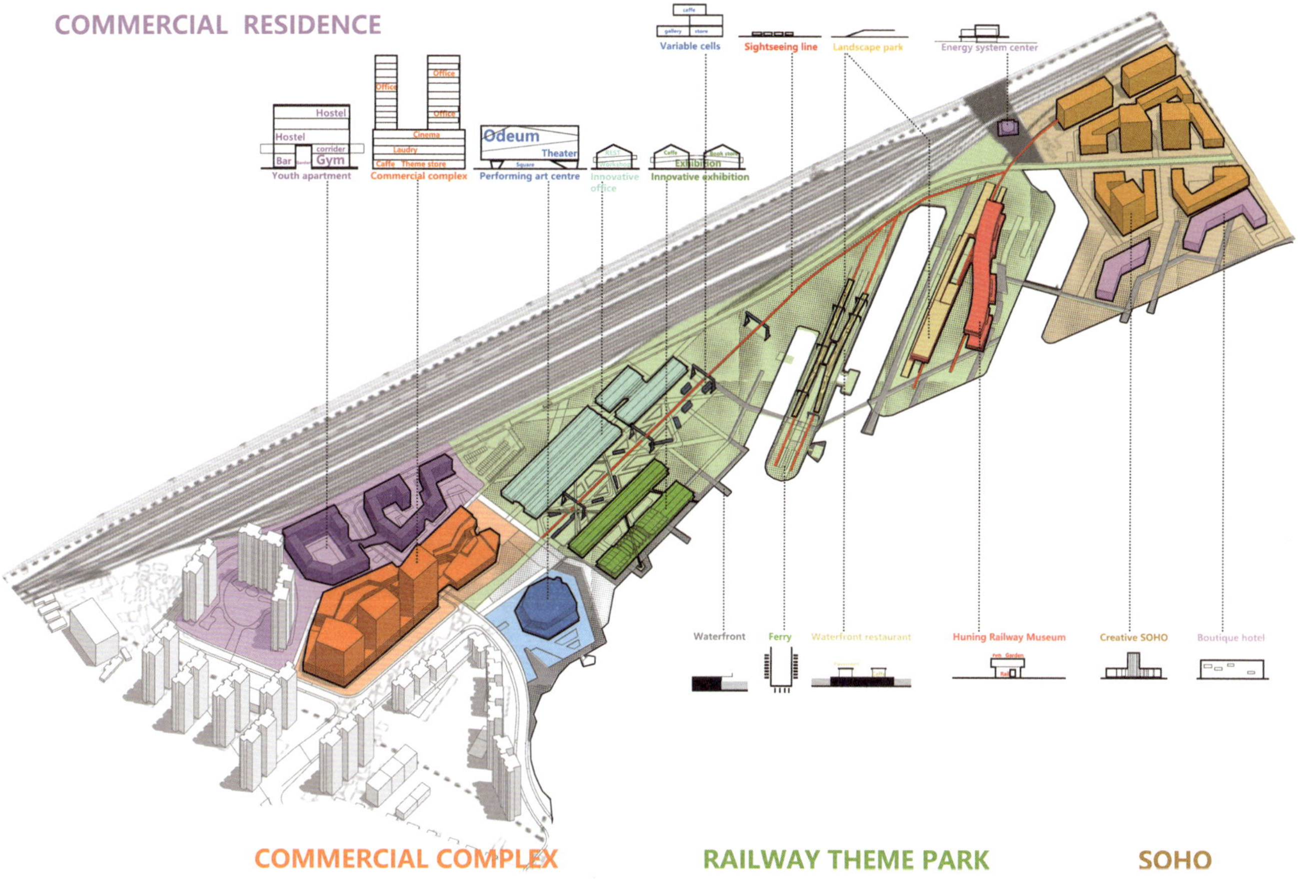

COMMERCIAL RESIDENCE
Hostel
Hostel
corrider
Bar
Gym
Youth apartment
Office
Office
Office
Cinema
Laudry
Caffe
Theme store
Commercial complex
Odeum
Theater
Square
Performing art centre
Innovative office
Caffe
Exhibition
Innovative exhibition
caffe
gallery
store
Variable cells
Sightseeing line
Landscape park
Energy system center
Waterfront
Ferry
Waterfront restaurant
Huning Railway Museum
Creative SOHO
Boutique hotel
COMMERCIAL COMPLEX
RAILWAY THEME PARK
SOHO

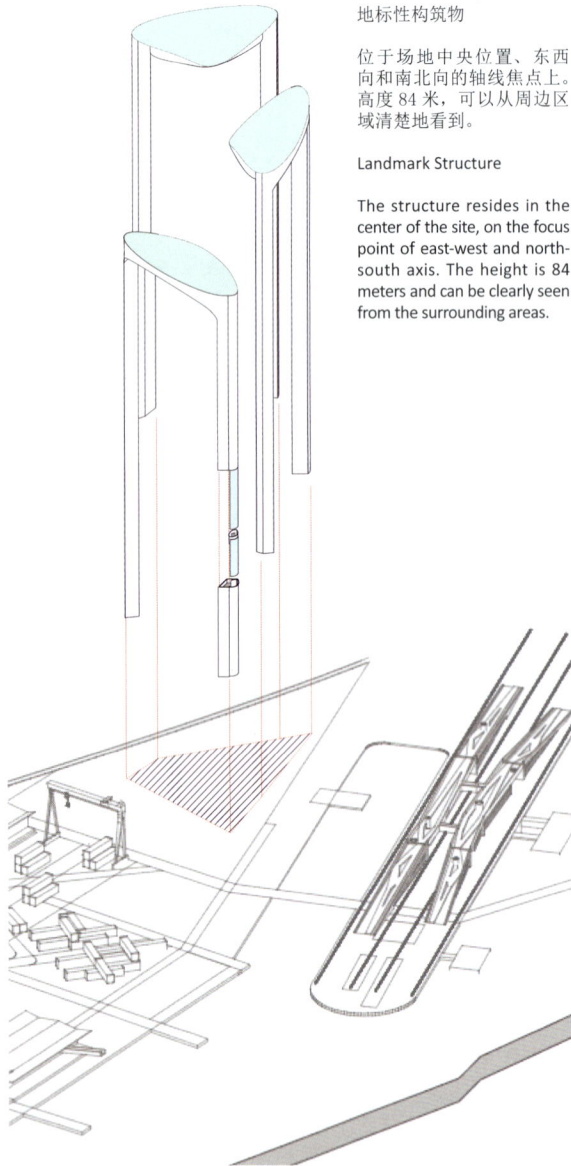

地标性构筑物

位于场地中央位置、东西向和南北向的轴线焦点上。高度84米，可以从周边区域清楚地看到。

Landmark Structure

The structure resides in the center of the site, on the focus point of east-west and north-south axis. The height is 84 meters and can be clearly seen from the surrounding areas.

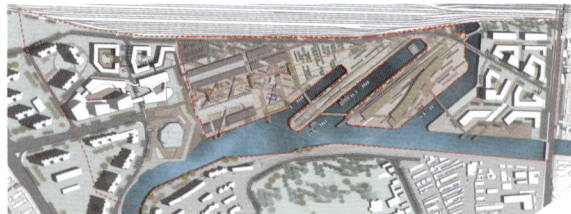

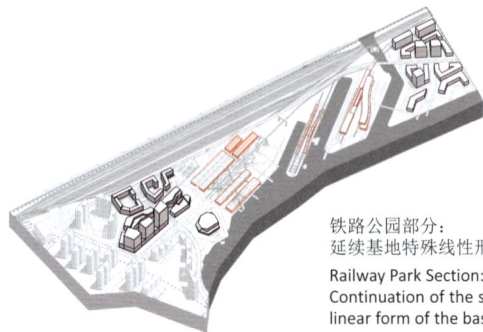

铁路公园部分：
延续基地特殊线性形态。

Railway Park Section:
Continuation of the special linear form of the base.

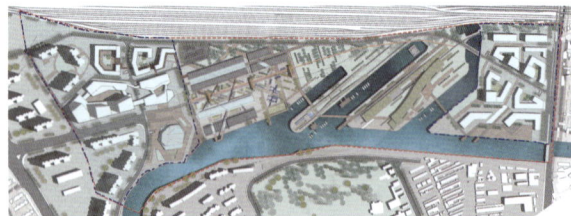

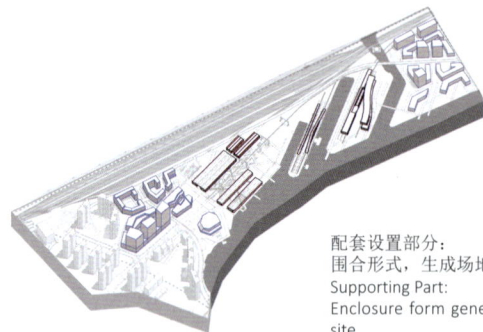

配套设置部分：
围合形式，生成场地。

Supporting Part:
Enclosure form generating site.

Process Management 过程管理

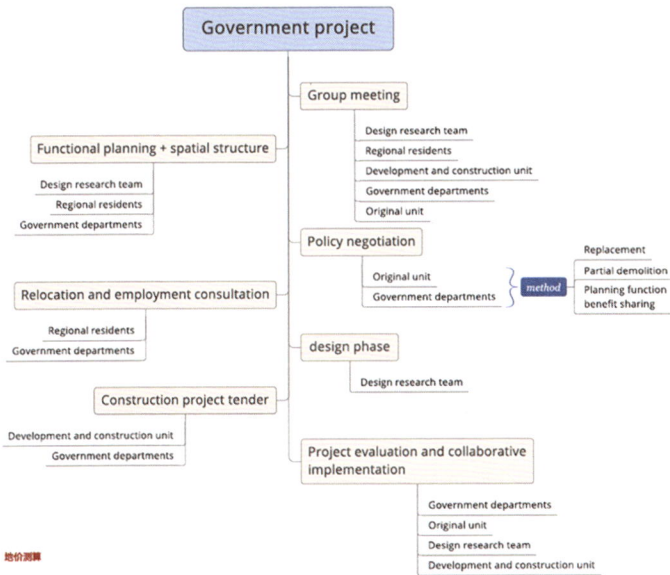

Government project

Group meeting
- Design research team
- Regional residents
- Development and construction unit
- Government departments
- Original unit

Functional planning + spatial structure
- Design research team
- Regional residents
- Government departments

Policy negotiation
- Original unit
- Government departments — method — Replacement / Partial demolition / Planning function benefit sharing

Relocation and employment consultation
- Regional residents
- Government departments

design phase
- Design research team

Construction project tender
- Development and construction unit
- Government departments

Project evaluation and collaborative implementation
- Government departments
- Original unit
- Design research team
- Development and construction unit

地价测算

样本地点	距场地中心距离	样本评估范围	地块加权平均价格
新体中心	4.5	5	4009.55
东方青龙北侧、湾城北路西侧QQ-070307-2	3	3	2276.21
东至青龙苑、南至新堂北路、西至横塘河东路、土	3.6	4	2065.29
中吴大道北侧、雕庄路东侧地块	3.8	4	2720.63
中吴大道南侧、晋陵南路东侧地块DN-080502-1	2.4	3	3002.26
北广场加油站东侧	1.7	3	3931.94
丽华北路西侧、河滨东路北侧	3.4	4	2760.20
延陵东路北侧、青洋路两侧	2.5	3	2576.73
火车站北广场	2.6	3	3931.94
延陵西路与南、北大街交叉口	3.5	4	3847.10
			3104.52

VALUE ASSESSMENT

Financial Value 经济价值
- ➤ 国民经济三次产业结构对比
- ➤ 工业主要行业对比
- ➤ 固定资产投资完成额趋势
- ➤ 进出口总额

Comparison of the three Industrial structure of the National economy
Comparison of Major Industrial
Trends in the volume of investment in fixed assets
total export-import volume

国民经济三次产业结构 Proportions in Gross Domestic Product

工业主要行业构成 Main Industry Structure

固定资产投资完成额 Realized Investment in Fixed Assets

进出口总额 Total Imports and Exports

Land Value 土地价值
- ➤ 人均拥有道路面积趋势
- ➤ 人均公园绿地面积趋势
- ➤ 建成区面积趋势
- ➤ 市民生活品质潜力指标

Per capita road area trend
the trend of park green area
the trend of area of built-up area
the potential index of quality of life of citizens

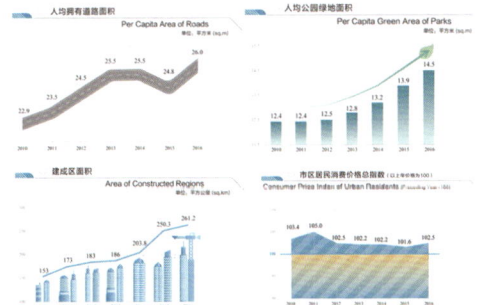

人均拥有道路面积 Per Capita Area of Roads

人均公园绿地面积 Per Capita Green Area of Parks

建成区面积 Area of Constructed Regions

市区居民消费价格总指数 Consumer Price Index of Urban Residents

生态分析 Analysis of Ecology

水源热泵系统 Water-source Heat Pump System

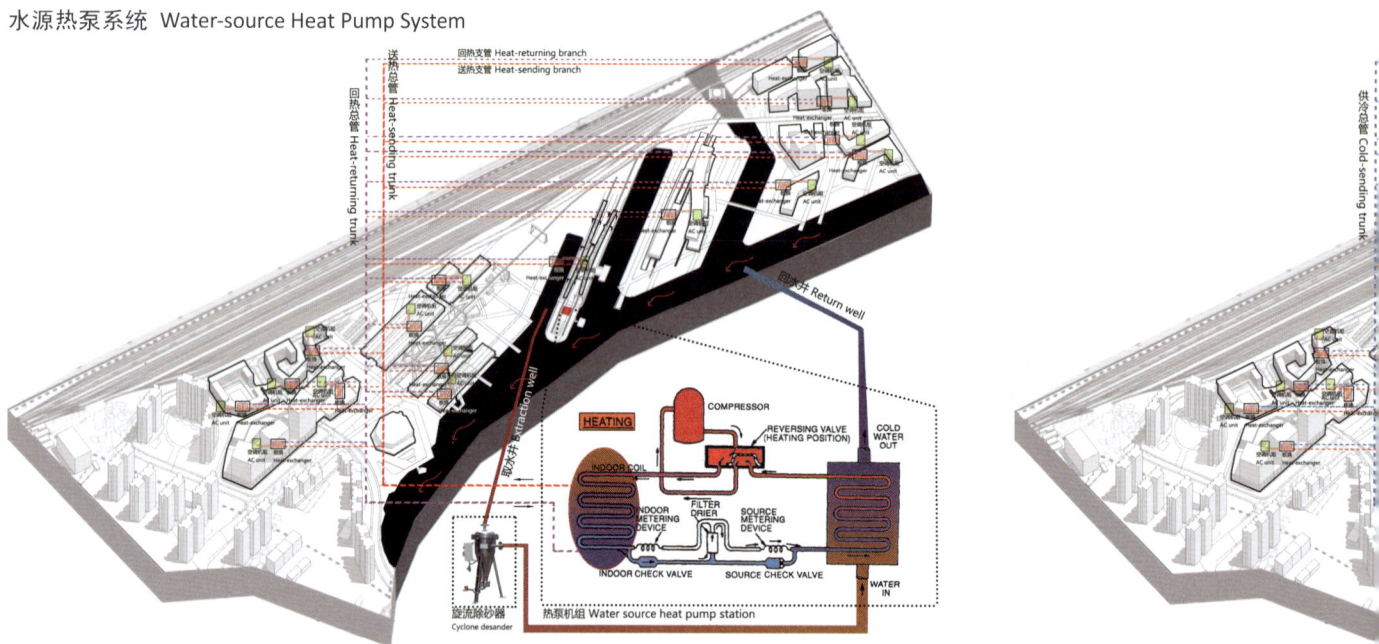

回热支管 Heat-returning branch
送热支管 Heat-sending branch
送热总管 Heat-sending trunk
回热总管 Heat-returning trunk
供冷总管 Cold-sending trunk
取水井 extraction well
回水井 Return well

HEATING
COMPRESSOR
REVERSING VALVE (HEATING POSITION)
COLD WATER OUT
INDOOR COIL
FILTER DRIER
INDOOR METERING DEVICE
SOURCE METERING DEVICE
INDOOR CHECK VALVE
SOURCE CHECK VALVE
WATER IN
旋流除砂器 Cyclone desander
热泵机组 Water source heat pump station

雨水回收系 Rainwater Cycling System

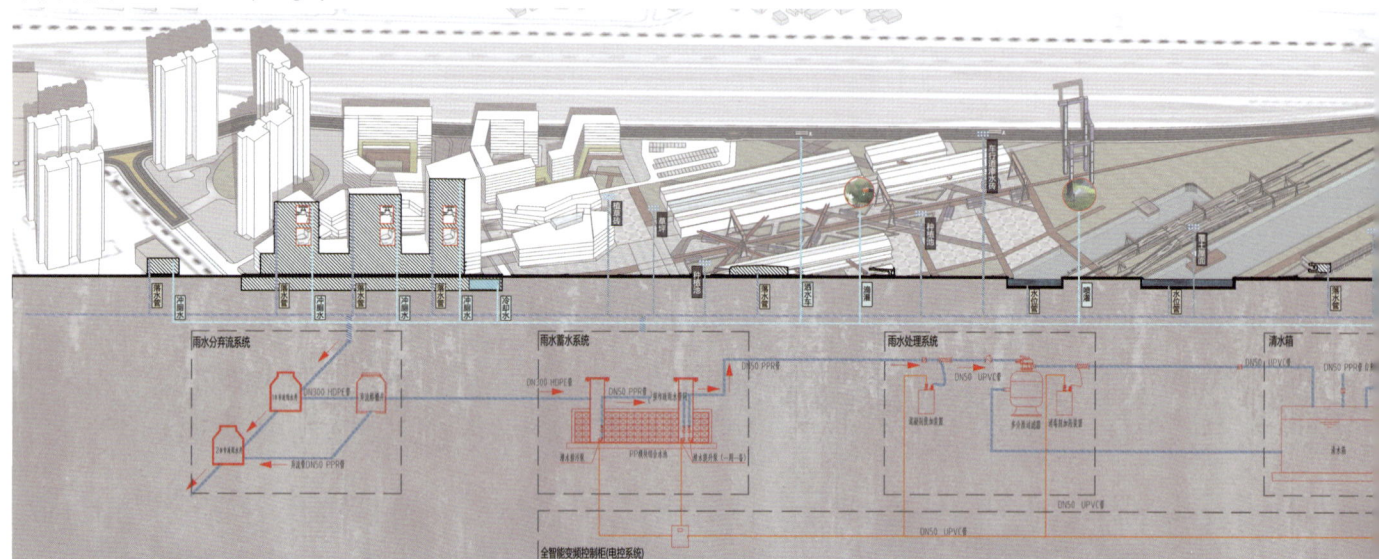

雨水分弃流系统
雨水蓄水系统
雨水处理系统
清水箱
全智能变频控制柜(电控系统)

室外风环境分析 Analysis of Wind Flows

风速云图 Wind speed cloud map

风速矢量图 Wind speed vector chart

风速等高面图 Wind speed contour map

建筑表面风力图 Building surface wind chart

1. The ventilation of the west side of the youth apartment yard is not smooth, need to open to the west.

2. The tangent direction of the street inside the commercial complex needs to be adjusted to ensure the continuity of ventilation in the west section.

3. The exterior space of the theme park can be allocated for different outdoor uses according to the influence of the wind speed: the open land on the west side is well ventilated and suitable for outdoor interaction; the east square of the railway museum is the wind shadow area, which is suitable for outdoor exhibition.

4. Creative soho outdoor corridor has a very high wind speed. We should pay attention to avoid the fjord effect caused by the change of the enclosed interface.

5. The core axis of the theme park and east-west canal are both good urban ventilation corridors in summer, which should be avoided from the interior of the base.

风速云图 Wind speed cloud map

风速矢量图 Wind speed vector chart

风速等高面图 Wind speed contour map

建筑表面风力图 Building surface wind chart

1. The dense building area on both sides of the base formed a good self-occlusion without bad wind environment such as the jet current area.

2. The deciduous broad-leaved forest on the north side of the base is planted in combination with evergreen broad-leaved forest to form winter monsoon occlusion and to reduce rail noise.

方案四　城市活力的绿色起搏器
Project 4　Green Pacemaker of Urban Vitality

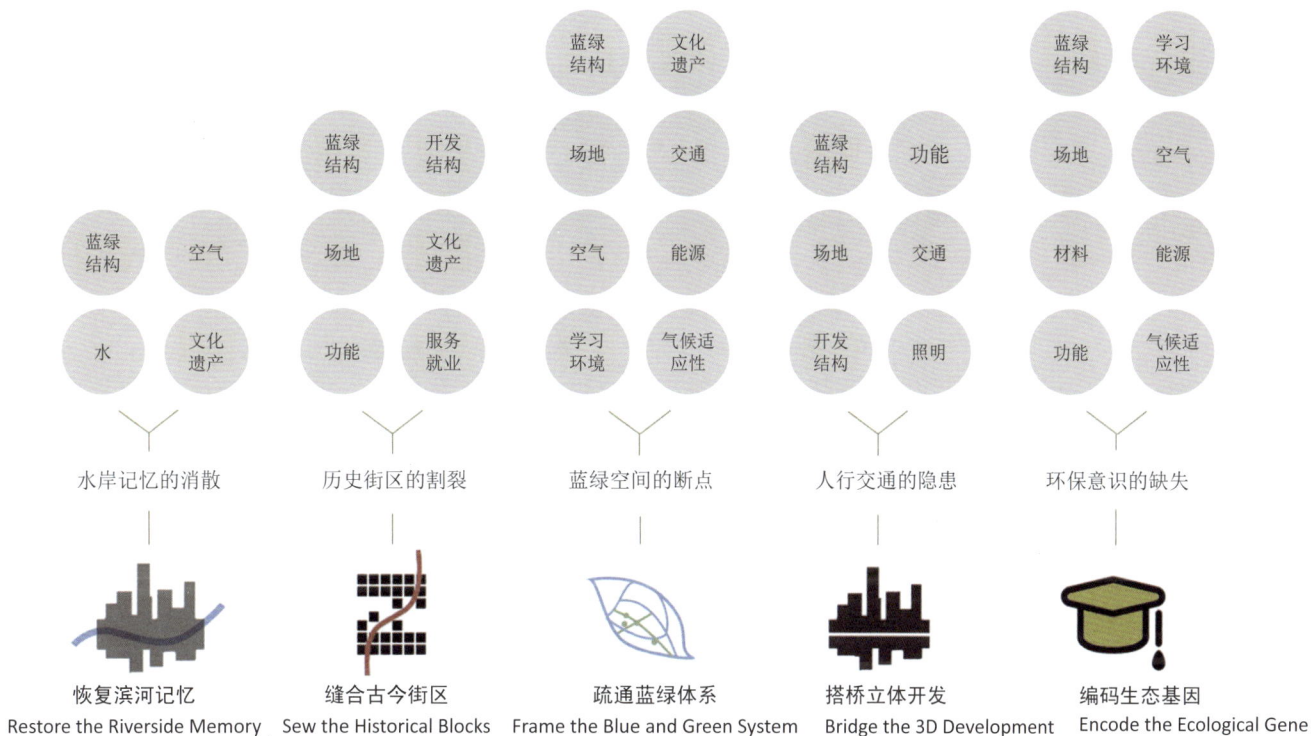

蓝绿结构	文化遗产		蓝绿结构	学习环境
场地	交通		场地	空气
空气	能源		材料	能源
学习环境	气候适应性		功能	气候适应性

水岸记忆的消散　　　历史街区的割裂　　　蓝绿空间的断点　　　人行交通的隐患　　　环保意识的缺失

恢复滨河记忆　　　缝合古今街区　　　疏通蓝绿体系　　　搭桥立体开发　　　编码生态基因

Restore the Riverside Memory　Sew the Historical Blocks　Frame the Blue and Green System　Bridge the 3D Development　Encode the Ecological Gene

人民公园
THE PEOPLE'S PARK

复兴后顾塘河
GUTANG RIVER AFTER RENAISSANCE

住宅小区
COMMUNITY

下沉绿地广场
SUNKEN GREEN SQUARE

购物中心
SHOPPING CENTER

N

商业建筑
COMMERCIAL BUILDINGS

办公建筑
OFFICE BUILDING

地铁换乘枢纽
JUNCTION OF
PARK AND SHIFT

下沉绿地广场
SUNKEN GREEN SQUARE

住宅小区
RESIDENCE COMMUNITY

特色酒店
CHARACTERISTIC HOTEL

商业建筑
COMMERCIAL BUILDINGS

公共活动中心
PUBLIC ACTIVITY CENTER

0 25   50   100 m

保留建筑
RESERVED BUILDING

总平面图   Master Plan

恢复滨河记忆
Restore the Riverside Memory

缝合历史街区
Sew the Historical Blocks

疏通蓝绿体系
Frame the Blue and Green System

搭桥立体开发
Bridge the 3D Development

编码生态基因
Encode the Ecological Gene

恢复滨河记忆 Restore the Riverside Memory

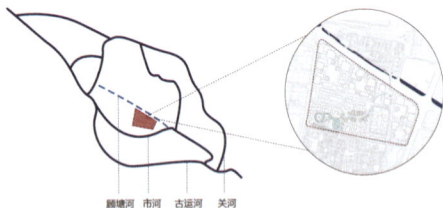

河道恢复 Renewing Channel

顾塘河　市河　古运河　关河

河道透视 Channel Perspective

常州是唯一一座京杭大运河穿越越府署驻所的老城，恢复顾塘河，不仅仅是找回一条河流，创造一片景观，更重要的目的是试图唤醒常州人基因深处的人文记忆，弥补即将断裂的场所精神。

Changzhou is the only old city where the Beijing-Hangzhou Grand Canal crosses the government headquarters. To restore the Gutang River is not only to recover a river and create a landscape, but also to awaken the deep and humanistic memory of Changzhou people to make up for the broken spirit of the place.

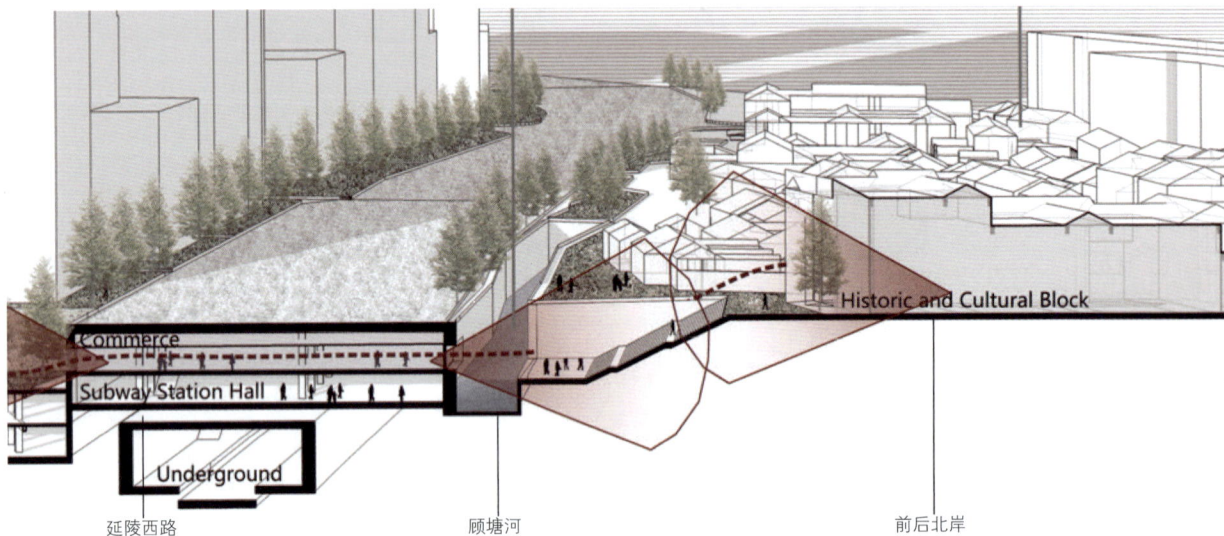

Commerce

Subway Station Hall

Underground

Historic and Cultural Block

延陵西路　　　　　顾塘河　　　　　前后北岸

开发结构 Development Structure

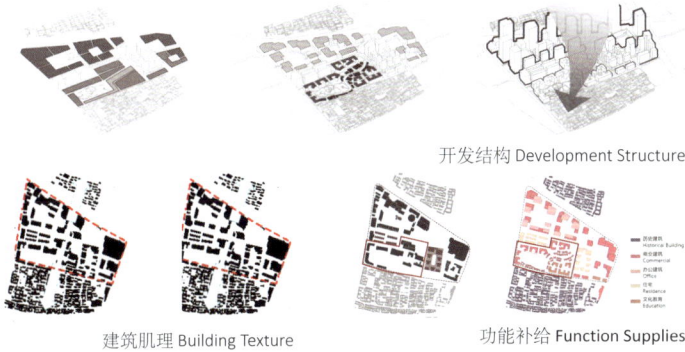

建筑肌理 Building Texture

功能补给 Function Supplies

基地位于青果巷和前后北岸这两个历史保护区之间，割裂了其肌理与空间体验，设计希望在保证城市中心地块高容积率的前提下，连接两片历史街区，同时串联约园及恢复的顾塘河。

The site is located between Qingguo Lane and Qianhoubei'an historical and cultural blocks, which has separated its texture and spatial experience. The design hopes to connect the two historical blocks on the premise of ensuring the high plot ratio of the urban central plot, and connect the Yue Garden and the restored Gutang River.

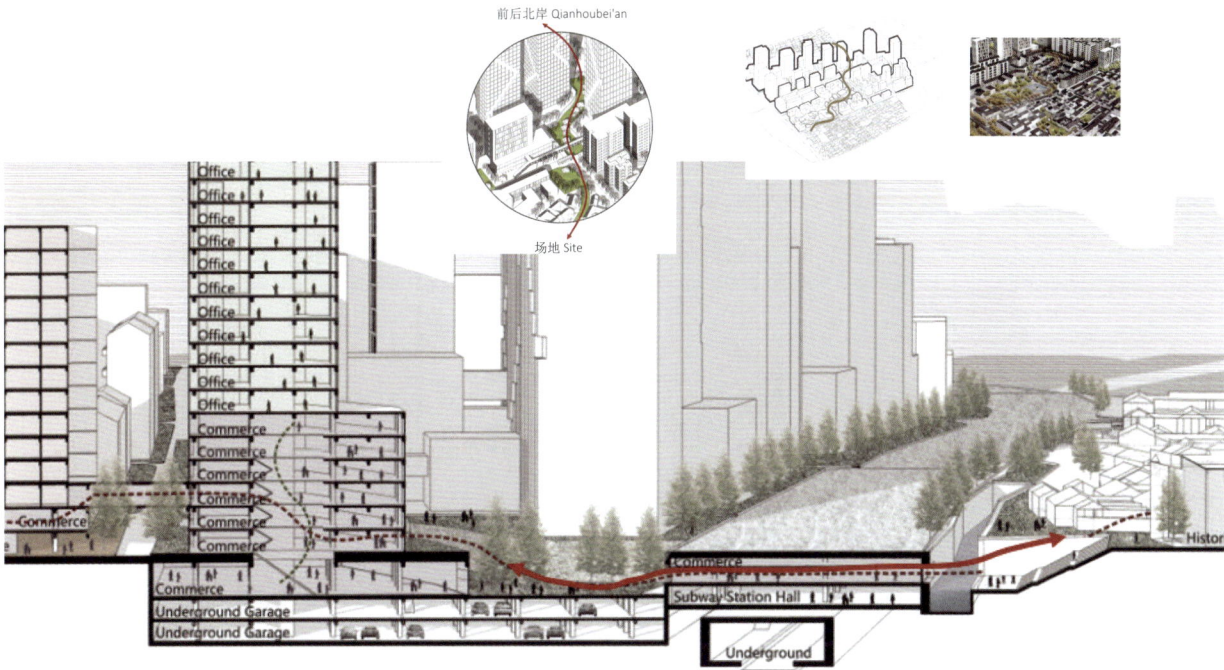

前后北岸 Qianhoubei'an

场地 Site

疏通蓝绿体系 Frame the Blue and Green System

水系分析 Water Analysis

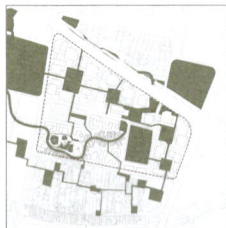

绿化分析 Green Analysis

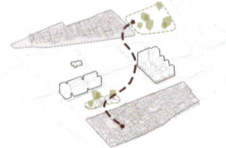

场地元素 Site Elements

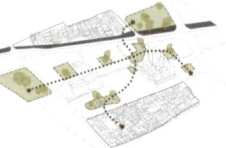

体系整合 System Intergration

场地内有较多破碎的绿地与水系，设计希望从宏观层面整合场地内外孤立的蓝绿元素，形成绿道连接场地内重要的历史元素，并将其纳入整个天宁区的公共空间系统。

There are a lot of broken greenbelt and water system in the site. The design hopes to integrate the isolated blue and green elements inside and outside the site from the macro level to form greenways to connect the important historical elements in the site and incorporate them into the public space system of the whole Tianning District.

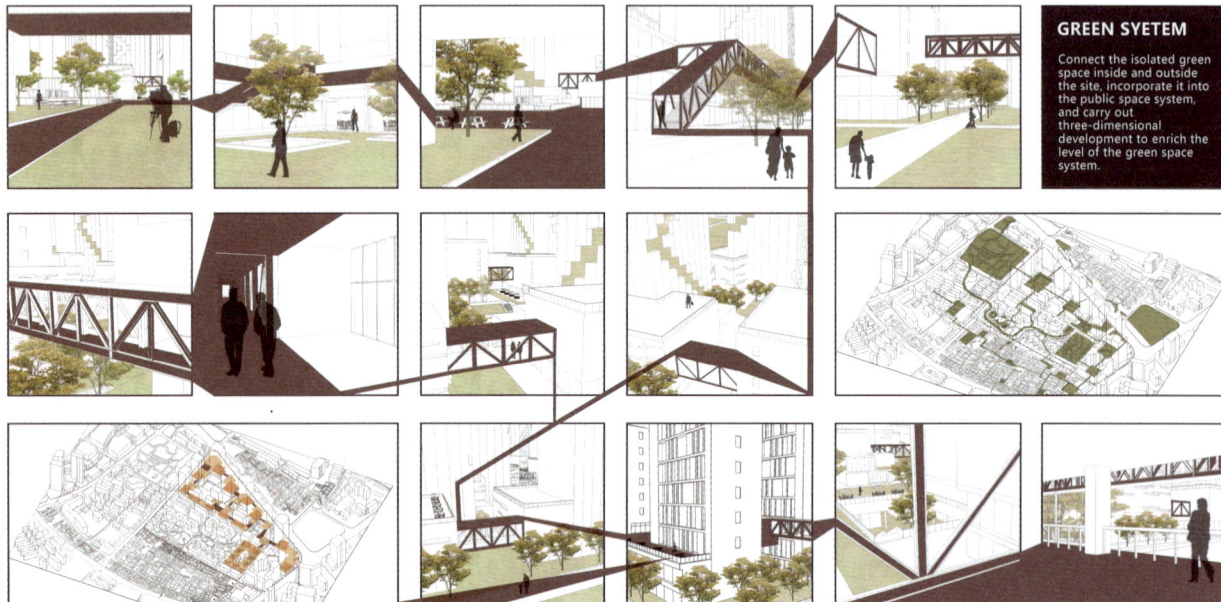

GREEN SYETEM

Connect the isolated green space inside and outside the site, incorporate it into the public space system, and carry out three-dimensional development to enrich the level of the green space system.

为了满足地块容积率要求，设计基本策略为在面对城市界面设置高大体量，面对历史保护区设置矮小体量，层层后退，确保主要绿道上肌理的统一性及人行体验的连续性。

In order to meet the requirements of plot volume ratio, the basic strategy of the design is to set up the high volume facing the urban interface and the short volume facing the historical protection area, and to step back layer by layer to ensure the unity of the main greenway texture and continuity of pedestrian experience.

机动车道 Moto Vehicle Lane
底层商业（局部架空）
Bottom Business (Partial Overhead)
步行道 Sidewalk

商业延伸空间
Business Extension Space
可进入的绿色空间
Accessible Green Space
慢行空间 Slow Space
天桥 Footbridge

步行道 Sidewalk
机动车道 Moto Vehicle Lane
公交站台 Bus Station
天桥 Footbridge

广告牌 Billboard
步行道 Sidewalk
非机动车道 Non-moto Vehicle Lane
公交站台 Bus Station
滨水步道 Waterfront Trail
机动车道 Moto Vehicle Lane
河道 River

街道剖面 Street Sections

垂直绿化
Vertical greening
垂直人行流线
Vertical Pedestrian streamline
垂直车行流线
Vertical car flowline

新建建筑
NEW BUILDINGS

绿化延伸
Greening extension

新建高层建筑
New High-rise Building
垂直绿化
Vertical greening

蓝绿体系
BLUE AND GREEN SYSTEM

绿地
Green land
水体
River

平台漫步流线
Platform Walking Streamline

漫步平台
RAMBLE PLATFORM

平台
Platform
廊道
Corridor

车行流线
Car flow line
地面花园漫步流线
Floor Garden Walking streamline

F1

商业
Commercial buildings
教育建筑
Educational buildings
保留建筑
Reserved building

下沉广场游憩流线
Sunken Square Walking Streamline

B1

商业
Commercial buildings
下沉绿地广场
Sunken Green Square
地下车库
Underground garage

B2

B3

地下车库
Underground garage

143

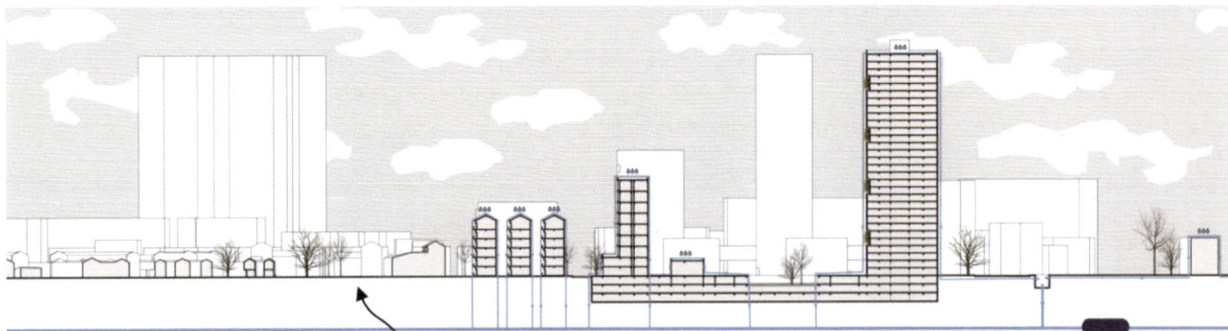

编码生态基因 Encode the Ecological Gene

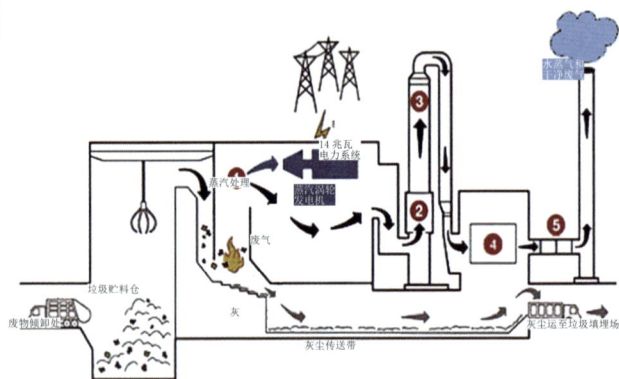

学习环境 Learning Setting

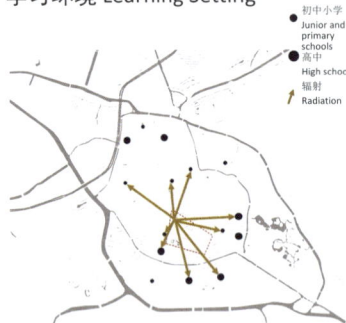

初中小学
Junior and
primary
schools
高中
High school
辐射
Radiation

设计希望利用地块周边丰富的学习资源，结合有利于学习的设置，给新一代常州人普及可持续发展城市的意识。

The design hopes to make use of the rich learning resources around the plot, combine with the settings conducive to learning, and popularize the awareness of sustainable development of the city to the new generation of Changzhou people.

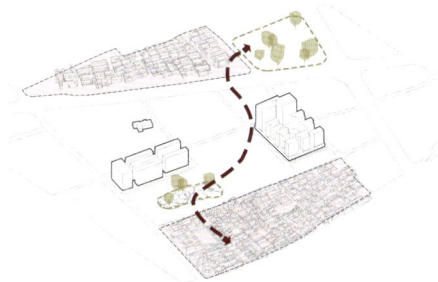

连接场地要素：青果巷、约园、前后北岸和文化宫地铁站
Connecting site elements: Qingguo Lane, Yue Garden, Qianhoubei'an and Cultural Palace subway station

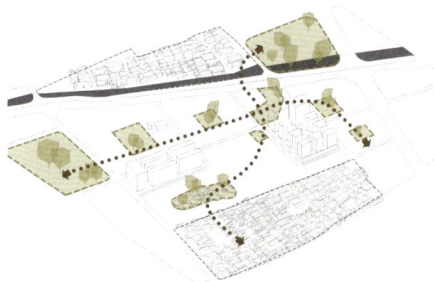

恢复顾塘河、增加街区绿化、完善蓝绿体系
Restore Gutang River, increase street greening, improve the blue and green system

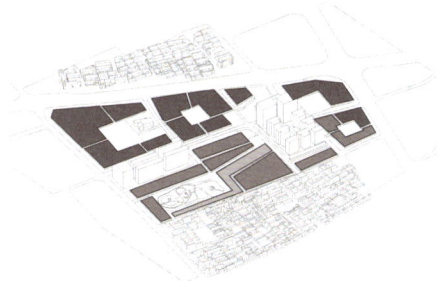

建筑占据、建筑体量由外围向历史区域递减
The building occupies, the building volume decreases from the periphery to the historical area

路径生成、调整体块形态
Path generation, adjust the overall block shape

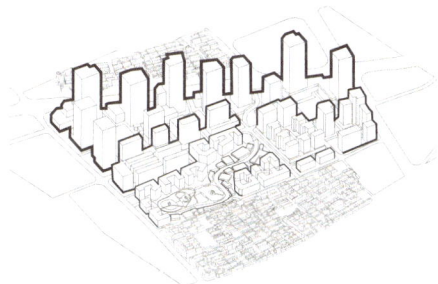

体量生成、保证高度层次
Volume generation, ensure a high level

小体量屋顶及中体量退台呼应历史建筑、平台连接高层
The small volume and the middle volume echo the historical building, and the platform connects the high-rises

水 + 公共服务

水系分析 Water Analysis

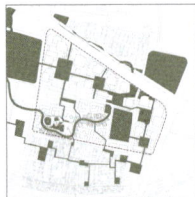

绿化分析 Green Analysis

蓝绿结构
场地

保留约园水系，恢复顾塘河，完善场地内外系统，修复滨水记忆；将人民公园、前后北岸以及青果巷的绿地系统纳入设计范围，整合绿化网络；整个蓝绿体系不仅是景观，还作为户外空间纳入公共空间系统。

Green and Blue Structure
Place

Retain the Yue Garden water system, restore the Gutang River, improve the water system to restore the waterfront memory. Integrate the green system of People's Park, Qianhoubei'an and Qingguo Lane and integrate the green space network. The whole blue-green system is not only the landscape, but also incorporated into the public space system.

人行流线 Pedestrian Flow

平台系统 Platform System

交通—
人行流线

改善人行环境，保证主要流线人车分流；利用地下空间与平台进行立体开发，促进商业发展。

Transportation-
Pedestrian Flow

Improve pedestrian environment, ensure the diversion line of people and vehicles diversion in the main flow; Use underground and platform for three-dimensional development, promote commercial development.

私家车流线 Private Car Flow

公交流线 Public Traffic Flow

交通—
车行流线

重新梳理车行系统，增建地下车库以解决停车问题；开设历史风貌区观光巴士，结合地铁 1 号和 2 号线，鼓励公共交通为主的出行方式。

Transportation-
Car Flow

Rearrange the vehicle system and add underground garage to solve the parking problem; Tourist buses with historical features will be opened, and metro line 1 and line 2 will be combined to encourage public transportation as the main mode of travel.

保留及拆除建筑 Preservation and Demolition of Buildings

功能分析 Function Analysis

功能
本地服务与就业

疏散错位功能，补给对位功能；保证就业。

Function
Local Supplier and Labor

Evacuate dislocation function, supply alignment function. Ensure the employment.

①商业 Commerce
②咖啡 Coffee
③展览 Exbihition
④辅助用房 Auxiliary
⑤餐饮 Restaurant
⑥厨房 Kitchen
⑦书店 Bookstore

0 25 50   100 m

一层平面图 Plan of F1

①商业 Commerce
②咖啡 Coffee
③辅助用房 Auxiliary
④餐饮 Restaurant
⑤书店 Bookstore

0　25　50　　100 m

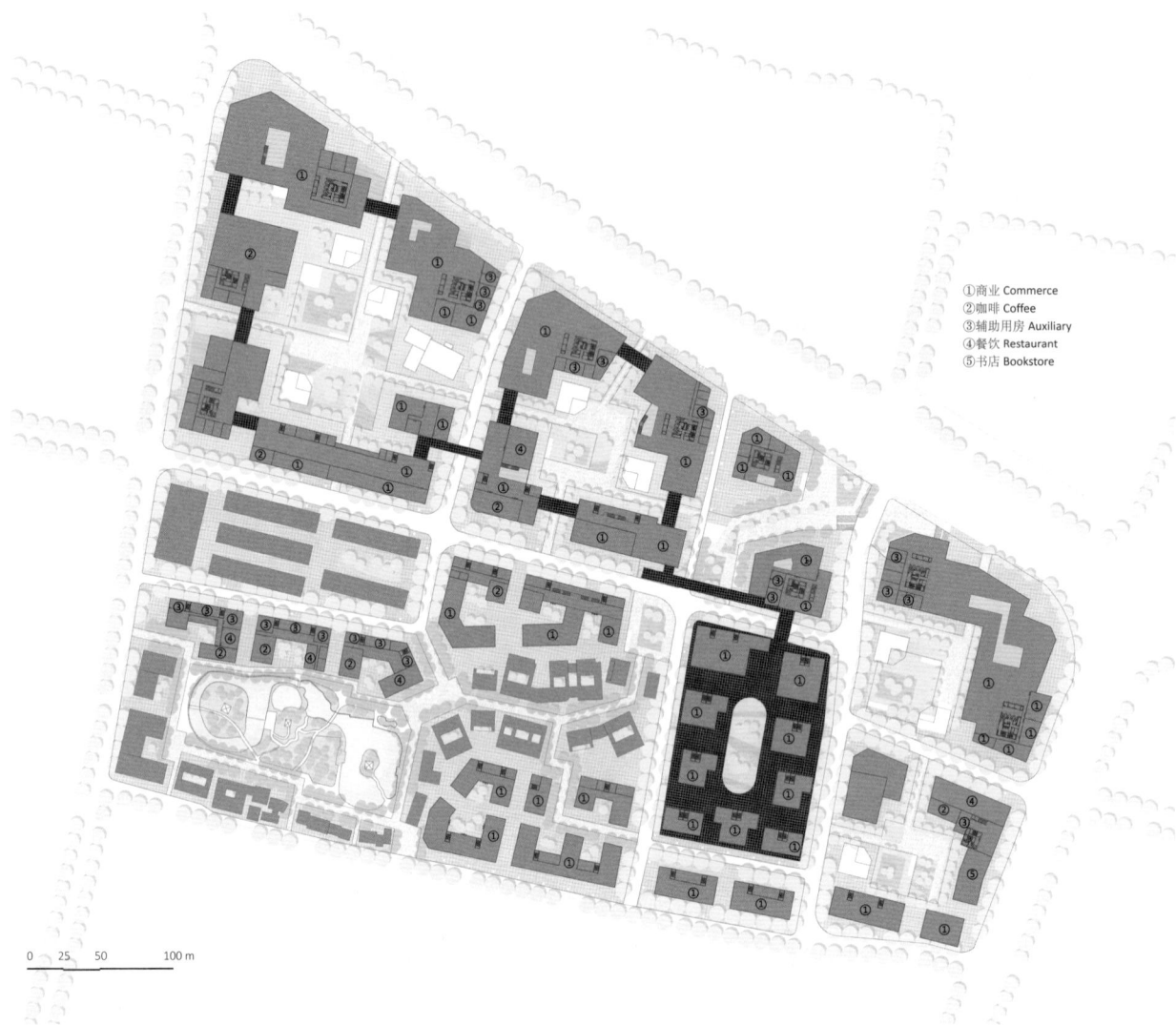

二层平面图　Plan of F2

①商业 Commerce
②设备 Equipment
③非机动车停车
Non-motor Vehicle Parking
④机动车停车
Motor Vehicle Parking
⑤餐饮 Restaurant
坡道 Ramp

0　25　50　　　100 m

一负层平面图　Plan of -F1

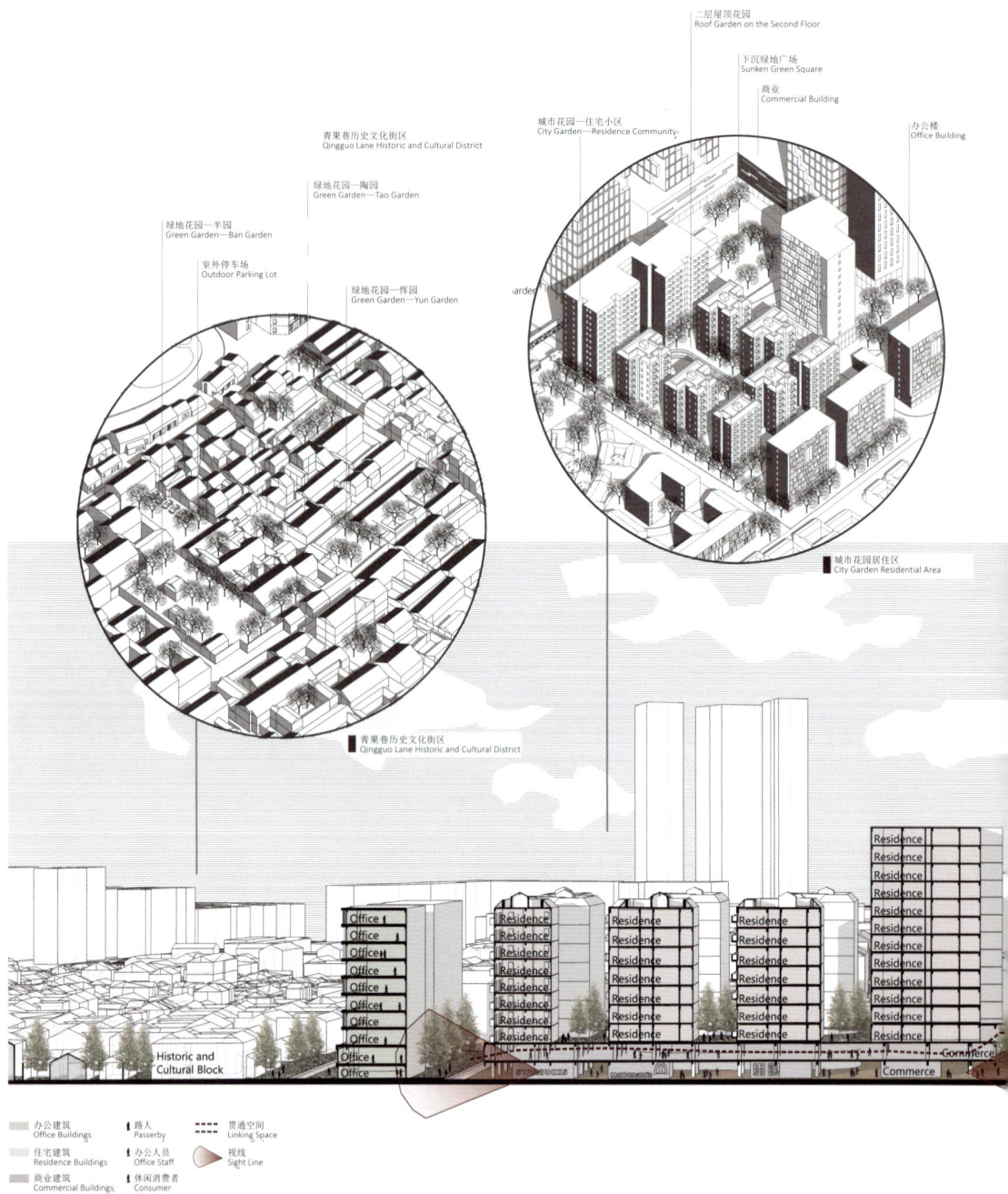

二层屋顶花园
Roof Garden on the Second Floor

下沉绿地广场
Sunken Green Square

商业
Commercial Building

办公楼
Office Building

城市花园—住宅小区
City Garden—Residence Community

青果巷历史文化街区
Qingguo Lane Historic and Cultural District

绿地花园—陶园
Green Garden—Tao Garden

绿地花园—半园
Green Garden—Ban Garden

室外停车场
Outdoor Parking Lot

绿地花园—恽园
Green Garden—Yun Garden

城市花园居住区
City Garden Residential Area

青果巷历史文化街区
Qingguo Lane Historic and Cultural District

办公建筑
Office Buildings

住宅建筑
Residence Buildings

商业建筑
Commercial Buildings

路人
Passerby

办公人员
Office Staff

休闲消费者
Consumer

贯通空间
Linking Space

视线
Sight Line

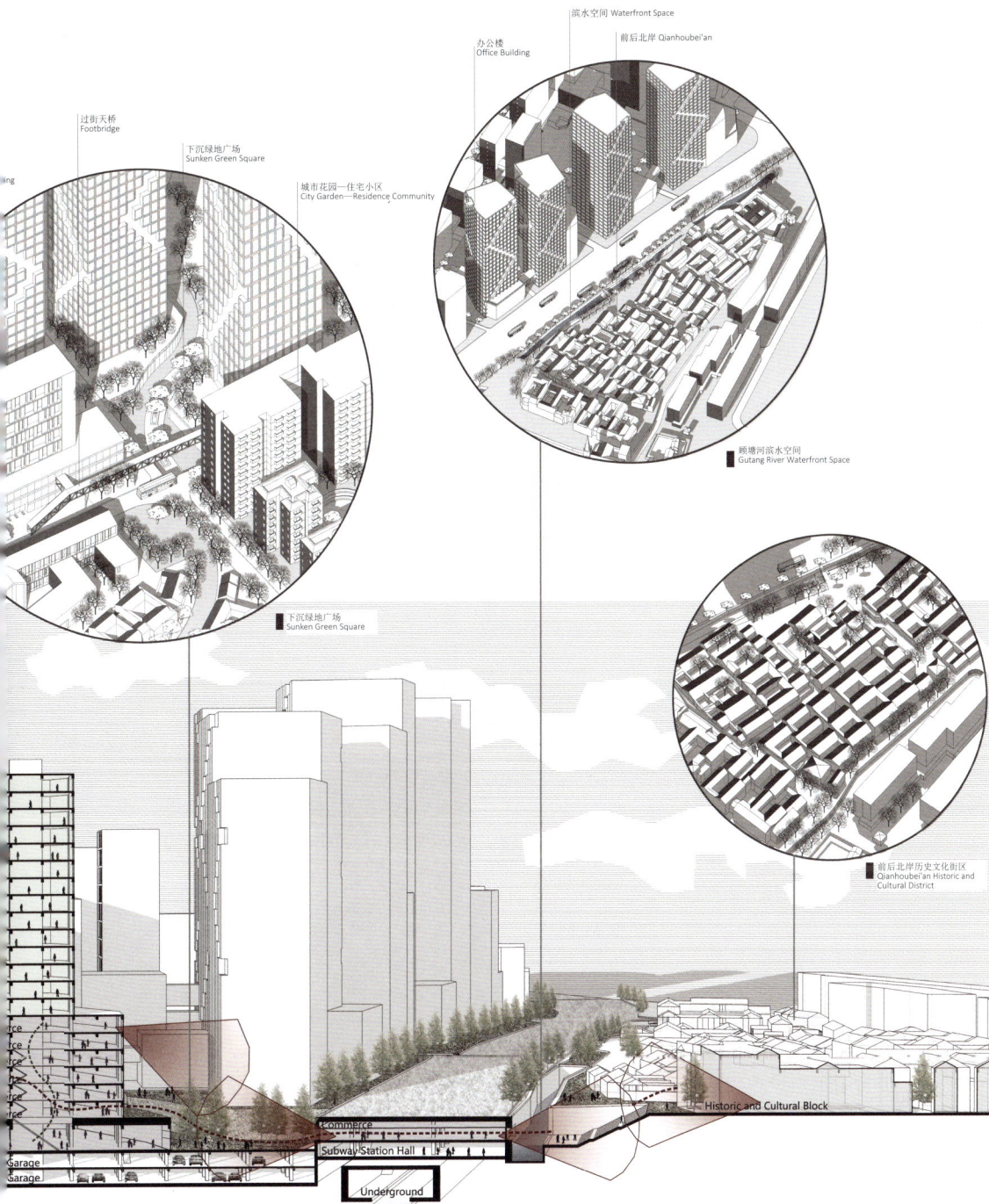

过街天桥
Footbridge

下沉绿地广场
Sunken Green Square

城市花园—住宅小区
City Garden—Residence Community

办公楼
Office Building

滨水空间 Waterfront Space

前后北岸 Qianhoubei'an

颐塘河滨水空间
Gutang River Waterfront Space

下沉绿地广场
Sunken Green Square

前后北岸历史文化街区
Qianhoubei'an Historic and
Cultural District

Historic and Cultural Block

Commerce

Subway Station Hall

Underground

Garage

Garage

水 + 城中村
Water + Urban Village
场地：茶山村 Site: Chashan Village

方案五　连接城 · 河 · 生境的村庄
Project 5　A Village Networked by Urban Biotope

- 生态需被重塑
  Reconstruct the Ecosystem

- 传统需被保留
  Preserve the Tradition

- 城村需被保留
  Link Village with the City

- 河流需被贯通
  Reconnect the River

水
+
城
中
村

现状 Present Situation

策略 Strategy

开发结构 Development Structure

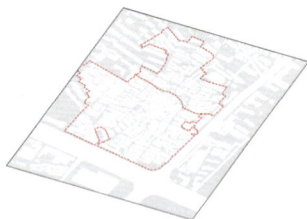

1. 重塑河道，塑造河岸多样化生态及景观。
2. 以河为媒，更新场所及建筑，提供新的发展可能。
3. 城中村内部局部更新放大，改善公共空间。
1. Reshape the river and shape the diverse ecology and landscape of the river bank.
2. Renew the site and buildings with the river as a medium to provide new development possibilities.
3. Partially update and enlarg inside the village, improve public space.

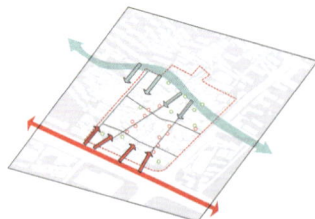

场地 Place

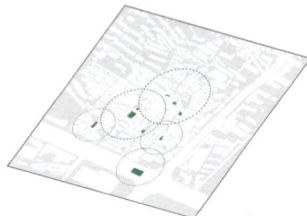

1. 重塑河道，塑造河岸景观，创造游憩场所。
2. 局部放大节点，改善公共空间。
3. 可设置专用的晒衣场，不占用公共活动空间。
1. Reshape the river, shape the riverbank landscape, and create a recreation place.
2. Locally amplify nodes to improve public space.
3. Set up a special clothes drying yard without occupying public activities space.

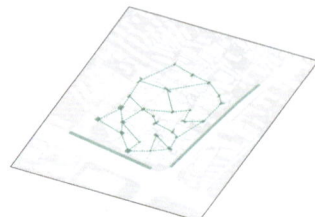

功能 Function

1. 以河为媒，连接村与城市，更新建筑和场地，形成城村融合的活力片区。
2. 沿面向城市界面的功能更新及立面翻新，为城村有机融合提供可能。
3. 更新后的节点与滨河区域提供新的功能与就业岗位，促进村民就业与对外联系。
1. Use the river as a medium to connect villages and cities, update buildings and venues, and form a vibrant area of city and village integration.
2. Functional update and refurbishment along the urban-facing interface, provide the possibility of organic integration of the village.
3. The updated nodes and riverfront areas provide new functions and jobs, and promote villagers' employment and external contacts.

学习环境 Learning Setting

对片区主要交通进行梳理，疏导出到达北处小学的通路，减轻主干道压力。
Care out the main traffic in the area, divert access to the primary school in the north, reduce the pressure on the main road.

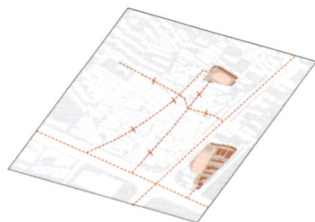

现状 Present Situation

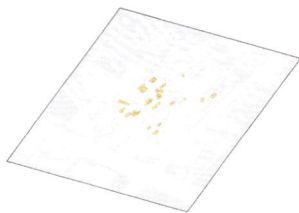

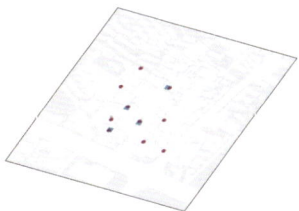

策略 Strategy

1. 对历史建筑进行修缮，还原历史风貌。
2. 将历史建筑改造为展示文物的公共空间。
3. 设计利于参观的引导路线，活化历史建筑。
1. Repair historical buildings and restore historical features.
2. Transform the historical buildings to public spaces for displaying cultural relics.
3. Design a guiding route that is conducive to the visit and activate the historic building.

文化遗产 Culture Heritage

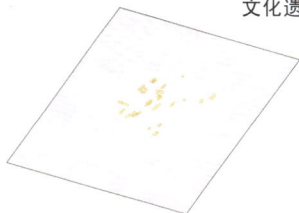

1. 疏导交通，加宽道路。
2. 明确机动车道路及步行通廊，人车分行。
1. Groom traffic and widen the road.
2. Defining motor vehicle roads and walking corridors, people and vehicles branches.

交通 Transportation

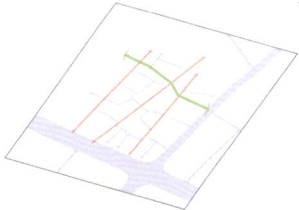

1. 重塑河道，用河串联起村落与城市，形成特色且多变的滨水空间，营造片区景观形象。
2. 重塑景观，塑造雨水花园等节点，形成逐步下渗的生态结构。
1. Reshape the river course, use the river to connect the village and the city in series, form a characteristic and changeable waterfront space, and create a landscape image of the district.
2. Reshape the landscape, shape the rainwater garden and other nodes to form a gradual infiltration of the ecological structure.

蓝绿结构 Blue and Green Structure

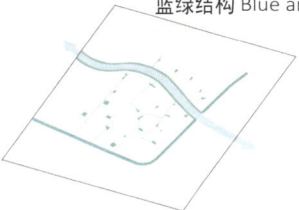

1. 重塑河道贯通水系，为片区提供水域来完善系统。
2. 沿河设绿化及雨水花园，稳固土壤，增加适应性。
3. 沿河逐步高差降低，解决内涝。
1. Reshape the river channel through the water system to provide water for the area to improve the system.
2. Set up green and rain gardens along the river to stabilize the soil and increase adaptability.
3. Gradually reduce the height difference along the river and solve the guilt.

气候适应性 Climate Adaptation

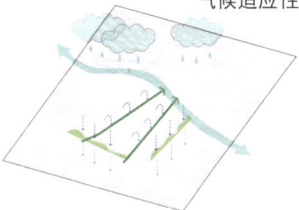

1. 设置垃圾回收政策，给予村民适量补贴鼓励村民有序分类处理垃圾。
2. 对于片区内建筑材料及建设环境进行管控，限制不环保建材的使用。
3. 改善垃圾回收站，并增加站点。
1. Set up a special garbage collection policy, and give the villagers appropriate subsidies to encourage the villagers to sort and dispose of garbage in an orderly manner.
2. Control the building materials and construction environment in the area to limit the use of non-environmental building materials.
3. Improve the garbage collection station and increase the site.

物质流动 Material Flow

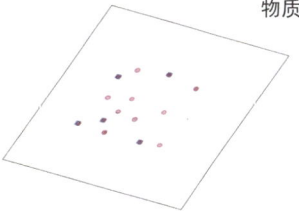

领域 Focus Areas	策略 Strategy
信息通信技术 Information and Communication Technology	城中村拥有与城市相同的信息通信技术，因此这方面不需要进行紧急改进处理 The City Village has the same information and communication technology as the city, so there is no need for urgent improvement in this area
噪声 Sound	沿主干道增设隔离绿化带，种植大乔木，减少噪音干扰 Add isolation green belt along the main road, plant large trees to reduce noise interference
本地服务与就业 Local Supplier and Labor	增加就业岗位，对沿街商业进行重塑。社区对片区商业进行集中管理，以及在片区内设置老年服务和医疗中心 Increase employment and reshape business along the street. The community centrally manages the business of the district and sets up elderly services and medical centers in the district
空气 Air	疏导道路，同时修整道路减少扬尘。重塑河道后通过生态手段对空气进行过滤。改造垃圾站，控制异味来源 Dredge the road and repair the road to reduce dust . After reshaping the river, the air is filtered by ecological means. Renovate the waste station in the area to control the source of odor
水 Water	设计水循环系统，部分回收利用。疏导排水体系，通过高差等措施将雨水引入河中，解决内涝 Design the water circulation system and partially recycle it. Drain the drainage system, introduce rainwater into the river through measures such as height difference, and solve the internal hemorrhoids
照明 Lighting	使用太阳能路灯，减少能源使用，改善片区照明条件。在各大主要道路上安装路灯方便夜间活动 Use solar street lights to reduce energy use and improve lighting conditions in the area. Installation of street lights on major roads is convenient for night activities
能源 Energy	政府加强基础设施建设。使用太阳能路灯，减少能源使用，改善片区照明条件。在片区内实行电器以旧换新政策，逐步淘汰老旧电器 The government has strengthened infrastructure construction. Use solar street lights to reduce energy use and improve lighting conditions in the area. Implement the trade-in policy in the area and gradually phase out old appliances
产品 Product	政府对片区增加风貌管控，对建筑材料做初步规定。可进行集中招标、统一建材等。减少产品使用带来的污染，实行以旧换新政策 The government has increased control over the area and made preliminary provisions on building materials. It can carry out centralized bidding to provide uniform building materials for the district, reduce the pollution caused by the use of products, and implement the trade-in policy

根据 CITYLAB 关注领域之间的协同与矛盾关系，将其总结为设计的四个关注要点。

According to the synergy and contradiction between the focus areas of interest in CITYLAB, summarize it as the four key points of design.

生态重塑 Reconstruct the Ecosystem

城村联系 Link Village with the City

历史保留 Preserve the Tradition

河流贯通 Reconnect the River

而这四点也就是设计的总体愿景。

These four points are also the overall vision of the design.

根据愿景从规划设计、技术层面以及建筑层面提出三层策略对其进行回应，构成方案架构。

According to the vision, from the planning and design, the technical level and the architectural level, propose a three-tier strategy to respond to it, forming a program structure.

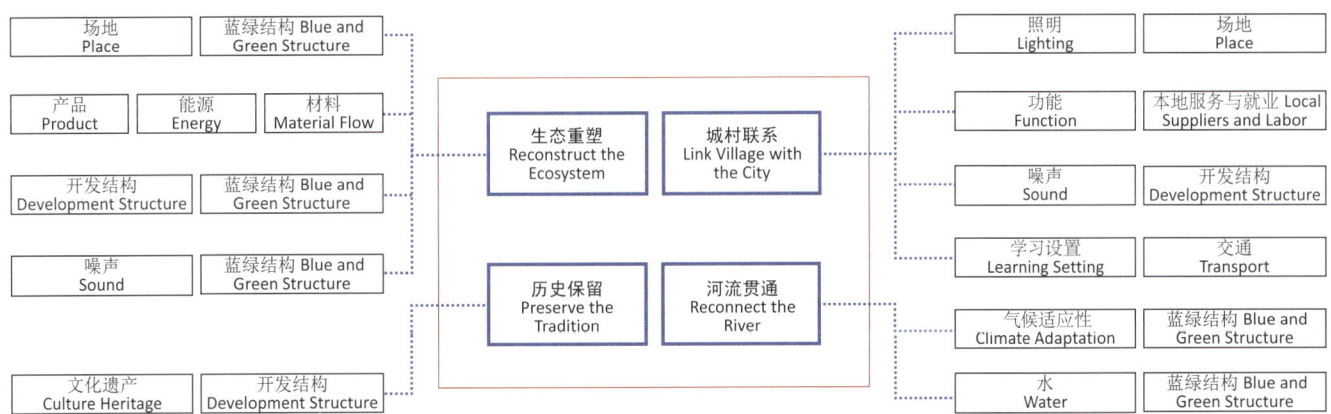

场地 Place	蓝绿结构 Blue and Green Structure				照明 Lighting	场地 Place
产品 Product	能源 Energy	材料 Material Flow			功能 Function	本地服务与就业 Local Suppliers and Labor
开发结构 Development Structure	蓝绿结构 Blue and Green Structure		生态重塑 Reconstruct the Ecosystem	城村联系 Link Village with the City	噪声 Sound	开发结构 Development Structure
噪声 Sound	蓝绿结构 Blue and Green Structure				学习设置 Learning Setting	交通 Transport
			历史保留 Preserve the Tradition	河流贯通 Reconnect the River	气候适应性 Climate Adaptation	蓝绿结构 Blue and Green Structure
文化遗产 Culture Heritage	开发结构 Development Structure				水 Water	蓝绿结构 Blue and Green Structure

蒲前中心小学
primary school

蒋氏宗祠
Ancestral Temple

龙游河
Longyou River

和平中路
Heping Road

常州市实验初级中学
Changzhou experimental
junior high school

蒲前老街 Puqian Old Street

垃圾回收点
Garbage Collection

村委会
Village Committee

地铁茶山站
Metro Chashan Station

中吴大道
Zhongwu Road

地铁大厦
Changzhou Metro Building

经济技术指标 Economic and Technical Norms	
规划用地面积: Planned land area:	14.6ha 14.6ha
总建筑面积: Building area:	125560m^2 125560m^2
容积率: Farr:	0.86 0.86
绿地率: Green rate:	18% 18%
建筑密度: Building Density:	38% 38%

总平面图　Master Plan

规划路线 Planning Route

整体规划设计分为三个阶段：

阶段1：点式激活。选取机会地块置入功能模块。
阶段2：线性更新。复原城市河流，沿着主要街巷和河流更新村庄。
阶段3：织补网络。依托线性功能外溢，逐渐织补城中村网络系统。

Step 1: Point to activate. Select the opportunity plot to place functional modules.
Step 2: Linear update. Restore the urban rivers, renovate the villages along major streets and rivers .
Step 3: Dam network. Relying on the linear function spillover, gradually weave the village network system in the city.

规划分析 Planning Analysis

结构分析 Structure Analysis
结构轴串点：依托河流和传统街道，串联起公共活力节点。
Structural axis string points: relying on rivers and traditional streets, connect public vitality nodes in series.

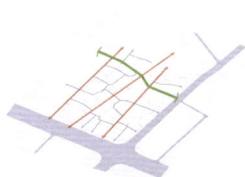

交通结构 Transport Structure
交通密织网：梳理主要街道巷道，使居民能高效利用慢行网络。
Traffic dense weaving network: combine the main street lanes, enable residents to efficiently use slow-moving networks.

功能结构 Function Structure
功能马赛克：摒弃机械分离的功能规划，倡导功能混合的"马赛克模型"。
Functional mosaic: abandon the functional planning of mechanical separation, advocate a "mosaic model" of functional mixing.

景观分析 Landscape Analysis
景观微渗透：针灸式置入微小绿地，将生态景观广泛渗透到城中村内部。
Landscape micro-infiltration: acupuncture is placed in tiny green spaces, and the ecological landscape is widely infiltrated into the inner village.

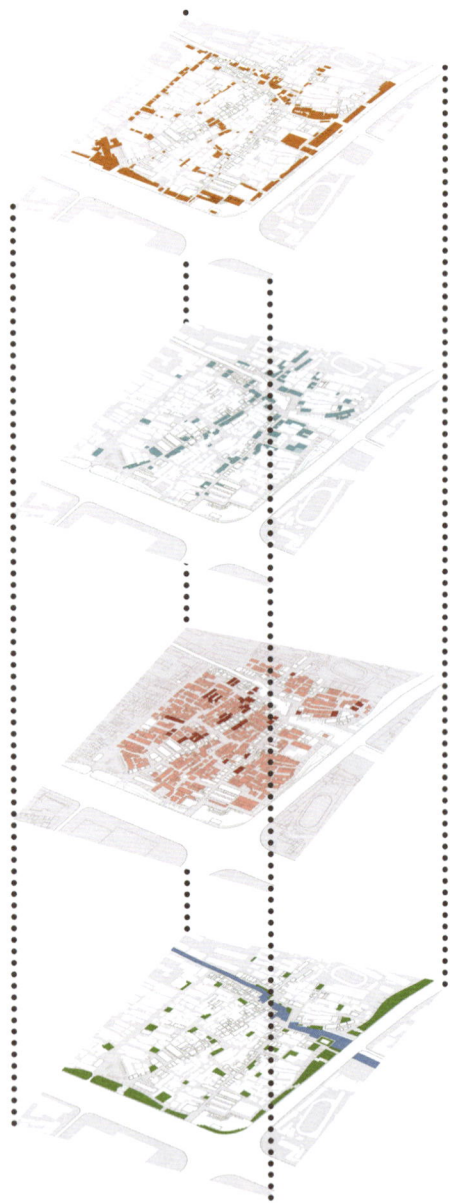

拆除违章搭建的棚户、质量较差的建筑、风貌较差的建筑、沿城市界面破旧低端的底商。

Demolish the shacks built in violation of regulations, poor quality buildings, poorly constructed buildings, and dilapidated low-end businesses along the urban interface.

改造沿着历史老街、与地铁相连街巷、沿河地区建筑。将这些建筑赋予功能。

Renovate the buildings along the historic old streets, connected to the subway, and along the river. Give these buildings a function.

保护文物保护建筑，保存当地民居对其进行修缮和整治，以达到面貌改善的目的。

Protect the cultural preservation building and preserve the local dwellings to repair and renovate them to achieve the purpose of improving the appearance.

在拆除部分建筑的空地上新增公共绿地，打造沿河、沿路的蓝绿系统。不仅为本地居民提供绿色生态空间，也改善城市形象。

New public green space will be added to the open space of some buildings to create a blue-green system along the river and along the road. It will not only provide green ecological space for local residents, but also improve the image of the city.

复原龙游河及其支流（三宝滨），完善城市水网体系，同时沿河形成城市绿轴，打造多样的公共活动场所及空间，提升环境品质与活力。

The Longyou River and its tributaries will be restored, the urban water network system will be improved, and the urban green axis will be formed along the river to create a variety of public activities and spaces to enhance environmental quality and vitality.

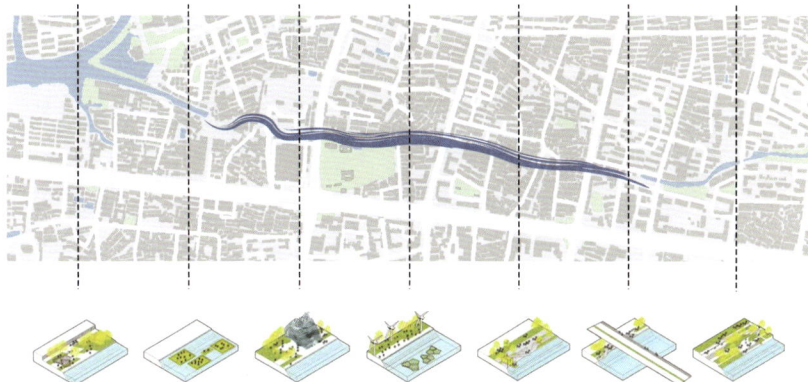

根据现场高程分析，可以明显地看出片区内低洼的地势，在河流存在时积水可顺应地势排入河中。但当河流消失，片区内就产生了严重的涝水问题。

According to the on-site elevation analysis, it can be clearly seen that the low-lying terrain in the area can be discharged into the river in response to the terrain when the river is present. But when the river disappears, there is a serious drowning problem in the area.

恢复河道，让自然被动式的排水体系得到重塑，在各绿化点处设计雨水花园，加强渗透；同时设置人工排水体系，最终在片区内形成完善的排水系统，改善区域生态与生活条件。

Restore the river channel, re-construct the natural passive drainage system, design rainwater gardens at various greening points to enhance penetration; at the same time set up artificial drainage system, and finally form a perfect drainage system in the area to improve regional ecological and living conditions

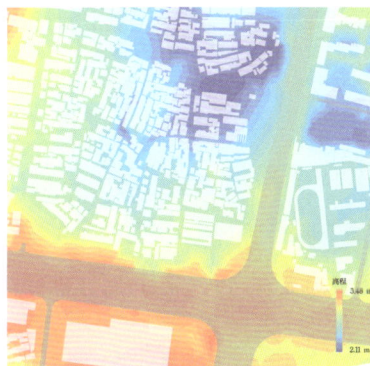

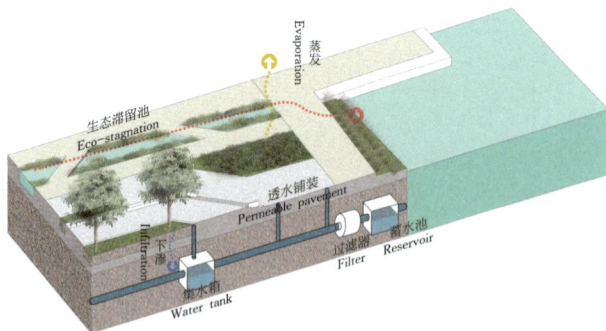

沿街节点：
沿街设计乔木、灌木等多种植被，种植形成雨水缓冲带，采用透水地砖进行雨水疏导，同时设计雨水生态滞留池对雨水进行截流。

A variety of vegetation such as trees and shrubs are planted along the street to form a rainwater buffer zone. The permeable floor tiles are used for rainwater drainage, and the rainwater ecological retention pool is designed to intercept the rainwater.

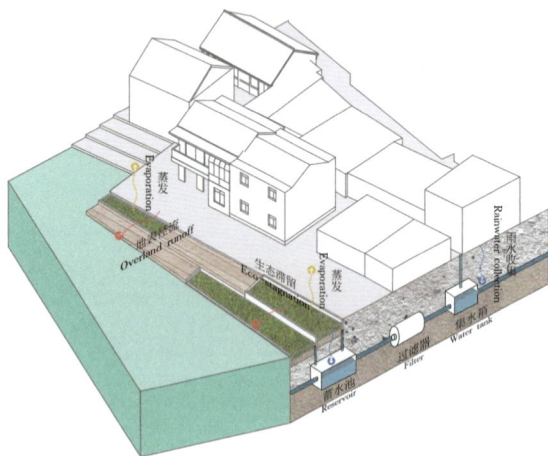

河流节点 1：
对地表径流进行生态滞留与渗透，对管道汇集的雨水进行过滤与蓄水。

Ecological retention and infiltration of surface runoff, filtration and storage of rainwater collected by pipelines.

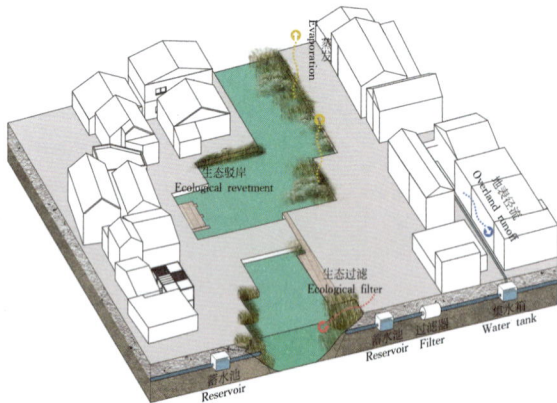

河流节点 2：
设计雨水管道对地表雨水径流进行汇集处理，沿河布置生态驳岸对未能集中的雨水生态过滤。

Design rainwater pipelines to collect surface rainwater runoff, and arrange ecological revetment along the river to filter the rainwater that is not concentrated.

沿街效果图 Street rendering

沿河效果图 1 Riverside rendering 1

沿河效果图 2 Riverside rendering 2

2.4m

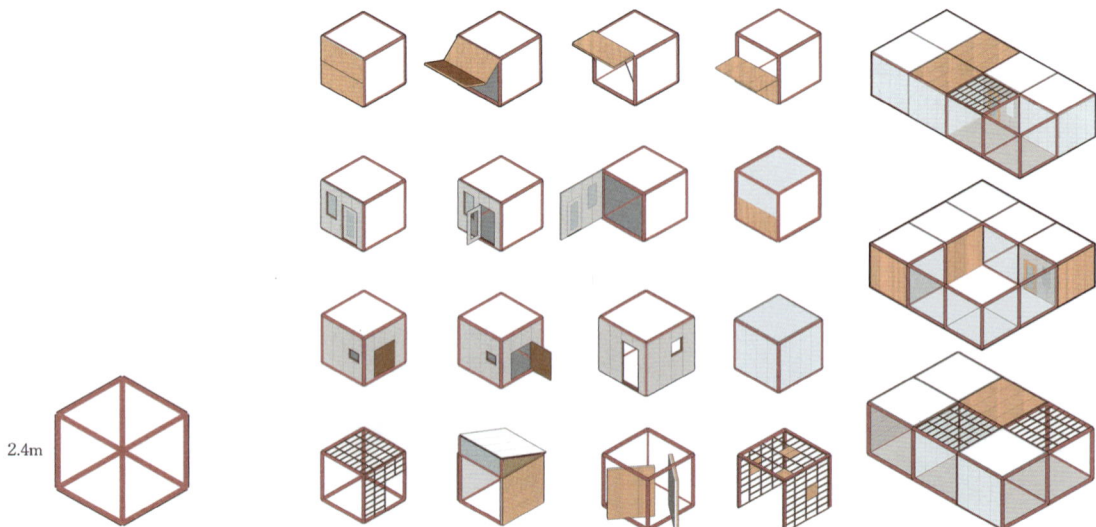

我们为城中村提供一种成长策略,利用 2.4 米 ×2.4 米的立方体为单位,对其进行不同功能下的使用方式分析,提供一系列使用方式。这种模块化措施造价低,施工速度快,可以灵活地根据使用者需求变更。

We provide a growth strategy for urban villages by using he 2.4 m × 2.4 m cube as the unit to analyze the usage modes under different functions. This modular measure has low cost and fast construction speed, and can be flexibly changed according to user requirements.

使用 2.4 米 ×2.4 米立方体,我们可创建一个具有全功能设施的预制洗手间。这些洗手间可以在每个家庭中实施,也可以放在院子里与多个家庭共用。本设计旨在解决城市村民的卫生问题,提高人们的生活质量。

Using the 2.4 m x 2.4 m blocks, we are able to create a prefabricated washroom with fully functional facilities. These washrooms can be implemented in each households or be placed in the yards to be shared with multiple households. This design is aimed to solve the hygienic issue and increase the life quality of the people in urban village.

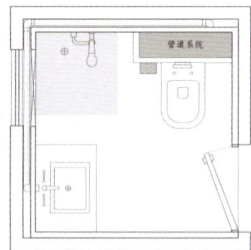

砖木结构房问题：
1. 屋面防水系统破损， 建筑无法满足使用需求。2. 屋架构多处节点松动，失去强度。3. 部分墙体破损、开裂。

Problems of Wood-brick Structure:
1. The roof waterproof system is damaged, and the building cannot meet the use demand. 2. Multiple parts of the framework are losing strength. 3. Parts of the wall are fractured and damaged.

砖混结构房问题：
1. 房屋排水系统差，导致雨水季节漏水涝水现象严重。2. 部分墙体破损开裂，无法满足结构荷载需求，严重影响美观。

Problems of Brick-cement Structure:
1. The poor run-off system of the housing causes the flooding during the rain season. 2. Parts of the walls are fractured and damaged, undermining the stability and aesthetics.

片区内老建筑均为明清与民国时期，多为一进的民宅，少数（蒋氏宗祠）为二进或以上的制式。随着城市化进程和人口增加，为了满足生活需求居民开始加建，破坏了原有的院落与城市肌理。

The old buildings in the area were all in the Ming and Qing Dynasties and the Republic of China. They were mostly private houses, and a few (Chiang Ancestral Hall) were two or more. With the urbanization process and population increase, residents began to build in order to meet the needs of life, destroying the original courtyard and urban texture.

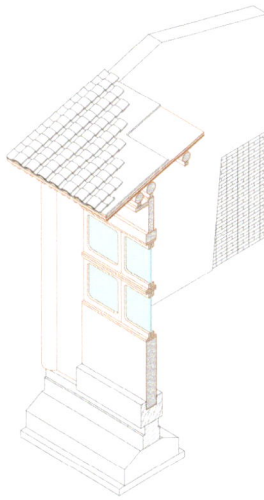

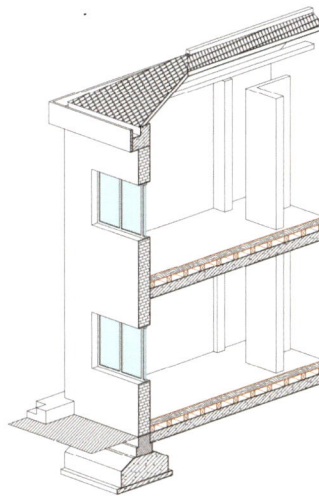

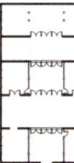

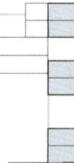

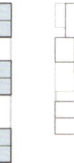

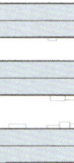

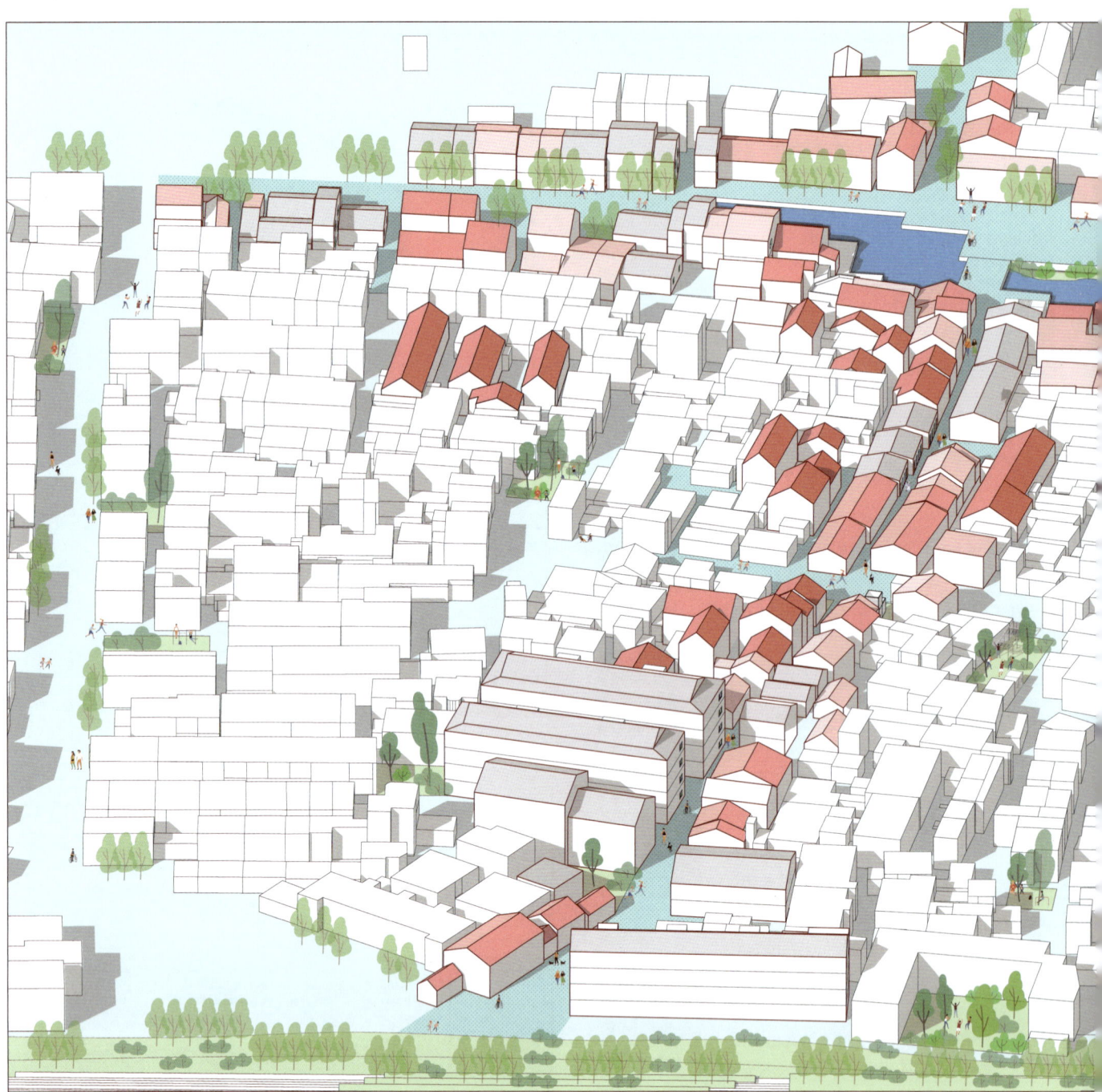

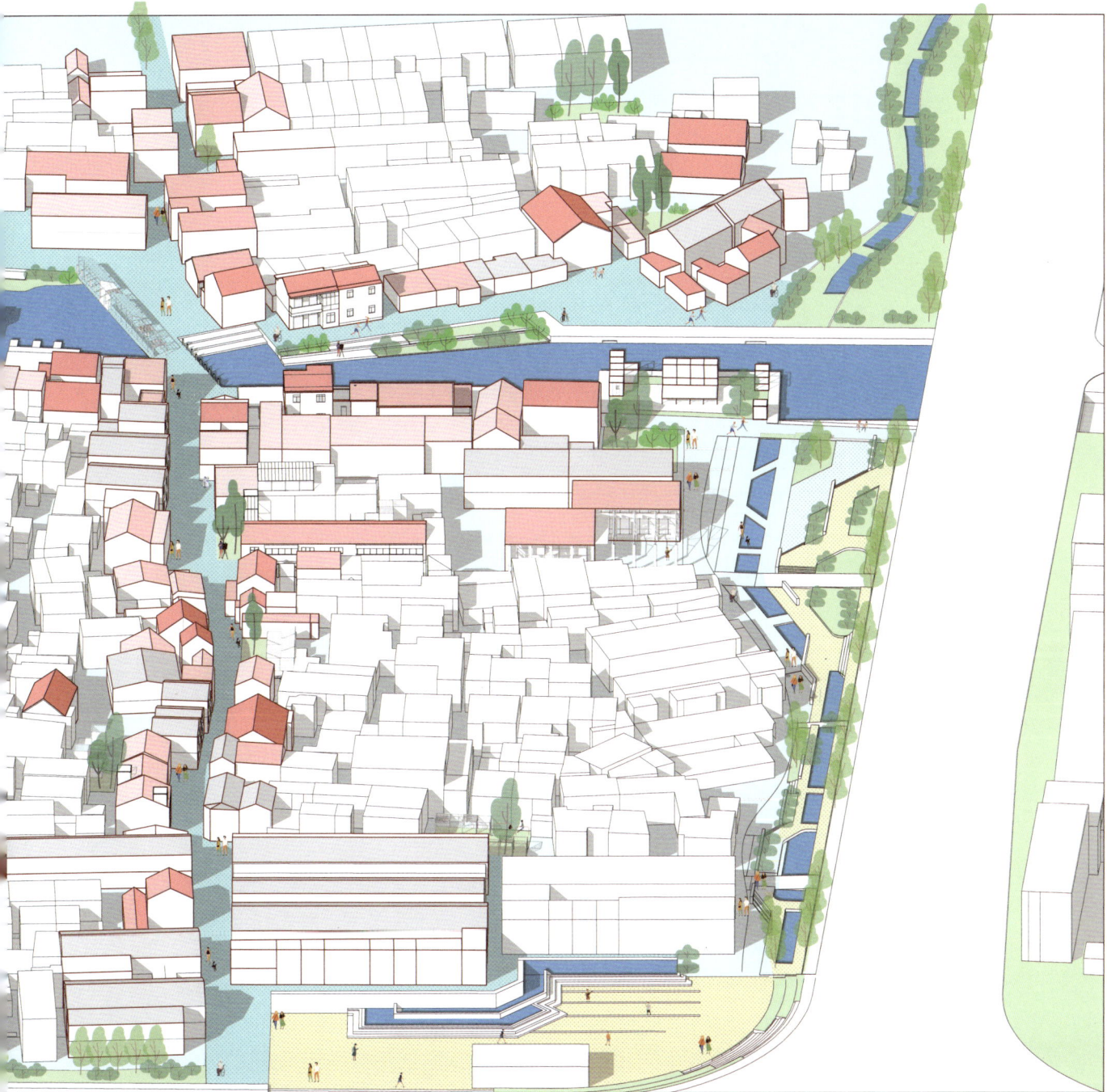

参考文献 References

[1] STAD S. Sustainable Urban-development Program[M]. Stockholm: Edita Bobergs., 2017
[2] Executive Office of Stockholm. Vision Stockholm Royal Seaport 2030[M]. EO Grafiska AB, 2010
[3] STAD S. Stockholm Royal Seaport Sustainability Report 2015[M]. Stockholm: Edita Bobergs, 2015
[4] STAD S. Stockholm Royal Seaport Sustainability Report 2017[M]. Stockholm: Edita Bobergs, 2017
[5] STAD S. Vision 2040: A Stockholm for Everyone[M]. Stockholm, 2015
[6] Louise H, Nils B, Karl H R. Can Stockholm Royal Seaport be part of the puzzle towards global sustainability?-From local to global sustainability using the same set of criteria[J]. Journal of Cleaner Production, 2017(140): 72-80
[7] Lagerqvist B. Heritage and Peacebuilding[M]. Britain：Boydell & Brewer, 2017: 221-234
[8] Zhang Yifan. Shorelines: Re-thinking and learning from the industrial heritage in Gothenburg[D]. Gothenburg: Chalmers University of Technology , 2014
[9] Lindholmen Science Park.From shipbuilding industry to Science Park［EB/OL].(2019).https://www.lindholmen.se/en/about-us/history,
[10] Gothenburg.Lindholmen – History, Vision and Role as an Accelerator［EB/OL].(2019).https://www.investingothenburg.com/news/lindholmen-history-vision-and-role-accelerator
[11] City of Gothenburg.Rivercity Gothenburg Vision[EB/OL].(2012).http://alvstaden.goteborg.se/
[12] Hoque A, Clarke A, Sultana T. Environmental sustainability practices in South Asian university campuses: an exploratory study on Bangladeshi universities[J]. Environment, Development and Sustainability, 2017, 19(6).
[13] Barthel S, Colding J, Ernstson H, et al. Albano Resilient Campus: A case-based exploration of urban social-ecological design (Q-book Albano)[S], 2010: 10.13140/RG.2.2.12457.85608
[14] Rawaf R. Social-Ecological Urbanism: Lessons in Design from the Albano Resilient Campus[R], 2017
[15] Colding J, Barthel S, Bendt P, et al. Urban green commons: Insights on urban common property systems[J]. Global Environmental Change, 2013(23): 1039-1051
[16] European commission. What is Horizon 2020[EB/OL], 2014
[17] GrowSmarter. GrowSmarter: Bringing together cities & industry to stimulate uptake of smart city solutions [EB/OL], 2015
[18] GrowSmarter. Technical factsheets: low energy districts[EB/OL], 2015
[19] GrowSmarter. Technical factsheets: integrated infrastructures[EB/OL], 2015
[20] GrowSmarter. Technical factsheets: sustainable urban mobility[EB/OL], 2015
[21] Holmstedt M, Cunningham A. Väsjö trafikanalys Sweco[R]. Sweden. SWECO, 2013-04-16
[22] Johansson M, Wiklund E,Hanson S. Trafikutredning Väsjön[R]. Sweden. SWECO, 2011

致　谢
Acknowledgements

与瑞典的接触和合作始于 2004 年 3 月韩冬青教授和我受邀访问瑞典皇家理工大学，斯堪的纳维亚半岛亲和的人性关怀和建设可持续性城市的努力给我们留下深刻的印象。之后伊沃·马丁奈克教授、罗纳德·维纳斯坦教授和何颖方女士于 2005 年 5 月回访东南大学建筑学院，双方合作成立"可持续性城市与建筑合作研究中心"，开始了之后长达十几年在科研、实践和人才培养方面的合作。

2018 年罗纳德·维纳斯坦教授签约东南大学作为建筑国际化示范学院的兼职教授，他介绍瑞典绿色建筑委员会 CITYLAB 行动机构与建筑学院开展联合研究与教学。这次以常州天宁区为研究对象的联合教学历时七个月，地跨中瑞两国四座城市，组织和参与方包括瑞典绿色建筑委员会 CITYLAB 在内的五个机构。

对于东南大学建筑学院硕士研究生一年级的学生来说，全面接触和学习世界上最前沿的可持续发展城市建设的理论和方法，实地参观斯德哥尔摩和哥德堡的先锋案例，体验和理解一个国家全民同心共同保护气候环境、建设可持续发展家园的意志、理念和行动策略，对照身边正处在急速变化之中的城乡环境，思考和寻找问题与可能的解决方案，七个月的联合教学带来的视野和认识的突破、思想的碰撞和一个前沿领域知识的全面接触，将在今后很长一段时间里持续产生影响，这是我们可以提供给学生的最好教学资源。

感谢瑞典绿色建筑委员会 CITYLAB 机构主任西格丽德·沃尔夫女士、高级顾问托马斯·古斯塔夫松先

The contact and cooperation with Sweden began in March 2004 when Professor Han Dongqing and I were invited to visit the Royal Institute of Technology (KTH). We were deeply impressed by Scandinavia's humanistic concern and its efforts to build sustainable environment. In 2005，Professor Ivo Martinac, Professor Ronald Wennersten and Ms. He Yingfang paid a visit to the School of Architecture at Southeast University in return, after which the two sides cooperatively established "Joint Research Center of Sustainable Urbanism and Architecture", thus more than a dozen years of cooperation in scientific research, practice and talent training began.

In 2018, Professor Ronald Wennersten signed a contract with Southeast University as a visiting professor in Architecture Internationalization Demonstration School at Southeast University. This introduced the CITYLAB of Sweden Green Building Council to conduct joint research and teaching with the School of Architecture at Southeast University. This joint teaching, taking Tianning District of Changzhou as the research case, lasted for seven months, geographically spanning four cities in China and Sweden, organized and participated by five institutions including CITYLAB of SGBC.

For first-year postgraduate students from the School of Architecture at Southeast University, comprehensive contacting with and learning the most cutting-edge theories and methods of sustainable urban development, visiting the pioneer cases in Stockholm and Gothenburg in person, experiencing and understanding the wills, ideas of the whole nation hold and the strategies they take together to protect global climate environment, and to build a sustainable hometown, reflecting on urban and rural environment in the rapid change around them, thinking of and searching for problems and possible solutions, all lead to the breakthrough of their vision and perception, the collision of their thoughts and a comprehensive contact with the cutting-edge knowledge, which will have a persistent impact in the future, and is the best teaching resource we can offer our students.

Special thanks to Head of CITYLAB, Ms. Sigrid Walve, CITYLAB Senior Advisor, Tomas Gustafsson, CITYLAB CEO, John Söderberg, CITYLAB Senior Expert, Ann-Kristin Belkert, CITYLAB Sunstainability Coordinator, Jenni Brink, Professor

生、首席执行官约翰·斯德伯格先生、高级专家安－克里斯汀·贝尔克特女士、可持续发展协调员珍妮·布林克女士，瑞典皇家理工大学埃里克·斯坦伯格教授、约翰·赫格斯特伦副教授，皇家海港埃米莉·泽特斯特伦女士，比耶金公司可持续发展顾问埃林·萨罗蒙森女士，教育住房公司项目经理约翰·布林先生，里克斯比根住房公司创新研究策略师彼得·塞尔伯格先生，斯德哥尔摩市新闻官员波·哈维斯特先生，SWECO国际中国区总监安娜·赫斯勒女士、尹莹博士，以及Kod 建筑事务所建筑师奥萨·卡尔斯特尼乌斯等专家在教学过程中的讲授、指导、支持和帮助。

这次联合教学得到江苏省城镇化和城乡规划研究中心、常州市规划局天宁分局、常州市规划设计研究院的通力合作和大力支持，他们分享的研究和实践成果为本次联合教学建构了完整的比较框架，也在学生们眼前展现了中国最发达地区在城乡环境可持续发展方面的建设理念和行动努力。

感谢江苏省自然资源厅陈小卉处长、江苏省城镇化和城乡规划研究中心叶兴平总规划师、陈国伟博士，常州市规划局天宁分局陆一中局长、汪曦晖副局长、屠泳博副局长，常州市规划设计研究院严玲副院长、黄勇总规划师、刘铭所长，中国生态城市研究院戴国雯所长在教学过程中的倾力付出和鼎力支持。

在本书的写作汇编过程中，东南大学建筑学院课题组全体老师和学生共同努力，使得这次教学活动的过程和成果得以完整呈现。特别感谢博士生季云竹、博士生戴天晨、硕士生段一行为本书成稿做出的贡献。

Erik Stenberg and Associate Professor Johan Högström from KTH, Sustainability Consultant, Ms. Emilie Zetterström from Royal Seaport, Ms. Elin Salomonsson from Bjerking AB, Project Manager Mr. Johan Bölin from Akademiska Hus, Research and Innovation Strategist Mr. Peter Selberg from Riksbyggen, Information Officer Mr. Bo Hallqvist of Stockholm City, Area Manager China Ms. Anna Hessle at SWECO International, Dr. Ying Ying at SWECO International, Architect Åsa Kallstenius from Kod Arkitekter, and other experts who taught, guided, supported and helped in the joint teaching.

The joint teaching was collaborated and substantially supported by Urbanization and Urban Rural Planning Research Center of Jiangsu, Changzhou Urban Planning Bureau Tianning Branch, Changzhou City Planning and Design Institute. The achievements of the research and practice they share contributed to constructing a complete comparison framework for the joint teaching, and to revealing the construction ideas and actions in the aspect of sustainable urban and rural environment development in the most developed areas in China.

Special thanks to the extreme devotion and full support in the joint teaching by Director of Natural Resources Department of Jiangsu, Professor Chen Xiaohui, Chief Planner Ye Xingping, Dr. Chen Guowei from Urbanization and Urban Rural Planning Research Center of Jiangsu, Director Lu Yizhong, Deputy Director Wang Xihui, Deputy Director Tu Yongbo from Changzhou Urban Planning Bureau Tianning Branch, Associate Dean Yan Ling, Chief Planner Huang Yong, Director Liu Ming from Changzhou City Planning and Design Institute, and Director Dai Guowen from China Eco-city Academy.

In the process of compiling this book, all teachers and students in the research group of the School of Architecture at Southeast University worked together to make sure the process and results of this joint teaching are completed presented. Special thanks to PhD candidates Ji Yunzhu, Dai Tianchen and postgraduate student Duan Yixing, for their contributions to the completion of this book.

张 彤
ZHANG Tong
2019-10-06

图书在版编目（CIP）数据

水域都市：中瑞联合可持续性城市发展研究与教学 ·
常州天宁 = AQUA-URBANISM: A Swedish CITYLAB Guided Joint
Research & Teaching Studio in Changzhou Tianning, China / 张彤等
著.-- 南京：东南大学出版社，2019.12
　ISBN 978-7-5641-8675-3

　Ⅰ. ①水… Ⅱ. ①张… Ⅲ. ①城市建筑–可持续性发展–研
究–常州 Ⅳ. ①F299.275.33

中国版本图书馆CIP数据核字（2019）第278090号

书　　　名：水域都市：中瑞联合可持续性城市发展研究与教学 · 常州天宁
　　　　　　SHUIYU DUSHI: ZHONGRUI LIANHE KECHIXUXING CHENGSHI FAZHAN
　　　　　　YANJIU YU JIAOXUE · CHANGZHOU TIANNING
著　　　者：张　彤　Ronald Wennersten　顾震弘　徐　瑾　殷　铭

责任编辑：戴　丽　魏晓平
责任印制：周荣虎
出版发行：东南大学出版社
地　　址：南京市四牌楼2号 邮编：210096
出 版 人：江建中
网　　址：http://www.seupress.com
电子邮箱：press@seupress.com
印　　刷：上海雅昌艺术印刷有限公司
经　　销：全国各地新华书店
开　　本：889 mm × 1194 mm 1/20
印　　张：8.6
字　　数：350千字
版　　次：2019年12月第1版
印　　次：2019年12月第1次印刷
书　　号：ISBN 978-7-5641-8675-3
定　　价：68.00元

（若有印装质量问题，请与营销部联系。电话：025-83791830）